MznLnx

Missing Links Exam Preps

Exam Prep for

Contemporary Marketing

Boone, Kurtz, 12th Edition

The MznLnx Exam Prep is your link from the texbook and lecture to your exams.
The MznLnx Exam Preps are unauthorized and comprehensive reviews of your textbooks.

All material provided by MznLnx and Rico Publications (c) 2010
Textbook publishers and textbook authors do not particpate in or contribute to these reviews.

MznLnx

Rico
Publications

Exam Prep for Contemporary Marketing
12th Edition
Boone, Kurtz

Publisher: Raymond Houge
Assistant Editor: Michael Rouger
Text and Cover Designer: Lisa Buckner
Marketing Manager: Sara Swagger
Project Manager, Editorial Production: Jerry Emerson
Art Director: Vernon Lowerui

Product Manager: Dave Mason
Editorial Assitant: Rachel Guzmanji
Pedagogy: Debra Long
Cover Image: Jim Reed/Getty Images
Text and Cover Printer: City Printing, Inc.
Compositor: Media Mix, Inc.

(c) 2010 Rico Publications

ALL RIGHTS RESERVED. No part of this work covered by the copyright may be reproduced or used in any form or by an means--graphic, electronic, or mechanical, including photocopying, recording, taping, Web distribution, information storage, and retrieval systems, or in any other manner--without the written permission of the publisher.

For more information about our products, contact us at:
Dave.Mason@RicoPublications.com

For permission to use material from this text or product, submit a request online to:
Dave.Mason@RicoPublications.com

Printed in the United States
ISBN:

Contents

CHAPTER 1
Marketing: Creating Satisfaction through Customer Relationships — 1

CHAPTER 2
Strategic Planning and the Marketing Process — 11

CHAPTER 3
The Marketing Environment, Ethics, and Social Responsibility — 22

CHAPTER 4
E-Commerce: Marketing in the Digital Age — 35

CHAPTER 5
Consumer Behavior — 43

CHAPTER 6
Business-to-Business (B2B) Marketing — 50

CHAPTER 7
Serving Global Markets — 56

CHAPTER 8
Marketing Research, Decision Support Systems, and Sales Forecasting — 65

CHAPTER 9
Market Segmentation, Targeting, and Positioning — 75

CHAPTER 10
Relationship Marketing, Customer Relationship Management (CRM) — 82

CHAPTER 11
Product and Service Strategies — 92

CHAPTER 12
Category and Brand Management, Product Identification — 99

CHAPTER 13
Marketing Channels and Supply Chain Management — 110

CHAPTER 14
Direct Marketing and Marketing Resellers: Retailers and Wholesalers — 119

CHAPTER 15
Integrated Marketing Communications — 130

CHAPTER 16
Advertising and Public Relations — 143

CHAPTER 17
Personal Selling and Sales Promotion — 151

CHAPTER 18
Price Concepts and Approaches — 158

CHAPTER 19
Pricing Strategies — 166

ANSWER KEY — 173

TO THE STUDENT

COMPREHENSIVE

The *MznLnx* Exam Prep series is designed to help you pass your exams. Editors at MznLnx review your textbooks and then prepare these practice exams to help you master the textbook material. Unlike study guides, workbooks, and practice tests provided by the texbook publisher and textbook authors, *MznLnx* gives you **all** of the material in each chapter in exam form, not just samples, so you can be sure to nail your exam.

MECHANICAL

The MznLnx Exam Prep series creates exams that will help you learn the subject matter as well as test you on your understanding. Each question is designed to help you master the concept. Just working through the exams, you gain an understanding of the subject--its a simple mechanical process that produces success.

INTEGRATED STUDY GUIDE AND REVIEW

MznLnx is not just a set of exams designed to test you, its also a comprehensive review of the subject content. Each exam question is also a review of the concept, making sure that you will get the answer correct without having to go to other sources of material. You learn as you go! Its the easiest way to pass an exam.

HUMOR

Studying can be tedious and dry. MznLnx's instructional design includes moderate humor within the exam questions on occassion, to break the tedium and revitalize the brain

Chapter 1. Marketing: Creating Satisfaction through Customer Relationships 1

1. _____ is a form of communication that typically attempts to persuade potential customers to purchase or to consume more of a particular brand of product or service. 'While now central to the contemporary global economy and the reproduction of global production networks, it is only quite recently that _____ has been more than a marginal influence on patterns of sales and production. The formation of modern _____ was intimately bound up with the emergence of new forms of monopoly capitalism around the end of the 19th and beginning of the 20th century as one element in corporate strategies to create, organize and where possible control markets, especially for mass produced consumer goods.
   - a. Advertising
   - b. AMAX
   - c. ACNielsen
   - d. ADTECH

2. _____ or _____ data refers to selected population characteristics as used in government, marketing or opinion research, or the _____ profiles used in such research. Note the distinction from the term 'demography' Commonly-used _____ include race, age, income, disabilities, mobility (in terms of travel time to work or number of vehicles available), educational attainment, home ownership, employment status, and even location.
   - a. African Americans
   - b. Demographic
   - c. Albert Einstein
   - d. AStore

3. _____ is a broad label that refers to any individuals or households that use goods and services generated within the economy. The concept of a _____ is used in different contexts, so that the usage and significance of the term may vary.

   A _____ is a person who uses any product or service.

   - a. 180SearchAssistant
   - b. Consumer
   - c. Power III
   - d. 6-3-5 Brainwriting

4. _____ is the study of when, why, how, where and what people do or do not buy products. It blends elements from psychology, sociology, social psychology, anthropology and economics. It attempts to understand the buyer decision making process, both individually and in groups. It studies characteristics of individual consumers such as demographics and behavioural variables in an attempt to understand people's wants. It also tries to assess influences on the consumer from groups such as family, friends, reference groups, and society in general.
   - a. Consumer behavior
   - b. Communal marketing
   - c. Consumer confidence
   - d. Multidimensional scaling

5. The loyalty business model is a business model used in strategic management in which company resources are employed so as to increase the loyalty of customers and other stakeholders in the expectation that corporate objectives will be met or surpassed. A typical example of this type of model is: quality of product or service leads to customer satisfaction, which leads to _____, which leads to profitability.

   Fredrick Reichheld (1996) expanded the loyalty business model beyond customers and employees.

   - a. Power III
   - b. 6-3-5 Brainwriting
   - c. 180SearchAssistant
   - d. Customer loyalty

Chapter 1. Marketing: Creating Satisfaction through Customer Relationships

6. _____ is a strategic planning method used to evaluate the Strengths, Weaknesses, Opportunities, and Threats involved in a project or in a business venture. It involves specifying the objective of the business venture or project and identifying the internal and external factors that are favorable and unfavorable to achieving that objective. The technique is credited to Albert Humphrey, who led a research project at Stanford University in the 1960s and 1970s using data from Fortune 500 companies.
   a. Market environment
   b. Lead scoring
   c. Product differentiation
   d. SWOT analysis

7. _____ in its literal sense is the process of transformation of local or regional phenomena into global ones. It can be described as a process by which the people of the world are unified into a single society and function together.

This process is a combination of economic, technological, sociocultural and political forces.

   a. Power III
   b. 6-3-5 Brainwriting
   c. 180SearchAssistant
   d. Globalization

8. A _____ is a subgroup of people or organizations sharing one or more characteristics that cause them to have similar product and/or service needs. A true _____ meets all of the following criteria: it is distinct from other segments (different segments have different needs), it is homogeneous within the segment (exhibits common needs); it responds similarly to a market stimulus, and it can be reached by a market intervention. The term is also used when consumers with identical product and/or service needs are divided up into groups so they can be charged different amounts.
   a. Commercial planning
   b. Customer insight
   c. Production orientation
   d. Market segment

9. _____s is the social science that studies the production, distribution, and consumption of goods and services. The term _____s comes from the Ancient Greek oá¼°κονομῖα from oá¼¶κος (oikos, 'house') + vÏŒμος (nomos, 'custom' or 'law'), hence 'rules of the house(hold)'. Current _____ models developed out of the broader field of political economy in the late 19th century, owing to a desire to use an empirical approach more akin to the physical sciences.
   a. Economic
   b. Industrial organization
   c. ACNielsen
   d. ADTECH

10. In economics, _____ is a measure of the relative satisfaction from consumption of various goods and services. Given this measure, one may speak meaningfully of increasing or decreasing _____, and thereby explain economic behavior in terms of attempts to increase one's _____. For illustrative purposes, changes in _____ are sometimes expressed in units called utils.
    a. Utility
    b. AMAX
    c. ADTECH
    d. ACNielsen

11. _____ is defined by the American _____ Association as the activity, set of institutions, and processes for creating, communicating, delivering, and exchanging offerings that have value for customers, clients, partners, and society at large. The term developed from the original meaning which referred literally to going to market, as in shopping, or going to a market to sell goods or services.

_____ practice tends to be seen as a creative industry, which includes advertising, distribution and selling.

Chapter 1. Marketing: Creating Satisfaction through Customer Relationships

a. Marketing myopia
b. Product naming
c. Customer acquisition management
d. Marketing

12. _____ often refers to either primary or secondary research. Secondary research involves a company using information compiled from various sources, which is about a new or existing product. The advantages of secondary research are that it is relatively cheap and easily accessible.
a. Mystery shoppers
b. Market Research
c. Mystery shopping
d. Questionnaire

13. A _____ dominated business thought from the beginning of capitalism to the mid 1950s, and some argue it still exists in some industries. Business concerned itself primarily with production, manufacturing, and efficiency issues. Say's Law encapsulated this viewpoint, stating: 'Supply creates its own demand'.
a. Blitz QFD
b. Marketing
c. Production orientation
d. Product differentiation

14. _____ are final goods specifically intended for the mass market. For instance, _____ do not include investment assets, like precious antiques, even though these antiques are final goods.

Manufactured goods are goods that have been processed by way of machinery.

a. Power III
b. Durable good
c. Free good
d. Consumer Goods

15. _____ is one of the four Ps of the marketing mix. The other three aspects are product, promotion, and place. It is also a key variable in microeconomic price allocation theory.
a. Price
b. Competitor indexing
c. Relationship based pricing
d. Pricing

16. _____ is a form of marketing developed from direct response marketing campaigns conducted in the 1970's and 1980's which emphasizes customer retention and satisfaction, rather than a dominant focus on 'point of sale' transactions.

_____ differs from other forms of marketing in that it recognizes the long term value to the firm of keeping customers, as opposed to direct or 'Intrusion' marketing, which focuses upon acquisition of new clients by targeting majority demographics based upon prospective client lists.

_____ refers to long-term and mutually beneficial arrangement wherein both buyer and seller focus on value enhancement through the certain of more satisfying exchange.This approach attempts to transcend the simple purchase exchange process with customer to make more meaningful and richer contact by providing a more holistic, personalized purchase, and use orn consumption experience to create stronger ties.

a. Global marketing
b. Relationship marketing
c. Diversity marketing
d. Guerrilla Marketing

17. An _____ is the manufacturing of a good or service within a category. Although _____ is a broad term for any kind of economic production, in economics and urban planning _____ is a synonym for the secondary sector, which is a type of economic activity involved in the manufacturing of raw materials into goods and products.

There are four key industrial economic sectors: the primary sector, largely raw material extraction industries such as mining and farming; the secondary sector, involving refining, construction, and manufacturing; the tertiary sector, which deals with services (such as law and medicine) and distribution of manufactured goods; and the quaternary sector, a relatively new type of knowledge _____ focusing on technological research, design and development such as computer programming, and biochemistry.

a. ACNielsen
b. ADTECH
c. Industry
d. AMAX

18. _____ is the ability of an individual or group to seclude themselves or information about themselves and thereby reveal themselves selectively. The boundaries and content of what is considered private differ among cultures and individuals, but share basic common themes. _____ is sometimes related to anonymity, the wish to remain unnoticed or unidentified in the public realm.

a. Privacy
b. 6-3-5 Brainwriting
c. Power III
d. 180SearchAssistant

19. _____ is one of the four elements of marketing mix. An organization or set of organizations (go-betweens) involved in the process of making a product or service available for use or consumption by a consumer or business user.

The other three parts of the marketing mix are product, pricing, and promotion.

a. Better Living Through Chemistry
b. Japan Advertising Photographers' Association
c. Comparison-Shopping agent
d. Distribution

20. _____ is a term used in marketing as well as the title of an important marketing paper written by Theodore Levitt. This paper was first published in 1960 in the Harvard Business Review; a journal of which he was an editor.

Some commentators have suggested that its publication marked the beginning of the modern marketing movement.

a. Business marketing
b. Corporate image
c. Marketing myopia
d. Marketing performance measurement and management

21. A _____ is a plan of action designed to achieve a particular goal.

_____ is different from tactics. In military terms, tactics is concerned with the conduct of an engagement while _____ is concerned with how different engagements are linked.

a. 180SearchAssistant
b. Power III
c. Strategy
d. 6-3-5 Brainwriting

Chapter 1. Marketing: Creating Satisfaction through Customer Relationships

22. _____ is a crime used to refer to fraud that involves someone pretending to be someone else in order to steal money or get other benefits. The term is relatively new and is actually a misnomer, since it is not inherently possible to steal an identity, only to use it. The person whose identity is used can suffer various consequences when he or she is held responsible for the perpetrator's actions.
   a. AMAX
   b. ADTECH
   c. ACNielsen
   d. Identity theft

23. _____ is the practice of individuals including commercial businesses, governments and institutions, facilitating the sale of their products or services to other companies or organizations that in turn resell them, use them as components in products or services they offer _____ is also called business-to-_____ for short. (Note that while marketing to government entities shares some of the same dynamics of organizational marketing, B2G Marketing is meaningfully different.)
   a. Mass marketing
   b. Business marketing
   c. Disruptive technology
   d. Law of disruption

24. _____ is a term commonly used to describe commerce transactions between businesses like the one between a manufacturer and a wholesaler or a wholesaler and a retailer i.e both the buyer and the seller are business entity.This is unlike business-to-consumers (B2C) which involve a business entity and end consumer, or business-to-government (B2G) which involve a business entity and government.

The volume of B2B transactions is much higher than the volume of B2C transactions. The primary reason for this is that in a typical supply chain there will be many B2B transactions involving subcomponent or raw materials, and only one B2C transaction, specifically sale of the finished product to the end customer.

   a. Disruptive technology
   b. Social marketing
   c. Customer relationship management
   d. Business-to-business

25. _____ or cause-related marketing refers to a type of marketing involving the cooperative efforts of a 'for profit' business and a non-profit organization for mutual benefit. The term is sometimes used more broadly and generally to refer to any type of marketing effort for social and other charitable causes, including in-house marketing efforts by non-profit organizations. _____ differs from corporate giving (philanthropy) as the latter generally involves a specific donation that is tax deductible, while _____ is a marketing relationship generally not based on a donation.
   a. Cause marketing
   b. Digital marketing
   c. Cause-related Marketing
   d. Global marketing

26. Electronic commerce, commonly known as _____ or eCommerce, consists of the buying and selling of products or services over electronic systems such as the Internet and other computer networks. The amount of trade conducted electronically has grown extraordinarily with wide-spread Internet usage. A wide variety of commerce is conducted in this way, spurring and drawing on innovations in electronic funds transfer, supply chain management, Internet marketing, online transaction processing, electronic data interchange (EDI), inventory management systems, and automated data collection systems.
   a. E-commerce
   b. AMAX
   c. ADTECH
   d. ACNielsen

27. _____ refer to a collection of facts usually collected as the result of experience, observation or experiment or a set of premises. This may consist of numbers, words particularly as measurements or observations of a set of variables. _____ are often viewed as a lowest level of abstraction from which information and knowledge are derived.
   a. Data
   b. Mean
   c. Pearson product-moment correlation coefficient
   d. Sample size

28. A _____ is a structured collection of records or data that is stored in a computer system. The structure is achieved by organizing the data according to a _____ model. The model in most common use today is the relational model.
   a. 6-3-5 Brainwriting
   b. Database
   c. Power III
   d. 180SearchAssistant

29. _____ refers to the evolving trend in marketing whereby marketing has moved from a transaction-based effort to a conversation. The definition of _____ comes from John Deighton at Harvard, who says _____ is the ability to address the customer, remember what the customer says and address the customer again in a way that illustrates that we remember what the customer has told us (Deighton 1996.) _____ is not synonymous with online marketing, although _____ processes are facilitated by internet technology.
   a. InfoNU
   b. Outsourcing relationship management
   c. Interactive marketing
   d. European Information Technology Observatory

30. A _____ is a collection of symbols, experiences and associations connected with a product, a service, a person or any other artifact or entity.

_____s have become increasingly important components of culture and the economy, now being described as 'cultural accessories and personal philosophies'.

Some people distinguish the psychological aspect of a _____ from the experiential aspect.

   a. Brand equity
   b. Brandable software
   c. Brand
   d. Store brand

31. The _____ is a database of consumer perception of brands created and managed by BrandAsset Consulting, a division of Young ' Rubicam Brands to provide information to enable firms to improve the marketing decision-making process and to manage brands better. _____ and _____ also describe the Y'R group managing the database.

_____ measures the value of a brand along four dimensions: 'Differentiation,' 'Relevance,' 'Esteem,' and 'Knowledge.' Differentiation and Relevance build up to 'Brand Strength.' Esteem and Knowledge are used to calculate 'Brand Stature.' _____ defines these terms as follows.

   a. Target audience
   b. Brand Asset Valuator
   c. Targeted advertising
   d. Hoover free flights promotion

32. The _____ is a very large set of interlinked hypertext documents accessed via the Internet. With a Web browser, one can view Web pages that may contain text, images, videos, and other multimedia and navigate between them using hyperlinks. Using concepts from earlier hypertext systems, the _____ was begun in 1992 by the English physicist Sir Tim Berners-Lee, now the Director of the _____ Consortium, and Robert Cailliau, a Belgian computer scientist, while both were working at CERN in Geneva, Switzerland.

Chapter 1. Marketing: Creating Satisfaction through Customer Relationships

a. 180SearchAssistant
b. Power III
c. 6-3-5 Brainwriting
d. World Wide Web

33. Human beings are also considered to be _____ because they have the ability to change raw materials into valuable _____. The term Human _____ can also be defined as the skills, energies, talents, abilities and knowledge that are used for the production of goods or the rendering of services. While taking into account human beings as _____, the following things have to be kept in mind:

- The size of the population
- The capabilities of the individuals in that population

Many _____ cannot be consumed in their original form. They have to be processed in order to change them into more usable commodities.

a. 6-3-5 Brainwriting
b. 180SearchAssistant
c. Power III
d. Resources

34. _____ is a method of direct marketing in which a salesperson solicits to prospective customers to buy products or services, either over the phone or through a subsequent face to face or Web conferencing appointment scheduled during the call.

_____ can also include recorded sales pitches programmed to be played over the phone via automatic dialing. _____ has come under fire in recent years, being viewed as an annoyance by many.

a. Directory Harvest Attack
b. Joe job
c. Telemarketing
d. Phishing

35. A _____ or pamphlet is a leaflet advertisement. _____s may advertise locations, events, hotels, products, services, etc. They are usually succinct in language and eye-catching in design.

a. Marketspace
b. Sweepstakes
c. Customer relationship management
d. Brochure

36. _____ is the provision of service to customers before, during and after a purchase.

According to Turban et al., '_____ is a series of activities designed to enhance the level of customer satisfaction - that is, the feeling that a product or service has met the customer expectation.'

Its importance varies by product, industry and customer.

a. COPC Inc.
b. Facing
c. Customer experience
d. Customer service

37. _____ is an advertisement in which a particular product specifically mentions a competitor by name for the express purpose of showing why the competitor is inferior to the product naming it.

This should not be confused with parody advertisements, where a fictional product is being advertised for the purpose of poking fun at the particular advertisement, nor should it be confused with the use of a coined brand name for the purpose of comparing the product without actually naming an actual competitor. ('Wikipedia tastes better and is less filling than the Encyclopedia Galactica.')

In the 1980s, during what has been referred to as the cola wars, soft-drink manufacturer Pepsi ran a series of advertisements where people, caught on hidden camera, in a blind taste test, chose Pepsi over rival Coca-Cola.

a. Cost per conversion
b. Heavy-up
c. Comparative advertising
d. GL-70

38. In marketing, customer _____, lifetime customer value (LCV), or _____ (LTV) and a new concept of 'customer life cycle management' is the present value of the future cash flows attributed to the customer relationship. Use of customer _____ as a marketing metric tends to place greater emphasis on customer service and long-term customer satisfaction, rather than on maximizing short-term sales.

Customer _____ has intuitive appeal as a marketing concept, because in theory it represents exactly how much each customer is worth in monetary terms, and therefore exactly how much a marketing department should be willing to spend to acquire each customer.

a. Sweepstakes
b. Value chain
c. Brand infiltration
d. Lifetime value

39. A personal and cultural _____ is a relative ethic _____, an assumption upon which implementation can be extrapolated. A _____ system is a set of consistent _____s and measures that is soo not true. A principle _____ is a foundation upon which other _____s and measures of integrity are based.

a. Supreme Court of the United States
b. Perceptual maps
c. Value
d. Package-on-Package

40. The _____ is a 1990 United States Federal law. It was signed into law on November 8, 1990 by the president.

The law gives the Food and Drug Administration (FDA) authority to require nutrition labeling of most foods regulated by the Agency; and to require that all nutrient content claims (for example, 'high fiber', 'low fat', etc).

a. Copyright infringement
b. Fair Debt Collection Practices Act
c. Trespass to land
d. Nutrition Labeling and Education Act

41. _____ refers to marketing strategies applied directly to a specific consumer.

Having the knowledge on the consumer preferences, there are suggested personalized products and promotions to each consumer.

The _____ is based in four main steps in order to fulfill its goals: Those stages are identify, differentiate, interact, and customize.

Chapter 1. Marketing: Creating Satisfaction through Customer Relationships 9

a. AMAX
b. ACNielsen
c. One-to-one marketing
d. ADTECH

42. In economics, an _____ is any good or commodity, transported from one country to another country in a legitimate fashion, typically for use in trade. _____ goods or services are provided to foreign consumers by domestic producers. _____ is an important part of international trade.
a. ADTECH
b. AMAX
c. Export
d. ACNielsen

43. In economics, business, retail, and accounting, a _____ is the value of money that has been used up to produce something, and hence is not available for use anymore. In economics, a _____ is an alternative that is given up as a result of a decision. In business, the _____ may be one of acquisition, in which case the amount of money expended to acquire it is counted as _____.
a. Transaction cost
b. Fixed costs
c. Variable cost
d. Cost

44. A _____ is a list of the general tasks and responsibilities of a position. Typically, it also includes to whom the position reports, specifications such as the qualifications needed by the person in the job, salary range for the position, etc. A _____ is usually developed by conducting a job analysis, which includes examining the tasks and sequences of tasks necessary to perform the job.
a. 180SearchAssistant
b. 6-3-5 Brainwriting
c. Job description
d. Power III

45. A _____ is a type of wholesale merchant business that buys goods and bulk products from importers, other wholesalers and then sells to retailers. _____s can deal in any commodity destined for the retail market. Typical categories are food, lumber, hardware, fuel, and textiles.
a. Chief privacy officer
b. Tacit collusion
c. Refusal to deal
d. Jobbing house

46. _____ refers to 'controlling human or societal behaviour by rules or restrictions.' _____ can take many forms: legal restrictions promulgated by a government authority, self-_____, social _____, co-_____ and market _____. One can consider _____ as actions of conduct imposing sanctions (such as a fine.) This action of administrative law, or implementing regulatory law, may be contrasted with statutory or case law.
a. Rule of four
b. Non-conventional trademark
c. CAN-SPAM
d. Regulation

47. _____ consists of the sale of goods or merchandise from a fixed location, such as a department store or kiosk in small or individual lots for direct consumption by the purchaser. _____ may include subordinated services, such as delivery. Purchasers may be individuals or businesses.
a. Thrifting
b. Warehouse store
c. Retailing
d. Charity shop

48. _____ is a concept that denotes the precise probability of specific eventualities. Technically, the notion of _____ is independent from the notion of value and, as such, eventualities may have both beneficial and adverse consequences. However, in general usage the convention is to focus only on potential negative impact to some characteristic of value that may arise from a future event.

a. 6-3-5 Brainwriting
c. Power III
b. Risk
d. 180SearchAssistant

49. _____ is a branch of philosophy which seeks to address questions about morality, such as how a moral outcome can be achieved in a specific situation (applied _____), how moral values should be determined (normative _____), what moral values people actually abide by (descriptive _____), what the fundamental semantic, ontological, and epistemic nature of _____ or morality is (meta-_____), and how moral capacity or moral agency develops and what its nature is (moral psychology.)

Socrates was one of the first Greek philosophers to encourage both scholars and the common citizen to turn their attention from the outside world to the condition of man. In this view, Knowledge having a bearing on human life was placed highest, all other knowledge being secondary.

a. ADTECH
c. AMAX
b. Ethics
d. ACNielsen

Chapter 2. Strategic Planning and the Marketing Process

1. _____ in organizations and public policy is both the organizational process of creating and maintaining a plan; and the psychological process of thinking about the activities required to create a desired goal on some scale. As such, it is a fundamental property of intelligent behavior. This thought process is essential to the creation and refinement of a plan, or integration of it with other plans, that is, it combines forecasting of developments with the preparation of scenarios of how to react to them.
   a. Power III
   b. 180SearchAssistant
   c. 6-3-5 Brainwriting
   d. Planning

2. _____ is an organization's process of defining its strategy and making decisions on allocating its resources to pursue this strategy, including its capital and people. Various business analysis techniques can be used in _____, including SWOT analysis (Strengths, Weaknesses, Opportunities, and Threats) and PEST analysis (Political, Economic, Social, and Technological analysis) or STEER analysis involving Socio-cultural, Technological, Economic, Ecological, and Regulatory factors and EPISTEL (Environment, Political, Informatic, Social, Technological, Economic and Legal)

   _____ is the formal consideration of an organization's future course. All _____ deals with at least one of three key questions:

   1. 'What do we do?'
   2. 'For whom do we do it?'
   3. 'How do we excel?'

   In business _____, the third question is better phrased 'How can we beat or avoid competition?'. (Bradford and Duncan, page 1.)

   a. Power III
   b. 6-3-5 Brainwriting
   c. Strategic planning
   d. 180SearchAssistant

3. _____ is a strategic planning method used to evaluate the Strengths, Weaknesses, Opportunities, and Threats involved in a project or in a business venture. It involves specifying the objective of the business venture or project and identifying the internal and external factors that are favorable and unfavorable to achieving that objective. The technique is credited to Albert Humphrey, who led a research project at Stanford University in the 1960s and 1970s using data from Fortune 500 companies.
   a. Market environment
   b. Lead scoring
   c. Product differentiation
   d. SWOT analysis

4. _____ is defined by the American _____ Association as the activity, set of institutions, and processes for creating, communicating, delivering, and exchanging offerings that have value for customers, clients, partners, and society at large. The term developed from the original meaning which referred literally to going to market, as in shopping, or going to a market to sell goods or services.

   _____ practice tends to be seen as a creative industry, which includes advertising, distribution and selling.

   a. Customer acquisition management
   b. Marketing myopia
   c. Product naming
   d. Marketing

5. The _____ is a 1990 United States Federal law. It was signed into law on November 8, 1990 by the president.

The law gives the Food and Drug Administration (FDA) authority to require nutrition labeling of most foods regulated by the Agency; and to require that all nutrient content claims (for example, 'high fiber', 'low fat', etc).

a. Nutrition Labeling and Education Act
b. Fair Debt Collection Practices Act
c. Copyright infringement
d. Trespass to land

6. A _____, broadcast market, media region, designated market area (DMA), Television Market Area (FCC term) or simply market is a region where the population can receive the same (or similar) television and radio station offerings, and may also include other types of media including newspapers and Internet content. They can coincide with metropolitan areas, though rural regions with few significant population centers can also be designated as markets. Conversely, very large metropolitan areas can sometimes be subdivided into multiple segments.

a. 180SearchAssistant
b. 6-3-5 Brainwriting
c. Power III
d. Media Market

7. Competitiveness is a comparative concept of the ability and performance of a firm, sub-sector or country to sell and supply goods and/or services in a given market. Although widely used in economics and business management, the usefulness of the concept, particularly in the context of national competitiveness, is vigorously disputed by economists, such as Paul Krugman.

The term may also be applied to markets, where it is used to refer to the extent to which the market structure may be regarded as perfectly _____.

a. Customs union
b. Geographical pricing
c. Free trade zone
d. Competitive

8. _____ is, in very basic words, a position a firm occupies against its competitors.

According to Michael Porter, the three methods for creating a sustainable _____ are through:

1. Cost leadership - Cost advantage occurs when a firm delivers the same services as its competitors but at a lower cost;

2.

a. 180SearchAssistant
b. Power III
c. 6-3-5 Brainwriting
d. Competitive advantage

9. A _____ is a process that can allow an organization to concentrate its limited resources on the greatest opportunities to increase sales and achieve a sustainable competitive advantage. A _____ should be centered around the key concept that customer satisfaction is the main goal.

A _____ is most effective when it is an integral component of corporate strategy, defining how the organization will successfully engage customers, prospects, and competitors in the market arena.

a. Cyberdoc　　　　　　　　　　　　　　b. Marketing strategy
c. Societal marketing　　　　　　　　　　d. Psychographic

10. Human beings are also considered to be _____ because they have the ability to change raw materials into valuable _____. The term Human _____ can also be defined as the skills, energies, talents, abilities and knowledge that are used for the production of goods or the rendering of services. While taking into account human beings as _____, the following things have to be kept in mind:

- The size of the population
- The capabilities of the individuals in that population

Many _____ cannot be consumed in their original form. They have to be processed in order to change them into more usable commodities.

a. 6-3-5 Brainwriting　　　　　　　　　　b. Resources
c. Power III　　　　　　　　　　　　　　d. 180SearchAssistant

11. A _____ is a plan of action designed to achieve a particular goal.

_____ is different from tactics. In military terms, tactics is concerned with the conduct of an engagement while _____ is concerned with how different engagements are linked.

a. Strategy　　　　　　　　　　　　　　b. Power III
c. 6-3-5 Brainwriting　　　　　　　　　　d. 180SearchAssistant

12.

Competitive advantage is, in very basic words, a position a firm occupies against its competitors. According to Michael Porter, the three methods for creating a _____ are through:

Cost leadership - Cost advantage occurs when a firm delivers the same services as its competitors but at a lower cost;

Differentiation - Differentiation advantage occurs when a firm delivers greater services for the same price of its competitors. They are collectively known as positional advantages because they denote the firm's position in its industry as a leader in either superior services or cost;

Focus (economics) - A focused approach requires the firm to concentrate on a narrow, exclusive competitive segment (market niche), hoping to achieve a local rather than industry wide competitive advantage. There are cost focus seekers, who aim to obtain a local cost advantage over competition and differentiation focuser, who are looking for a local difference.

a. Sustainable competitive advantage　　　b. 6-3-5 Brainwriting
c. Power III　　　　　　　　　　　　　　d. 180SearchAssistant

Chapter 2. Strategic Planning and the Marketing Process

13. _____ is a business term meaning the market segment to which a particular good or service is marketed. It is mainly defined by age, gender, geography, socio-economic grouping, technographic, or any other combination of demographics. It is generally studied and mapped by an organization through lists and reports containing demographic information that may have an effect on the marketing of key products or services.

   a. Brando
   b. Distribution
   c. Category Development Index
   d. Market specialization

14. _____ is a form of intellectual property which gives the creator of an original work exclusive rights for a certain time period in relation to that work, including its publication, distribution and adaptation; after which time the work is said to enter the public domain. _____ applies to any expressible form of an idea or information that is substantive and discrete. Some jurisdictions also recognize 'moral rights' of the creator of a work, such as the right to be credited for the work.

   a. Reasonable person standard
   b. Collective mark
   c. Copyright
   d. Celler-Kefauver Act

15. The _____ is a United States copyright law that implements two 1996 treaties of the World Intellectual Property Organization (WIPO.) It criminalizes production and dissemination of technology, devices whether or not there is actual infringement of copyright itself. In addition, the _____ heightens the penalties for copyright infringement on the Internet.

   a. Regulatory
   b. Digital Millennium Copyright Act
   c. Copyright infringement
   d. Priority right

16. The _____ is generally accepted as the use and specification of the four p's describing the strategic position of a product in the marketplace. One version of the origins of the _____ starts in 1948 when James Culliton said that a marketing decision should be a result of something similar to a recipe. This version continued in 1953 when Neil Borden, in his American Marketing Association presidential address, took the recipe idea one step further and coined the term 'Marketing-Mix'.

   a. 180SearchAssistant
   b. 6-3-5 Brainwriting
   c. Power III
   d. Marketing mix

17. _____ is one of the four elements of marketing mix. An organization or set of organizations (go-betweens) involved in the process of making a product or service available for use or consumption by a consumer or business user.

The other three parts of the marketing mix are product, pricing, and promotion.

   a. Better Living Through Chemistry
   b. Distribution
   c. Japan Advertising Photographers' Association
   d. Comparison-Shopping agent

18. _____ is the use of an object (typically referred to as an RFID tag) applied to or incorporated into a product, animal, or person for the purpose of identification and tracking using radio waves. Some tags can be read from several meters away and beyond the line of sight of the reader.

Most RFID tags contain at least two parts.

   a. Power III
   b. 180SearchAssistant
   c. 6-3-5 Brainwriting
   d. Radio-frequency identification

Chapter 2. Strategic Planning and the Marketing Process

19. _____ is one of the four Ps of the marketing mix. The other three aspects are product, promotion, and place. It is also a key variable in microeconomic price allocation theory.
   a. Competitor indexing
   b. Price
   c. Pricing
   d. Relationship based pricing

20. _____ , according to The American Marketing Association, is 'a planning process designed to assure that all brand contacts received by a customer or prospect for a product, service, or organization are relevant to that person and consistent over time.' (Marketing Power Dictionary)

   _____ is a term used to describe a holistic approach to marketing. It aims to ensure consistency of message and the complementary use of media. The concept includes online and offline marketing channels.

   a. ADTECH
   b. ACNielsen
   c. Integrated marketing communications
   d. AMAX

21. _____ refers to messages and related media used to communicate with a market. Those who practice advertising, branding, direct marketing, graphic design, marketing, packaging, promotion, publicity, sponsorship, public relations, sales, sales promotion and online marketing are termed marketing communicators, _____ managers, or more briefly as marcom managers.
   a. Merchandising
   b. Merchandise
   c. Sales promotion
   d. Marketing communication

22. _____ involves disseminating information about a product, product line, brand, or company. It is one of the four key aspects of the marketing mix. (The other three elements are product marketing, pricing, and distribution). P>_____ is generally sub-divided into two parts:

   - Above the line _____: Promotion in the media (e.g. TV, radio, newspapers, Internet and Mobile Phones) in which the advertiser pays an advertising agency to place the ad
   - Below the line _____: All other _____. Much of this is intended to be subtle enough for the consumer to be unaware that _____ is taking place. E.g. sponsorship, product placement, endorsements, sales _____, merchandising, direct mail, personal selling, public relations, trade shows

   a. Davie Brown Index
   b. Promotion
   c. Bottling lines
   d. Cashmere Agency

23. _____, also referred to as i-marketing, web marketing, online marketing is the marketing of products or services over the Internet.

   The Internet has brought many unique benefits to marketing, one of which being lower costs for the distribution of information and media to a global audience. The interactive nature of _____, both in terms of providing instant response and eliciting responses, is a unique quality of the medium.

   a. ADTECH
   b. AMAX
   c. ACNielsen
   d. Internet marketing

Chapter 2. Strategic Planning and the Marketing Process

24. An _____ is the manufacturing of a good or service within a category. Although _____ is a broad term for any kind of economic production, in economics and urban planning _____ is a synonym for the secondary sector, which is a type of economic activity involved in the manufacturing of raw materials into goods and products.

There are four key industrial economic sectors: the primary sector, largely raw material extraction industries such as mining and farming; the secondary sector, involving refining, construction, and manufacturing; the tertiary sector, which deals with services (such as law and medicine) and distribution of manufactured goods; and the quaternary sector, a relatively new type of knowledge _____ focusing on technological research, design and development such as computer programming, and biochemistry.

   a. ACNielsen
   c. ADTECH
   b. AMAX
   d. Industry

25. The _____ is a marketing term and refers to all of the forces outside of marketing that affect marketing management's ability to build and maintain successful relationships with target customers. The _____ consists of both the macroenvironment and the microenvironment.

The microenvironment refers to the forces that are close to the company and affect its ability to serve its customers.

   a. Customer franchise
   c. Psychographic
   b. Business-to-consumer
   d. Market environment

26. In business, a _____ is a product or a business unit that generates unusually high profit margins: so high that it is responsible for a large amount of a company's operating profit. This profit far exceeds the amount necessary to maintain the _____ business, and the excess is used by the business for other purposes.

A firm is said to be acting as a _____ when its earnings per share (EPS) is equal to its dividends per share (DPS), or in other words, when a firm pays out 100% of its free cash flow (FCF) to its shareholders as dividends at the end of each accounting term.

   a. Corporate transparency
   c. Goal setting
   b. Cash cow
   d. Crisis management

27. A _____ is a type of business entity in which partners (owners) share with each other the profits or losses of the business undertaking in which all have invested. _____s are often favored over corporations for taxation purposes, as the _____ structure does not generally incur a tax on profits before it is distributed to the partners (i.e. there is no dividend tax levied.) However, depending on the _____ structure and the jurisdiction in which it operates, owners of a _____ may be exposed to greater personal liability than they would as shareholders of a corporation.
   a. Competition law
   c. Partnership
   b. Fair Debt Collection Practices Act
   d. Brand piracy

28. _____ is understood as a business unit within the overall corporate identity which is distinguishable from other business because it serves a defined external market where management can conduct strategic planning in relation to products and markets. When companies become really large, they are best thought of as being composed of a number of businesses (or _____s.)

Chapter 2. Strategic Planning and the Marketing Process 17

In the broader domain of strategic management, the phrase '_____' came into use in the 1960s, largely as a result of General Electric's many units.

a. Business strategy
c. Corporate strategy
b. Cost leadership
d. Strategic business unit

29. _____ is difficult to define. For example, in 1952, Alfred Kroeber and Clyde Kluckhohn compiled a list of 164 definitions of '_____' in _____: A Critical Review of Concepts and Definitions. However, the word '_____' is most commonly used in three basic senses:

- excellence of taste in the fine arts and humanities
- an integrated pattern of human knowledge, belief, and behavior that depends upon the capacity for symbolic thought and social learning
- the set of shared attitudes, values, goals, and practices that characterizes an institution, organization or group.

When the concept first emerged in eighteenth- and nineteenth-century Europe, it connoted a process of cultivation or improvement, as in agriculture or horticulture. In the nineteenth century, it came to refer first to the betterment or refinement of the individual, especially through education, and then to the fulfillment of national aspirations or ideals.

a. AStore
c. Albert Einstein
b. African Americans
d. Culture

30. A _____ is a collection of symbols, experiences and associations connected with a product, a service, a person or any other artifact or entity.

_____s have become increasingly important components of culture and the economy, now being described as 'cultural accessories and personal philosophies'.

Some people distinguish the psychological aspect of a _____ from the experiential aspect.

a. Store brand
c. Brand equity
b. Brandable software
d. Brand

31. The _____ is a database of consumer perception of brands created and managed by BrandAsset Consulting, a division of Young ' Rubicam Brands to provide information to enable firms to improve the marketing decision-making process and to manage brands better. _____ and _____ also describe the Y'R group managing the database.

_____ measures the value of a brand along four dimensions: 'Differentiation,' 'Relevance,' 'Esteem,' and 'Knowledge.' Differentiation and Relevance build up to 'Brand Strength.' Esteem and Knowledge are used to calculate 'Brand Stature.' _____ defines these terms as follows.

Chapter 2. Strategic Planning and the Marketing Process

a. Hoover free flights promotion
b. Brand Asset Valuator
c. Targeted advertising
d. Target audience

32. _____ often refers to either primary or secondary research. Secondary research involves a company using information compiled from various sources, which is about a new or existing product. The advantages of secondary research are that it is relatively cheap and easily accessible.
a. Mystery shopping
b. Questionnaire
c. Market Research
d. Mystery shoppers

33. A _____ or trade mark, identified by the symbols â„¢ (not yet registered) and Â® (registered) business organization or other legal entity to identify that the products and/or services to consumers with which the _____ appears originate from a unique source of origin, and to distinguish its products or services from those of other entities. A _____ is a type of intellectual property, and typically a name, word, phrase, logo, symbol, design, image, or a combination of these elements. There is also a range of non-conventional _____s comprising marks which do not fall into these standard categories.
a. Risk management
b. 180SearchAssistant
c. Power III
d. Trademark

34. A _____ is a formal statement of a set of business goals, the reasons why they are believed attainable, and the plan for reaching those goals. It may also contain background information about the organization or team attempting to reach those goals.

The business goals may be defined for for-profit or for non-profit organizations.

a. Logistics management
b. Digital strategy
c. Product marketing
d. Business plan

35. _____ is a term used in business for a short document that summarises a longer report, proposal or group of related reports in such a way that readers can rapidly become acquainted with a large body of material without having to read it all. It will usually contain a brief statement of the problem or proposal covered in the major document(s), background information, concise analysis and main conclusions. It is intended as an aid to decision making by business managers.
a. ADTECH
b. AMAX
c. ACNielsen
d. Executive summary

36. A _____ is a written document that details the necessary actions to achieve one or more marketing objectives. It can be for a product or service, a brand, or a product line. _____s cover between one and five years.
a. Marketing strategy
b. Marketing plan
c. Disruptive technology
d. Prosumer

37. A _____ is a brief statement of the purpose of a company, organization. It is ideally used to guide the actions of the organization.

Chapter 2. Strategic Planning and the Marketing Process 19

_____s often contain the following:

- Purpose of the organization
- The organization's primary stakeholders: clients, stockholders, etc.
- Responsibilities of the organization towards these stockholders
- Products and services offered

Generally shorter _____s are more effective than longer ones.

In developing a _____:

- Encourage input as feasible from employees, volunteers, and other stakeholders
- Publicize it broadly

The _____ can be used to resolve differences between business stakeholders. Stakeholders include: employees including managers and executives, stockholders, board of directors, customers, suppliers, distributors, creditors, governments (local, state, federal, etc.), unions, competitors, NGO's, and the general public.

a. 180SearchAssistant
b. 6-3-5 Brainwriting
c. Power III
d. Mission statement

38. In economics, an _____ is any good or commodity, transported from one country to another country in a legitimate fashion, typically for use in trade. _____ goods or services are provided to foreign consumers by domestic producers. _____ is an important part of international trade.
a. ACNielsen
b. Export
c. AMAX
d. ADTECH

39. _____ is a trademark law concept permitting the owner of a famous trademark to forbid others from using that mark in a way that would lessen its uniqueness. In most cases, _____ involves an unauthorized use of another's trademark on products that do not compete with, and have little connection with, those of the trademark owner. For example, a famous trademark used by one company to refer to hair care products might be diluted if another company began using a similar mark to refer to breakfast cereals or spark plugs.
a. Trademark Dilution
b. Trademark attorney
c. Federal Bureau of Investigation
d. Trespass to land

40. _____ is a broad label that refers to any individuals or households that use goods and services generated within the economy. The concept of a _____ is used in different contexts, so that the usage and significance of the term may vary.

A _____ is a person who uses any product or service.

Chapter 2. Strategic Planning and the Marketing Process

a. Power III
b. 180SearchAssistant
c. Consumer
d. 6-3-5 Brainwriting

41. _____ are final goods specifically intended for the mass market. For instance, _____ do not include investment assets, like precious antiques, even though these antiques are final goods.

Manufactured goods are goods that have been processed by way of machinery.

a. Power III
b. Durable good
c. Free good
d. Consumer Goods

42. Core competency is something that a firm can do well and that meets the following three conditions:

1. It provides consumer benefits
2. It is not easy for competitors to imitate
3. It can be leveraged widely to many products and markets.

A core competency can take various forms, including technical/subject matter know how, a reliable process, and/or close relationships with customers and suppliers (Mascarenhas et al. 1998.) It may also include product development or culture, such as employee dedication.

_____ are particular strengths relative to other organizations in the industry which provide the fundamental basis for the provision of added value.

a. Core competencies
b. 6-3-5 Brainwriting
c. Power III
d. 180SearchAssistant

43. _____ is a marketing term, and involves evaluating the situation and trends in a particular company's market. _____ is often called the 'three c's', which refers to the three major elements that must be studied:

- Customers
- Costs
- Competition

The number of 'c's' is sometimes extended to four, five, or even six, with 'Collaboration', 'Company', and 'Competitive advantage'.

- Marketing mix
- SWOT analysis

a. 180SearchAssistant
b. Power III
c. Situation analysis
d. 6-3-5 Brainwriting

44. _____ generally refers to a list of all planned expenses and revenues. It is a plan for saving and spending. A _____ is an important concept in microeconomics, which uses a _____ line to illustrate the trade-offs between two or more goods.
   a. 180SearchAssistant
   b. Power III
   c. Budget
   d. 6-3-5 Brainwriting

Chapter 3. The Marketing Environment, Ethics, and Social Responsibility

1. _____ is a form of intellectual property which gives the creator of an original work exclusive rights for a certain time period in relation to that work, including its publication, distribution and adaptation; after which time the work is said to enter the public domain. _____ applies to any expressible form of an idea or information that is substantive and discrete. Some jurisdictions also recognize 'moral rights' of the creator of a work, such as the right to be credited for the work.
   a. Reasonable person standard
   b. Copyright
   c. Collective mark
   d. Celler-Kefauver Act

2. The _____ is a United States copyright law that implements two 1996 treaties of the World Intellectual Property Organization (WIPO.) It criminalizes production and dissemination of technology, devices whether or not there is actual infringement of copyright itself. In addition, the _____ heightens the penalties for copyright infringement on the Internet.
   a. Copyright infringement
   b. Priority right
   c. Digital Millennium Copyright Act
   d. Regulatory

3. _____ is defined by the American _____ Association as the activity, set of institutions, and processes for creating, communicating, delivering, and exchanging offerings that have value for customers, clients, partners, and society at large. The term developed from the original meaning which referred literally to going to market, as in shopping, or going to a market to sell goods or services.

   _____ practice tends to be seen as a creative industry, which includes advertising, distribution and selling.

   a. Marketing myopia
   b. Customer acquisition management
   c. Product naming
   d. Marketing

4. The _____ is a marketing term and refers to all of the forces outside of marketing that affect marketing management's ability to build and maintain successful relationships with target customers. The _____ consists of both the macroenvironment and the microenvironment.

   The microenvironment refers to the forces that are close to the company and affect its ability to serve its customers.

   a. Psychographic
   b. Business-to-consumer
   c. Customer franchise
   d. Market environment

5. _____ is a term commonly used to describe commerce transactions between businesses like the one between a manufacturer and a wholesaler or a wholesaler and a retailer i.e both the buyer and the seller are business entity. This is unlike business-to-consumers (B2C) which involve a business entity and end consumer, or business-to-government (B2G) which involve a business entity and government.

   The volume of B2B transactions is much higher than the volume of B2C transactions. The primary reason for this is that in a typical supply chain there will be many B2B transactions involving subcomponent or raw materials, and only one B2C transaction, specifically sale of the finished product to the end customer.

   a. Disruptive technology
   b. Social marketing
   c. Customer relationship management
   d. Business-to-business

Chapter 3. The Marketing Environment, Ethics, and Social Responsibility

6. Electronic commerce, commonly known as _____ or eCommerce, consists of the buying and selling of products or services over electronic systems such as the Internet and other computer networks. The amount of trade conducted electronically has grown extraordinarily with wide-spread Internet usage. A wide variety of commerce is conducted in this way, spurring and drawing on innovations in electronic funds transfer, supply chain management, Internet marketing, online transaction processing, electronic data interchange (EDI), inventory management systems, and automated data collection systems.

   a. ACNielsen
   b. AMAX
   c. E-commerce
   d. ADTECH

7. _____ is a process of gathering, analyzing, and dispensing information for tactical or strategic purposes. The _____ process entails obtaining both factual and subjective information on the business environments in which a company is operating or considering entering.

There are three ways of scanning the business environment:

- Ad-hoc scanning - Short term, infrequent examinations usually initiated by a crisis
- Regular scanning - Studies done on a regular schedule (say, once a year)
- Continuous scanning(also called continuous learning) - continuous structured data collection and processing on a broad range of environmental factors

Most commentators feel that in today's turbulent business environment the best scanning method available is continuous scanning.This allows the firm to :

-act quickly-take advantage of opportunities before competitors do-respond to environmental threats before significant damage is done

The Macro Environment

_____ usually refers just to the macro environment, but it can also include:-industry -competitor analysis -marketing research(consumer analysis) -New Product Development(product innovations)- the company's internal environment

Macro _____ involves analysing:

- The Economy

GDP per capitaeconomic growthunemployment]] rateinflation]] rateconsumer and investor confidenceinventory levelscurrency exchange ratesmerchandise trade balancefinancial and political health of trading partnersbalance of paymentsfuture trends

- Government

Chapter 3. The Marketing Environment, Ethics, and Social Responsibility

political climate - amount of government activitypolitical stability and riskgovernment debtbudget deficit or surpluscorporate and personal tax ratespayroll taxesimport tariffs and quotasexport restrictionsrestrictions on international financial flows

- Legal

minimum wage lawsenvironmental protection lawsworker safety lawsunion lawscopyright and patent lawsanti- monopoly lawsSunday closing lawsmunicipal licenceslaws that favour business investment

- Technology

efficiency of infrastructure, including: roads, ports, airports, rolling stock, hospitals, education, healthcare, communication, etc.industrial productivitynew manufacturing processesnew products and services of competitorsnew products and services of supply chain partnersany new technology that could impact the companycost and accessibility of electrical power

- Ecology
    - ecological concerns that affect the firms production processes
    - ecological concerns that affect customers' buying habits
    - ecological concerns that affect customers' perception of the company or product
- Socio-Cultural
    - demographic factors such as:
        - population size and distribution
        - age distribution
        - education levels
        - income levels
        - ethnic origins
        - religious affiliations
    - attitudes towards:
        - materialism, capitalism, free enterprise
        - individualism, role of family, role of government, collectivism
        - role of church and religion
        - consumerism
        - environmentalism
        - importance of work, pride of accomplishment
    - cultural structures including:
        - diet and nutrition
        - housing conditions
- Potential Suppliers
    - Labour supply
        - quantity of labour available
        - quality of labour available
        - stability of labour supply
        - wage expectations
        - employee turn-over rate
        - strikes and labour relations
        - educational facilities
    - Material suppliers
        - quality, quantity, price, and stability of material inputs
        - delivery delays
        - proximity of bulky or heavy material inputs
        - level of competition among suppliers
    - Service Providers
        - quantity, quality, price, and stability of service facilitators
        - special requirements
- Stakeholders
    - Lobbyists
    - Shareholders
    - Employees
    - Partners

Scanning these macro environmental variables for threats and opportunities requires that each issue be rated on two dimensions. It must be rated on its potential impact on the company, and rated on its likeliness of occurrence.

a. ACNielsen
b. Environmental scanning
c. ADTECH
d. AMAX

8. An _____ is the manufacturing of a good or service within a category. Although _____ is a broad term for any kind of economic production, in economics and urban planning _____ is a synonym for the secondary sector, which is a type of economic activity involved in the manufacturing of raw materials into goods and products.

There are four key industrial economic sectors: the primary sector, largely raw material extraction industries such as mining and farming; the secondary sector, involving refining, construction, and manufacturing; the tertiary sector, which deals with services (such as law and medicine) and distribution of manufactured goods; and the quaternary sector, a relatively new type of knowledge _____ focusing on technological research, design and development such as computer programming, and biochemistry.

a. ACNielsen
b. ADTECH
c. AMAX
d. Industry

9. _____ is a marketing term, and involves evaluating the situation and trends in a particular company's market. _____ is often called the 'three c's', which refers to the three major elements that must be studied:

- Customers
- Costs
- Competition

The number of 'c's' is sometimes extended to four, five, or even six, with 'Collaboration', 'Company', and 'Competitive advantage'.

- Marketing mix
- SWOT analysis

a. Power III
b. 6-3-5 Brainwriting
c. 180SearchAssistant
d. Situation analysis

10. The _____ is a 1990 United States Federal law. It was signed into law on November 8, 1990 by the president.

The law gives the Food and Drug Administration (FDA) authority to require nutrition labeling of most foods regulated by the Agency; and to require that all nutrient content claims (for example, 'high fiber', 'low fat', etc).

a. Copyright infringement
b. Trespass to land
c. Fair Debt Collection Practices Act
d. Nutrition Labeling and Education Act

Chapter 3. The Marketing Environment, Ethics, and Social Responsibility

11. A _____ or trade mark, identified by the symbols ™ (not yet registered) and ® (registered) business organization or other legal entity to identify that the products and/or services to consumers with which the _____ appears originate from a unique source of origin, and to distinguish its products or services from those of other entities. A _____ is a type of intellectual property, and typically a name, word, phrase, logo, symbol, design, image, or a combination of these elements. There is also a range of non-conventional _____s comprising marks which do not fall into these standard categories.
   a. Risk management
   b. Power III
   c. 180SearchAssistant
   d. Trademark

12. _____ is a rivalry between individuals, groups, nations for territory, a niche, or allocation of resources. It arises whenever two or more parties strive for a goal which cannot be shared. _____ occurs naturally between living organisms which co-exist in the same environment.
   a. Non-price competition
   b. Price fixing
   c. Competition
   d. Price competition

13. Competitiveness is a comparative concept of the ability and performance of a firm, sub-sector or country to sell and supply goods and/or services in a given market. Although widely used in economics and business management, the usefulness of the concept, particularly in the context of national competitiveness, is vigorously disputed by economists, such as Paul Krugman .

The term may also be applied to markets, where it is used to refer to the extent to which the market structure may be regarded as perfectly _____.

   a. Free trade zone
   b. Customs union
   c. Geographical pricing
   d. Competitive

14. _____ is a process by which government's control over businesses and individuals is reduced or eliminated. It is the removal of some governmental controls over a market. _____ does not mean elimination of laws against fraud, but eliminating or reducing government control of how business is done, thereby moving toward a more free market.
   a. Power III
   b. Consumer spending
   c. Deregulation
   d. Value added

15. The most narrow form of competition is _____, where products which perform the same function compete against each other. For example, one brand of pick-up trucks competes with several other brands of pick-up trucks.
   a. Price competition
   b. Price fixing
   c. Non-price competition
   d. Direct competition

16. _____ is a branch of philosophy which seeks to address questions about morality, such as how a moral outcome can be achieved in a specific situation (applied _____), how moral values should be determined (normative _____), what moral values people actually abide by (descriptive _____), what the fundamental semantic, ontological, and epistemic nature of _____ or morality is (meta-_____), and how moral capacity or moral agency develops and what its nature is (moral psychology.)

Socrates was one of the first Greek philosophers to encourage both scholars and the common citizen to turn their attention from the outside world to the condition of man. In this view, Knowledge having a bearing on human life was placed highest, all other knowledge being secondary.

a. AMAX b. ADTECH
c. ACNielsen d. Ethics

17. An _____ is a market form in which a market or industry is dominated by a small number of sellers (oligopolists.) Because there are few participants in this type of market, each oligopolist is aware of the actions of the others. The decisions of one firm influence, and are influenced by, the decisions of other firms.
a. Oligopoly b. ADTECH
c. AMAX d. ACNielsen

18. A _____ is a plan of action designed to achieve a particular goal.

_____ is different from tactics. In military terms, tactics is concerned with the conduct of an engagement while _____ is concerned with how different engagements are linked.

a. Power III b. Strategy
c. 6-3-5 Brainwriting d. 180SearchAssistant

19. _____ is a broad label that refers to any individuals or households that use goods and services generated within the economy. The concept of a _____ is used in different contexts, so that the usage and significance of the term may vary.

A _____ is a person who uses any product or service.

a. 180SearchAssistant b. Power III
c. 6-3-5 Brainwriting d. Consumer

20. _____ are final goods specifically intended for the mass market. For instance, _____ do not include investment assets, like precious antiques, even though these antiques are final goods.

Manufactured goods are goods that have been processed by way of machinery.

a. Power III b. Durable good
c. Free good d. Consumer Goods

21. _____ is one of the four Ps of the marketing mix. The other three aspects are product, promotion, and place. It is also a key variable in microeconomic price allocation theory.
a. Competitor indexing b. Price
c. Relationship based pricing d. Pricing

22. The _____ of 1936 (or Anti-Price Discrimination Act, 15 U.S.C. § 13) is a United States federal law that prohibits what were considered, at the time of passage, to be anticompetitive practices by producers, specifically price discrimination. It grew out of practices in which chain stores were allowed to purchase goods at lower prices than other retailers.
a. Trademark infringement b. Fair Debt Collection Practices Act
c. Registered trademark symbol d. Robinson-Patman Act

Chapter 3. The Marketing Environment, Ethics, and Social Responsibility

23. _____ refers to 'controlling human or societal behaviour by rules or restrictions.' _____ can take many forms: legal restrictions promulgated by a government authority, self-_____, social _____, co-_____ and market _____. One can consider _____ as actions of conduct imposing sanctions (such as a fine.) This action of administrative law, or implementing regulatory law, may be contrasted with statutory or case law.
   a. Rule of four
   b. Non-conventional trademark
   c. CAN-SPAM
   d. Regulation

24. _____ is the ability of an individual or group to seclude themselves or information about themselves and thereby reveal themselves selectively. The boundaries and content of what is considered private differ among cultures and individuals, but share basic common themes. _____ is sometimes related to anonymity, the wish to remain unnoticed or unidentified in the public realm.
   a. Power III
   b. Privacy
   c. 6-3-5 Brainwriting
   d. 180SearchAssistant

25. The _____ is an independent agency of the United States government, established in 1914 by the _____ Act. Its principal mission is the promotion of 'consumer protection' and the elimination and prevention of what regulators perceive to be harmfully 'anti-competitive' business practices, such as coercive monopoly.

The _____ Act was one of President Wilson's major acts against trusts.

   a. Power III
   b. 6-3-5 Brainwriting
   c. Federal Trade Commission
   d. 180SearchAssistant

26. The _____ of 1914 (15 U.S.C §§ 41-58, as amended) established the Federal Trade Commission (FTC), a bipartisan body of five members appointed by the President of the United States for seven year terms. This Commission was authorized to issue Cease and Desist orders to large corporations to curb unfair trade practices. This Act also gave more flexibility to the US congress for judicial matters.
   a. Gripe site
   b. Comparative negligence
   c. Product liability
   d. Federal Trade Commission Act

27. _____ is a method of direct marketing in which a salesperson solicits to prospective customers to buy products or services, either over the phone or through a subsequent face to face or Web conferencing appointment scheduled during the call.

_____ can also include recorded sales pitches programmed to be played over the phone via automatic dialing. _____ has come under fire in recent years, being viewed as an annoyance by many.

   a. Phishing
   b. Directory Harvest Attack
   c. Telemarketing
   d. Joe job

28. _____ is a fee paid on borrowed assets. It is the price paid for the use of borrowed money, or, money earned by deposited funds. Assets that are sometimes lent with _____ include money, shares, consumer goods through hire purchase, major assets such as aircraft, and even entire factories in finance lease arrangements.
   a. AMAX
   b. ADTECH
   c. ACNielsen
   d. Interest

Chapter 3. The Marketing Environment, Ethics, and Social Responsibility

29. _____ is the practice of individuals including commercial businesses, governments and institutions, facilitating the sale of their products or services to other companies or organizations that in turn resell them, use them as components in products or services they offer _____ is also called business-to-_____ for short. (Note that while marketing to government entities shares some of the same dynamics of organizational marketing, B2G Marketing is meaningfully different.)

a. Mass marketing
b. Business marketing
c. Law of disruption
d. Disruptive technology

30. A _____ is a collection of symbols, experiences and associations connected with a product, a service, a person or any other artifact or entity.

_____s have become increasingly important components of culture and the economy, now being described as 'cultural accessories and personal philosophies'.

Some people distinguish the psychological aspect of a _____ from the experiential aspect.

a. Store brand
b. Brand equity
c. Brandable software
d. Brand

31. The _____ is a database of consumer perception of brands created and managed by BrandAsset Consulting, a division of Young ' Rubicam Brands to provide information to enable firms to improve the marketing decision-making process and to manage brands better. _____ and _____ also describe the Y'R group managing the database.

_____ measures the value of a brand along four dimensions: 'Differentiation,' 'Relevance,' 'Esteem,' and 'Knowledge.' Differentiation and Relevance build up to 'Brand Strength.' Esteem and Knowledge are used to calculate 'Brand Stature.' _____ defines these terms as follows.

a. Targeted advertising
b. Target audience
c. Hoover free flights promotion
d. Brand Asset Valuator

32. A _____, broadcast market, media region, designated market area (DMA), Television Market Area (FCC term) or simply market is a region where the population can receive the same (or similar) television and radio station offerings, and may also include other types of media including newspapers and Internet content. They can coincide with metropolitan areas, though rural regions with few significant population centers can also be designated as markets. Conversely, very large metropolitan areas can sometimes be subdivided into multiple segments.

a. 6-3-5 Brainwriting
b. Power III
c. Media Market
d. 180SearchAssistant

33. The term _____ refers to economy-wide fluctuations in production or economic activity over several months or years. These fluctuations occur around a long-term growth trend, and typically involve shifts over time between periods of relatively rapid economic growth (expansion or boom), and periods of relative stagnation or decline (contraction or recession.)

These fluctuations are often measured using the growth rate of real gross domestic product.

Chapter 3. The Marketing Environment, Ethics, and Social Responsibility

a. Perfect competition
c. Market structure

b. Monopolistic competition
d. Business cycle

34. _____s is the social science that studies the production, distribution, and consumption of goods and services. The term _____s comes from the Ancient Greek οἰκονομῐ́α from οἶκος (oikos, 'house') + νόμος (nomos, 'custom' or 'law'), hence 'rules of the house(hold)'. Current _____ models developed out of the broader field of political economy in the late 19th century, owing to a desire to use an empirical approach more akin to the physical sciences.
   a. Economic
   c. Industrial organization
   b. ACNielsen
   d. ADTECH

35. In economics, the term _____ describes the reduction of a country's gross domestic product (GDP) for at least two quarters. The usual dictionary definition is 'a period of reduced economic activity', a business cycle contraction.

The United States-based National Bureau of Economic Research (NBER) defines economic _____ as: 'a significant decline in [the] economic activity spread across the country, lasting more than a few months, normally visible in real GDP growth, real personal income, employment (non-farm payrolls), industrial production, and wholesale-retail sales.' The NBER's Business Cycle Dating Committee is generally seen as the authority for dating US _____s.

   a. Recession
   c. Macroeconomics
   b. Law of demand
   d. Leading indicator

36. A _____ is a company or individual that purchases goods or services with the intention of reselling them rather than consuming or using them. This is usually done for profit (but could be resold at a loss.) One example can be found in the industry of telecommunications, where companies buy excess amounts of transmission capacity or call time from other carriers and resell it to smaller carriers.
   a. Jobbing house
   c. Value-based pricing
   b. Reseller
   d. Discontinuation

37. _____ is a form of communication that typically attempts to persuade potential customers to purchase or to consume more of a particular brand of product or service. 'While now central to the contemporary global economy and the reproduction of global production networks, it is only quite recently that _____ has been more than a marginal influence on patterns of sales and production. The formation of modern _____ was intimately bound up with the emergence of new forms of monopoly capitalism around the end of the 19th century and beginning of the 20th century as one element in corporate strategies to create, organize and where possible control markets, especially for mass produced consumer goods.
   a. Advertising
   c. AMAX
   b. ADTECH
   d. ACNielsen

38. _____ is a contract between two parties, one being the employer and the other being the employee. An employee may be defined as: 'A person in the service of another under any contract of hire, express or implied, oral or written, where the employer has the power or right to control and direct the employee in the material details of how the work is to be performed.' Black's Law Dictionary page 471 (5th ed. 1979.)
   a. ADTECH
   c. ACNielsen
   b. AMAX
   d. Employment

Chapter 3. The Marketing Environment, Ethics, and Social Responsibility

39. In economics, _____ is a rise in the general level of prices of goods and services in an economy over a period of time. The term '_____' once referred to increases in the money supply (monetary _____); however, economic debates about the relationship between money supply and price levels have led to its primary use today in describing price _____. Inflation can also be described as a decline in the real value of money--a loss of purchasing power in the medium of exchange which is also the monetary unit of account.

a. ADTECH
b. ACNielsen
c. Industrial organization
d. Inflation

40. _____ is income after subtracting taxes and normal expenses (such as rent or mortgage and food) to maintain a certain standard of living. It is the amount of an individual's income available for spending after the essentials (such as food, clothing, and shelter) have been taken care of:

_____ = Gross income - taxes - necessities

Despite the formal definitions above, disposable income is commonly used to denote _____. The meaning should therefore be interpreted from context.

a. Power III
b. Discretionary income
c. 6-3-5 Brainwriting
d. 180SearchAssistant

41. Human beings are also considered to be _____ because they have the ability to change raw materials into valuable _____. The term Human _____ can also be defined as the skills, energies, talents, abilities and knowledge that are used for the production of goods or the rendering of services. While taking into account human beings as _____, the following things have to be kept in mind:

- The size of the population
- The capabilities of the individuals in that population

Many _____ cannot be consumed in their original form. They have to be processed in order to change them into more usable commodities.

a. Resources
b. 6-3-5 Brainwriting
c. Power III
d. 180SearchAssistant

42. _____ is a strategic planning method used to evaluate the Strengths, Weaknesses, Opportunities, and Threats involved in a project or in a business venture. It involves specifying the objective of the business venture or project and identifying the internal and external factors that are favorable and unfavorable to achieving that objective. The technique is credited to Albert Humphrey, who led a research project at Stanford University in the 1960s and 1970s using data from Fortune 500 companies.

a. Market environment
b. Lead scoring
c. Product differentiation
d. SWOT analysis

Chapter 3. The Marketing Environment, Ethics, and Social Responsibility

43. _____ is the study of when, why, how, where and what people do or do not buy products. It blends elements from psychology, sociology, social psychology, anthropology and economics. It attempts to understand the buyer decision making process, both individually and in groups. It studies characteristics of individual consumers such as demographics and behavioural variables in an attempt to understand people's wants. It also tries to assess influences on the consumer from groups such as family, friends, reference groups, and society in general.

a. Communal marketing
b. Consumer behavior
c. Multidimensional scaling
d. Consumer confidence

44. _____ is the equation of personal happiness with consumption and the purchase of material possessions.

The term is often associated with criticisms of consumption starting with Thorstein Veblen.

Veblen's subject of examination, the newly emergent middle class arising at the turn of the twentieth century, comes to full fruition by the end of the twentieth century through the process of globalization.

In economics, _____ refers to economic policies placing emphasis on consumption.

a. 180SearchAssistant
b. 6-3-5 Brainwriting
c. Power III
d. Consumerism

45. _____ is the area of applied ethics which deals with the moral principles behind the operation and regulation of marketing. Some areas of _____ overlap with media ethics.

Possible frameworks:

- Value-oriented framework, analyzing ethical problems on the basis of the values which they infringe (e.g. honesty, autonomy, privacy, transparency.) An example of such an approach is the AMA Statement of Ethics.
- Stakeholder-oriented framework, analysing ethical problems on the basis of whom they affect (e.g. consumers, competitors, society as a whole.)
- Process-oriented framework, analysing ethical problems in terms of the categories used by marketing specialists (e.g. research, price, promotion, placement.)

None of these frameworks allows, by itself, a convenient and complete categorization of the great variety of issues in _____.

Contrary to popular impressions, not all marketing is adversarial, and not all marketing is stacked in favour of the marketer.

a. Power III
b. 180SearchAssistant
c. 6-3-5 Brainwriting
d. Marketing ethics

46. _____ is the use of an object (typically referred to as an RFID tag) applied to or incorporated into a product, animal, or person for the purpose of identification and tracking using radio waves. Some tags can be read from several meters away and beyond the line of sight of the reader.

Most RFID tags contain at least two parts.

a. 180SearchAssistant
b. Power III
c. 6-3-5 Brainwriting
d. Radio-frequency identification

47. _____ often refers to either primary or secondary research. Secondary research involves a company using information compiled from various sources, which is about a new or existing product. The advantages of secondary research are that it is relatively cheap and easily accessible.

a. Mystery shopping
b. Questionnaire
c. Market Research
d. Mystery shoppers

48. _____ is the process of a product becoming obsolete and/or non-functional after a certain period or amount of use in a way that is planned or designed by the manufacturer. _____ has potential benefits for a producer because the product fails and the consumer is under pressure to purchase again, whether from the same manufacturer (a replacement part or a newer model), or from a competitor which might also rely on _____. The purpose of _____ is to hide the real cost per use from the consumer, and charge a higher price than they would otherwise be willing to pay (or would be unwilling to spend all at once.)

a. 180SearchAssistant
b. 6-3-5 Brainwriting
c. Power III
d. Planned obsolescence

49. According to the American Marketing Association, _____ is the marketing of products that are presumed to be environmentally safe. Thus _____ incorporates a broad range of activities, including product modification, changes to the production process, packaging changes, as well as modifying advertising. Yet defining _____ is not a simple task where several meanings intersect and contradict each other; an example of this will be the existence of varying social, environmental and retail definitions attached to this term.

a. Customer Interaction Tracker
b. Value proposition
c. Commercialization
d. Green marketing

Chapter 4. E-Commerce: Marketing in the Digital Age

1. Electronic commerce, commonly known as _____ or eCommerce, consists of the buying and selling of products or services over electronic systems such as the Internet and other computer networks. The amount of trade conducted electronically has grown extraordinarily with wide-spread Internet usage. A wide variety of commerce is conducted in this way, spurring and drawing on innovations in electronic funds transfer, supply chain management, Internet marketing, online transaction processing, electronic data interchange (EDI), inventory management systems, and automated data collection systems.
   a. E-commerce
   b. ADTECH
   c. AMAX
   d. ACNielsen

2. An _____ is the manufacturing of a good or service within a category. Although _____ is a broad term for any kind of economic production, in economics and urban planning _____ is a synonym for the secondary sector, which is a type of economic activity involved in the manufacturing of raw materials into goods and products.

   There are four key industrial economic sectors: the primary sector, largely raw material extraction industries such as mining and farming; the secondary sector, involving refining, construction, and manufacturing; the tertiary sector, which deals with services (such as law and medicine) and distribution of manufactured goods; and the quaternary sector, a relatively new type of knowledge _____ focusing on technological research, design and development such as computer programming, and biochemistry.

   a. ACNielsen
   b. ADTECH
   c. AMAX
   d. Industry

3. _____ is a form of intellectual property which gives the creator of an original work exclusive rights for a certain time period in relation to that work, including its publication, distribution and adaptation; after which time the work is said to enter the public domain. _____ applies to any expressible form of an idea or information that is substantive and discrete. Some jurisdictions also recognize 'moral rights' of the creator of a work, such as the right to be credited for the work.
   a. Collective mark
   b. Reasonable person standard
   c. Celler-Kefauver Act
   d. Copyright

4. The _____ is a United States copyright law that implements two 1996 treaties of the World Intellectual Property Organization (WIPO.) It criminalizes production and dissemination of technology, devices whether or not there is actual infringement of copyright itself. In addition, the _____ heightens the penalties for copyright infringement on the Internet.
   a. Priority right
   b. Copyright infringement
   c. Regulatory
   d. Digital Millennium Copyright Act

5. The _____ is a 1990 United States Federal law. It was signed into law on November 8, 1990 by the president.

   The law gives the Food and Drug Administration (FDA) authority to require nutrition labeling of most foods regulated by the Agency; and to require that all nutrient content claims (for example, 'high fiber', 'low fat', etc).

   a. Fair Debt Collection Practices Act
   b. Nutrition Labeling and Education Act
   c. Copyright infringement
   d. Trespass to land

Chapter 4. E-Commerce: Marketing in the Digital Age

6. _____ refers to the evolving trend in marketing whereby marketing has moved from a transaction-based effort to a conversation. The definition of _____ comes from John Deighton at Harvard, who says _____ is the ability to address the customer, remember what the customer says and address the customer again in a way that illustrates that we remember what the customer has told us (Deighton 1996.) _____ is not synonymous with online marketing, although _____ processes are facilitated by internet technology.
   a. European Information Technology Observatory
   b. InfoNU
   c. Outsourcing relationship management
   d. Interactive marketing

7. _____ is defined by the American _____ Association as the activity, set of institutions, and processes for creating, communicating, delivering, and exchanging offerings that have value for customers, clients, partners, and society at large. The term developed from the original meaning which referred literally to going to market, as in shopping, or going to a market to sell goods or services.

   _____ practice tends to be seen as a creative industry, which includes advertising, distribution and selling.

   a. Product naming
   b. Customer acquisition management
   c. Marketing myopia
   d. Marketing

8. _____ refers to marketing strategies applied directly to a specific consumer.

Having the knowledge on the consumer preferences, there are suggested personalized products and promotions to each consumer.

The _____ is based in four main steps in order to fulfill its goals: Those stages are identify, differentiate, interact, and customize.

   a. AMAX
   b. One-to-one marketing
   c. ACNielsen
   d. ADTECH

9. _____, also referred to as i-marketing, web marketing, online marketing is the marketing of products or services over the Internet.

The Internet has brought many unique benefits to marketing, one of which being lower costs for the distribution of information and media to a global audience. The interactive nature of _____, both in terms of providing instant response and eliciting responses, is a unique quality of the medium.

   a. AMAX
   b. ACNielsen
   c. ADTECH
   d. Internet marketing

10. _____ or personalisation is tailoring a consumer product, electronic or written medium to a user based on personal details or characteristics they provide. More recently, it has especially been applied in the context of the World Wide Web.

Web pages are personalized based on the interests of an individual.

a. Sexism,
c. Flighting

b. Personalization
d. Complex sale

11. In economics, an _____ is any good or commodity, transported from one country to another country in a legitimate fashion, typically for use in trade. _____ goods or services are provided to foreign consumers by domestic producers. _____ is an important part of international trade.
   a. ADTECH
   b. ACNielsen
   c. AMAX
   d. Export

12. The _____ is a very large set of interlinked hypertext documents accessed via the Internet. With a Web browser, one can view Web pages that may contain text, images, videos, and other multimedia and navigate between them using hyperlinks. Using concepts from earlier hypertext systems, the _____ was begun in 1992 by the English physicist Sir Tim Berners-Lee, now the Director of the _____ Consortium, and Robert Cailliau, a Belgian computer scientist, while both were working at CERN in Geneva, Switzerland.
   a. Power III
   b. 180SearchAssistant
   c. World Wide Web
   d. 6-3-5 Brainwriting

13. An _____ is a private network that uses Internet protocols, network connectivity, and possibly the public telecommunication system to securely share part of an organization's information or operations with suppliers, vendors, partners, customers or other businesses. An _____ can be viewed as part of a company's intranet that is extended to users outside the company (e.g.: normally over the Internet.) It has also been described as a 'state of mind' in which the Internet is perceived as a way to do business with a preapproved set of other companies business-to-business (B2B), in isolation from all other Internet users.
   a. Extranet
   b. ADTECH
   c. ACNielsen
   d. AMAX

14. _____ is an advertisement in which a particular product specifically mentions a competitor by name for the express purpose of showing why the competitor is inferior to the product naming it.

This should not be confused with parody advertisements, where a fictional product is being advertised for the purpose of poking fun at the particular advertisement, nor should it be confused with the use of a coined brand name for the purpose of comparing the product without actually naming an actual competitor. ('Wikipedia tastes better and is less filling than the Encyclopedia Galactica.')

In the 1980s, during what has been referred to as the cola wars, soft-drink manufacturer Pepsi ran a series of advertisements where people, caught on hidden camera, in a blind taste test, chose Pepsi over rival Coca-Cola.

   a. Cost per conversion
   b. Heavy-up
   c. Comparative advertising
   d. GL-70

15. A _____ is an entity that provides services to other entities. Usually this refers to a business that provides subscription or web service to other businesses or individuals. Examples of these services include Internet access, Mobile phone operator, and web application hosting.
   a. Service provider
   b. Cross-selling
   c. Freebie marketing
   d. Yield management

Chapter 4. E-Commerce: Marketing in the Digital Age

16. A _____ is a list of the general tasks and responsibilities of a position. Typically, it also includes to whom the position reports, specifications such as the qualifications needed by the person in the job, salary range for the position, etc. A _____ is usually developed by conducting a job analysis, which includes examining the tasks and sequences of tasks necessary to perform the job.

   a. Power III
   c. 6-3-5 Brainwriting
   b. Job description
   d. 180SearchAssistant

17. A _____ is a collection of symbols, experiences and associations connected with a product, a service, a person or any other artifact or entity.

_____s have become increasingly important components of culture and the economy, now being described as 'cultural accessories and personal philosophies'.

Some people distinguish the psychological aspect of a _____ from the experiential aspect.

   a. Brand
   c. Brandable software
   b. Store brand
   d. Brand equity

18. The _____ is a database of consumer perception of brands created and managed by BrandAsset Consulting, a division of Young ' Rubicam Brands to provide information to enable firms to improve the marketing decision-making process and to manage brands better. _____ and _____ also describe the Y'R group managing the database.

_____ measures the value of a brand along four dimensions: 'Differentiation,' 'Relevance,' 'Esteem,' and 'Knowledge.' Differentiation and Relevance build up to 'Brand Strength.' Esteem and Knowledge are used to calculate 'Brand Stature.' _____ defines these terms as follows.

   a. Target audience
   c. Targeted advertising
   b. Hoover free flights promotion
   d. Brand Asset Valuator

19. A _____ is a type of wholesale merchant business that buys goods and bulk products from importers, other wholesalers and then sells to retailers. _____s can deal in any commodity destined for the retail market. Typical categories are food, lumber, hardware, fuel, and textiles.

   a. Chief privacy officer
   c. Tacit collusion
   b. Refusal to deal
   d. Jobbing house

20. The term _____ is primarily used by mass media to describe any form of synchronous conferencing, occasionally even asynchronous conferencing. The term can thus mean any technology ranging from real-time online chat over instant messaging and online forums to fully immersive graphical social environments.

Online chat is a way of communicating by sending text messages to people in the same chat-room in real-time.

   a. Chat room
   c. Power III
   b. 6-3-5 Brainwriting
   d. 180SearchAssistant

Chapter 4. E-Commerce: Marketing in the Digital Age

21. In economics, business, retail, and accounting, a _____ is the value of money that has been used up to produce something, and hence is not available for use anymore. In economics, a _____ is an alternative that is given up as a result of a decision. In business, the _____ may be one of acquisition, in which case the amount of money expended to acquire it is counted as _____.
   a. Cost
   b. Variable cost
   c. Transaction cost
   d. Fixed costs

22. _____ is a term commonly used to describe commerce transactions between businesses like the one between a manufacturer and a wholesaler or a wholesaler and a retailer i.e both the buyer and the seller are business entity.This is unlike business-to-consumers (B2C) which involve a business entity and end consumer, or business-to-government (B2G) which involve a business entity and government.

The volume of B2B transactions is much higher than the volume of B2C transactions. The primary reason for this is that in a typical supply chain there will be many B2B transactions involving subcomponent or raw materials, and only one B2C transaction, specifically sale of the finished product to the end customer.

   a. Disruptive technology
   b. Social marketing
   c. Customer relationship management
   d. Business-to-business

23. _____ describes activities of businesses serving end consumers with products and/or services.

An example of a B2C transaction would be a person buying a pair of shoes from a retailer. The transactions that led to the shoes being available for purchase, that is the purchase of the leather, laces, rubber, etc.

   a. Corporate capabilities package
   b. Demand generation
   c. Societal marketing
   d. Business-to-consumer

24. _____ is the examining of goods or services from retailers with the intent to purchase at that time. _____ is an activity of selection and/or purchase. In some contexts it is considered a leisure activity as well as an economic one.
   a. Shopping
   b. Hawkers
   c. Khodebshchik
   d. Discount store

25. _____ is a broad label that refers to any individuals or households that use goods and services generated within the economy. The concept of a _____ is used in different contexts, so that the usage and significance of the term may vary.

A _____ is a person who uses any product or service.

   a. 6-3-5 Brainwriting
   b. Power III
   c. 180SearchAssistant
   d. Consumer

26. _____ are final goods specifically intended for the mass market. For instance, _____ do not include investment assets, like precious antiques, even though these antiques are final goods.

Manufactured goods are goods that have been processed by way of machinery.

a. Free good
b. Durable good
c. Power III
d. Consumer Goods

27. _____ is one of the four Ps of the marketing mix. The other three aspects are product, promotion, and place. It is also a key variable in microeconomic price allocation theory.
a. Price
b. Relationship based pricing
c. Pricing
d. Competitor indexing

28. _____ refer to a collection of facts usually collected as the result of experience, observation or experiment or a set of premises. This may consist of numbers, words particularly as measurements or observations of a set of variables. _____ are often viewed as a lowest level of abstraction from which information and knowledge are derived.
a. Pearson product-moment correlation coefficient
b. Mean
c. Data
d. Sample size

29. _____ is the ability of an individual or group to seclude themselves or information about themselves and thereby reveal themselves selectively. The boundaries and content of what is considered private differ among cultures and individuals, but share basic common themes. _____ is sometimes related to anonymity, the wish to remain unnoticed or unidentified in the public realm.
a. Privacy
b. Power III
c. 6-3-5 Brainwriting
d. 180SearchAssistant

30. _____ is a term used to describe a process of preparing and collecting data - for example as part of a process improvement or similar project.

_____ usually takes place early on in an improvement project, and is often formalised through a _____ Plan which often contains the following activity.

1. Pre collection activity - Agree goals, target data, definitions, methods
2. Collection - _____
3. Present Findings - usually involves some form of sorting analysis and/or presentation.

A formal _____ process is necessary as it ensures that data gathered is both defined and accurate and that subsequent decisions based on arguments embodied in the findings are valid. The process provides both a baseline from which to measure from and in certain cases a target on what to improve. Types of _____ 1-By mail questionnaires 2-By personal interview

- Six sigma
- Sampling (statistics)

a. 6-3-5 Brainwriting
b. 180SearchAssistant
c. Data collection
d. Power III

31. _____ is computer software that is installed surreptitiously on a personal computer to intercept or take partial control over the user's interaction with the computer, without the user's informed consent.

While the term _____ suggests software that secretly monitors the user's behavior, the functions of _____ extend well beyond simple monitoring. _____ programs can collect various types of personal information, such as Internet surfing habits, sites that have been visited, but can also interfere with user control of the computer in other ways, such as installing additional software, and redirecting Web browser activity.

a. 6-3-5 Brainwriting
b. Power III
c. 180SearchAssistant
d. Spyware

32. A _____ or banner ad is a form of advertising on the World Wide Web. This form of online advertising entails embedding an advertisement into a web page. It is intended to attract traffic to a website by linking to the website of the advertiser.

a. Consumer privacy
b. Spamvertising
c. Disintermediation
d. Web banner

33. _____ is the study of when, why, how, where and what people do or do not buy products. It blends elements from psychology, sociology, social psychology, anthropology and economics. It attempts to understand the buyer decision making process, both individually and in groups. It studies characteristics of individual consumers such as demographics and behavioural variables in an attempt to understand people's wants. It also tries to assess influences on the consumer from groups such as family, friends, reference groups, and society in general.

a. Consumer behavior
b. Communal marketing
c. Consumer confidence
d. Multidimensional scaling

34. _____ are used for a variety of social and professional groups interacting via the Internet. It does not necessarily mean that there is a strong bond among the members, although Howard Rheingold, author of the book of the same name, mentions that _____ form 'when people carry on public discussions long enough, with sufficient human feeling, to form webs of personal relationships'. An email distribution list may have hundreds of members and the communication which takes place may be merely informational (questions and answers are posted), but members may remain relative strangers and the membership turnover rate could be high.

a. Virtual communities
b. 6-3-5 Brainwriting
c. Power III
d. 180SearchAssistant

35. _____ are a form of online advertising on the World Wide Web intended to attract web traffic or capture email addresses. It works when certain web sites open a new web browser window to display advertisements. The pop-up window containing an advertisement is usually generated by JavaScript, but can be generated by other means as well.

a. Project Portfolio Management
b. Pop-up ads
c. Power III
d. Customer intelligence

36. In the Mediterranean Basin and the Near East, a _____ is a small, separated garden pavilion open on some or all sides. _____s were common in Persia, India, Pakistan, and in the Ottoman Empire from the 13th century onward. Today, there are many _____s in and around the Topkapı Palace in Istanbul, and they are still a relatively common sight in Greece.

a. Power III
b. 180SearchAssistant
c. Kiosk
d. 6-3-5 Brainwriting

37. A _____ is a repository usually within the Usenet system, for messages posted from many users in different locations. The term may be confusing to some, because it is usually a discussion group. _____s are technically distinct from, but functionally similar to, discussion forums on the World Wide Web.
   a. Power III
   b. 6-3-5 Brainwriting
   c. 180SearchAssistant
   d. Newsgroup

38. A _____ is a type of website, usually maintained by an individual with regular entries of commentary, descriptions of events, or other material such as graphics or video. Entries are commonly displayed in reverse-chronological order. '_____' can also be used as a verb, meaning to maintain or add content to a _____.
   a. Power III
   b. 6-3-5 Brainwriting
   c. Blog
   d. 180SearchAssistant

39. In marketing a _____ is a ticket or document that can be exchanged for a financial discount or rebate when purchasing a product. Customarily, _____s are issued by manufacturers of consumer packaged goods or by retailers, to be used in retail stores as a part of sales promotions. They are often widely distributed through mail, magazines, newspapers, the Internet, and mobile devices such as cell phones.
   a. Merchandise
   b. Marketing communication
   c. Merchandising
   d. Coupon

40. _____ is a way of measuring the success of an online advertising campaign. A CTR is obtained by dividing the number of users who clicked on an ad on a web page by the number of times the ad was delivered (impressions.) For example, if a banner ad was delivered 100 times (impressions delivered) and one person clicked on it (clicks recorded), then the resulting CTR would be 1 percent.
   a. Web analytics
   b. Display advertising
   c. JICIMS
   d. Click-through rate

Chapter 5. Consumer Behavior

1. A _____ or trade mark, identified by the symbols ā„¢ (not yet registered) and Â® (registered) business organization or other legal entity to identify that the products and/or services to consumers with which the _____ appears originate from a unique source of origin, and to distinguish its products or services from those of other entities. A _____ is a type of intellectual property, and typically a name, word, phrase, logo, symbol, design, image, or a combination of these elements. There is also a range of non-conventional _____s comprising marks which do not fall into these standard categories.
   - a. Power III
   - b. 180SearchAssistant
   - c. Risk management
   - d. Trademark

2. _____ is a broad label that refers to any individuals or households that use goods and services generated within the economy. The concept of a _____ is used in different contexts, so that the usage and significance of the term may vary.

   A _____ is a person who uses any product or service.

   - a. Consumer
   - b. 6-3-5 Brainwriting
   - c. Power III
   - d. 180SearchAssistant

3. _____ is the study of when, why, how, where and what people do or do not buy products. It blends elements from psychology, sociology, social psychology, anthropology and economics. It attempts to understand the buyer decision making process, both individually and in groups. It studies characteristics of individual consumers such as demographics and behavioural variables in an attempt to understand people's wants. It also tries to assess influences on the consumer from groups such as family, friends, reference groups, and society in general.
   - a. Consumer behavior
   - b. Multidimensional scaling
   - c. Consumer confidence
   - d. Communal marketing

4. In algebra, a _____ is a function depending on n that associates a scalar, det(A), to an n×n square matrix A. The fundamental geometric meaning of a _____ is a scale factor for measure when A is regarded as a linear transformation. _____s are important both in calculus, where they enter the substitution rule for several variables, and in multilinear algebra.

   For a fixed nonnegative integer n, there is a unique _____ function for the n×n matrices over any commutative ring R. In particular, this function exists when R is the field of real or complex numbers.

   - a. Motion Picture Association of America's film-rating system
   - b. Package-on-Package
   - c. Black Friday
   - d. Determinant

5. _____ are final goods specifically intended for the mass market. For instance, _____ do not include investment assets, like precious antiques, even though these antiques are final goods.

   Manufactured goods are goods that have been processed by way of machinery.

   - a. Consumer Goods
   - b. Power III
   - c. Free good
   - d. Durable good

Chapter 5. Consumer Behavior

6. _____ refer to a collection of facts usually collected as the result of experience, observation or experiment or a set of premises. This may consist of numbers, words particularly as measurements or observations of a set of variables. _____ are often viewed as a lowest level of abstraction from which information and knowledge are derived.
   a. Sample size
   b. Data
   c. Pearson product-moment correlation coefficient
   d. Mean

7. _____ is one of the four Ps of the marketing mix. The other three aspects are product, promotion, and place. It is also a key variable in microeconomic price allocation theory.
   a. Relationship based pricing
   b. Price
   c. Competitor indexing
   d. Pricing

8. _____ is difficult to define. For example, in 1952, Alfred Kroeber and Clyde Kluckhohn compiled a list of 164 definitions of '_____' in _____: A Critical Review of Concepts and Definitions. However, the word '_____' is most commonly used in three basic senses:

   - excellence of taste in the fine arts and humanities
   - an integrated pattern of human knowledge, belief, and behavior that depends upon the capacity for symbolic thought and social learning
   - the set of shared attitudes, values, goals, and practices that characterizes an institution, organization or group.

   When the concept first emerged in eighteenth- and nineteenth-century Europe, it connoted a process of cultivation or improvement, as in agriculture or horticulture. In the nineteenth century, it came to refer first to the betterment or refinement of the individual, especially through education, and then to the fulfillment of national aspirations or ideals.

   a. Culture
   b. AStore
   c. African Americans
   d. Albert Einstein

9. A personal and cultural _____ is a relative ethic _____, an assumption upon which implementation can be extrapolated. A _____ system is a set of consistent _____s and measures that is soo not true. A principle _____ is a foundation upon which other _____s and measures of integrity are based.
   a. Perceptual maps
   b. Value
   c. Supreme Court of the United States
   d. Package-on-Package

10. In sociology, anthropology and cultural studies, a _____ is a group of people with a culture (whether distinct or hidden) which differentiates them from the larger culture to which they belong. If a particular _____ is characterized by a systematic opposition to the dominant culture, it may be described as a counterculture. As Ken Gelder notes, _____s are social, with their own shared conventions, values and rituals, but they can also seem 'immersed' or self-absorbed--another feature that distinguishes them from countercultures.
    a. 6-3-5 Brainwriting
    b. Subculture
    c. Power III
    d. 180SearchAssistant

11. The _____ of 1936 (or Anti-Price Discrimination Act, 15 U.S.C. § 13) is a United States federal law that prohibits what were considered, at the time of passage, to be anticompetitive practices by producers, specifically price discrimination. It grew out of practices in which chain stores were allowed to purchase goods at lower prices than other retailers.

Chapter 5. Consumer Behavior

a. Registered trademark symbol
b. Fair Debt Collection Practices Act
c. Trademark infringement
d. Robinson-Patman Act

12. A _____ is a sociological concept referring to a group to which an individual or another group is compared.

_____s are used in order to evaluate and determine the nature of a given individual or other group's characteristics and sociological attributes. It is the group to which the individual relates or aspires relate himself or self psychologically.

a. Mociology
b. Power III
c. Reference group
d. Minority

13. _____ is a term commonly used to describe commerce transactions between businesses like the one between a manufacturer and a wholesaler or a wholesaler and a retailer i.e both the buyer and the seller are business entity.This is unlike business-to-consumers (B2C) which involve a business entity and end consumer, or business-to-government (B2G) which involve a business entity and government.

The volume of B2B transactions is much higher than the volume of B2C transactions. The primary reason for this is that in a typical supply chain there will be many B2B transactions involving subcomponent or raw materials, and only one B2C transaction, specifically sale of the finished product to the end customer.

a. Social marketing
b. Customer relationship management
c. Disruptive technology
d. Business-to-business

14. Electronic commerce, commonly known as _____ or eCommerce, consists of the buying and selling of products or services over electronic systems such as the Internet and other computer networks. The amount of trade conducted electronically has grown extraordinarily with wide-spread Internet usage. A wide variety of commerce is conducted in this way, spurring and drawing on innovations in electronic funds transfer, supply chain management, Internet marketing, online transaction processing, electronic data interchange (EDI), inventory management systems, and automated data collection systems.

a. AMAX
b. ADTECH
c. ACNielsen
d. E-commerce

15. _____ is a concept that arose out of the theory of two-step flow of communication propounded by Paul Lazarsfeld and Elihu Katz. This theory is one of several models that try to explain the diffusion of innovations, ideas, or commercial products.

The opinion leader is the agent who is an active media user and who interprets the meaning of media messages or content for lower-end media users.

a. Opinion leadership
b. Elasticity
c. ACNielsen
d. Intellectual property

16. A _____ is a type of wholesale merchant business that buys goods and bulk products from importers, other wholesalers and then sells to retailers. _____s can deal in any commodity destined for the retail market. Typical categories are food, lumber, hardware, fuel, and textiles.

a. Tacit collusion
b. Refusal to deal
c. Chief privacy officer
d. Jobbing house

17. _____ is a strategic planning method used to evaluate the Strengths, Weaknesses, Opportunities, and Threats involved in a project or in a business venture. It involves specifying the objective of the business venture or project and identifying the internal and external factors that are favorable and unfavorable to achieving that objective. The technique is credited to Albert Humphrey, who led a research project at Stanford University in the 1960s and 1970s using data from Fortune 500 companies.

a. Market environment
b. SWOT analysis
c. Product differentiation
d. Lead scoring

18. _____ consists of the sale of goods or merchandise from a fixed location, such as a department store or kiosk in small or individual lots for direct consumption by the purchaser. _____ may include subordinated services, such as delivery. Purchasers may be individuals or businesses.

a. Thrifting
b. Warehouse store
c. Charity shop
d. Retailing

19. Maslow's _____ is a theory in psychology, proposed by Abraham Maslow in his 1943 paper A Theory of Human Motivation, which he subsequently extended to include his observations of humans' innate curiosity.

Maslow studied what he called exemplary people such as Albert Einstein, Jane Addams, Eleanor Roosevelt, and Frederick Douglass rather than mentally ill or neurotic people, writing that 'the study of crippled, stunted, immature, and unhealthy specimens can yield only a cripple psychology and a cripple philosophy.' Maslow also studied the healthiest one percent of the college student population. In his book, The Farther Reaches of Human Nature, Maslow writes, 'By ordinary standards of this kind of laboratory research...

a. Hierarchy of needs
b. Power III
c. 6-3-5 Brainwriting
d. 180SearchAssistant

20. An _____ is the manufacturing of a good or service within a category. Although _____ is a broad term for any kind of economic production, in economics and urban planning _____ is a synonym for the secondary sector, which is a type of economic activity involved in the manufacturing of raw materials into goods and products.

There are four key industrial economic sectors: the primary sector, largely raw material extraction industries such as mining and farming; the secondary sector, involving refining, construction, and manufacturing; the tertiary sector, which deals with services (such as law and medicine) and distribution of manufactured goods; and the quaternary sector, a relatively new type of knowledge _____ focusing on technological research, design and development such as computer programming, and biochemistry.

a. ADTECH
b. AMAX
c. ACNielsen
d. Industry

21. _____ is a term that has been used in various psychology theories, often in slightly different ways (e.g., Goldstein, Maslow, Rogers.) The term was originally introduced by the organismic theorist Kurt Goldstein for the motive to realise all of one's potentialities. In his view, it is the master motive--indeed, the only real motive a person has, all others being merely manifestations of it.

Chapter 5. Consumer Behavior

a. Self-actualization
b. 6-3-5 Brainwriting
c. Power III
d. 180SearchAssistant

22. A _____ is a collection of symbols, experiences and associations connected with a product, a service, a person or any other artifact or entity.

_____s have become increasingly important components of culture and the economy, now being described as 'cultural accessories and personal philosophies'.

Some people distinguish the psychological aspect of a _____ from the experiential aspect.

a. Brand equity
b. Brandable software
c. Store brand
d. Brand

23. The _____ is a database of consumer perception of brands created and managed by BrandAsset Consulting, a division of Young ' Rubicam Brands to provide information to enable firms to improve the marketing decision-making process and to manage brands better. _____ and _____ also describe the Y'R group managing the database.

_____ measures the value of a brand along four dimensions: 'Differentiation,' 'Relevance,' 'Esteem,' and 'Knowledge.' Differentiation and Relevance build up to 'Brand Strength.' Esteem and Knowledge are used to calculate 'Brand Stature.' _____ defines these terms as follows.

a. Hoover free flights promotion
b. Brand Asset Valuator
c. Targeted advertising
d. Target audience

24. In psychology, philosophy, and the cognitive sciences, _____ is the process of attaining awareness or understanding of sensory information. It is a task far more complex than was imagined in the 1950s and 1960s, when it was predicted that building perceiving machines would take about a decade, a goal which is still very far from fruition. The word _____ comes from the Latin words _____, percepio, meaning 'receiving, collecting, action of taking possession, apprehension with the mind or senses.'

_____ is one of the oldest fields in psychology.

a. Power III
b. Perception
c. 180SearchAssistant
d. Groupthink

25. _____ is defined by the American _____ Association as the activity, set of institutions, and processes for creating, communicating, delivering, and exchanging offerings that have value for customers, clients, partners, and society at large. The term developed from the original meaning which referred literally to going to market, as in shopping, or going to a market to sell goods or services.

_____ practice tends to be seen as a creative industry, which includes advertising, distribution and selling.

a. Marketing myopia
b. Product naming
c. Customer acquisition management
d. Marketing

Chapter 5. Consumer Behavior

26. The _____ is a marketing term and refers to all of the forces outside of marketing that affect marketing management's ability to build and maintain successful relationships with target customers. The _____ consists of both the macroenvironment and the microenvironment.

The microenvironment refers to the forces that are close to the company and affect its ability to serve its customers.

    a. Business-to-consumer   b. Psychographic
    c. Customer franchise   d. Market environment

27. In marketing a _____ is a ticket or document that can be exchanged for a financial discount or rebate when purchasing a product. Customarily, _____s are issued by manufacturers of consumer packaged goods or by retailers, to be used in retail stores as a part of sales promotions. They are often widely distributed through mail, magazines, newspapers, the Internet, and mobile devices such as cell phones.

    a. Merchandising   b. Merchandise
    c. Marketing communication   d. Coupon

28. A _____ is a process that can allow an organization to concentrate its limited resources on the greatest opportunities to increase sales and achieve a sustainable competitive advantage. A _____ should be centered around the key concept that customer satisfaction is the main goal.

A _____ is most effective when it is an integral component of corporate strategy, defining how the organization will successfully engage customers, prospects, and competitors in the market arena.

    a. Psychographic   b. Societal marketing
    c. Cyberdoc   d. Marketing strategy

29. In operant conditioning, _____ occurs when an event following a response causes an increase in the probability of that response occurring in the future. Response strength can be assessed by measures such as the frequency with which the response is made (for example, a pigeon may peck a key more times in the session), or the speed with which it is made (for example, a rat may run a maze faster.) The environment change contingent upon the response is called a reinforcer.

    a. Relationship Management Application   b. Generic brands
    c. Completely randomized designs   d. Reinforcement

30. _____ or self identity refers to the global understanding a sentient being has of him or herself. It presupposes but can be distinguished from self-consciousness, which is simply an awareness of one's self. It is also more general than self-esteem, which is the purely evaluative element of the _____.

    a. Self-concept   b. Power III
    c. Need for cognition   d. 180SearchAssistant

31. _____ often refers to either primary or secondary research. Secondary research involves a company using information compiled from various sources, which is about a new or existing product. The advantages of secondary research are that it is relatively cheap and easily accessible.

    a. Mystery shopping   b. Questionnaire
    c. Mystery shoppers   d. Market Research

Chapter 5. Consumer Behavior

32. _____ is a form of intellectual property which gives the creator of an original work exclusive rights for a certain time period in relation to that work, including its publication, distribution and adaptation; after which time the work is said to enter the public domain. _____ applies to any expressible form of an idea or information that is substantive and discrete. Some jurisdictions also recognize 'moral rights' of the creator of a work, such as the right to be credited for the work.
   a. Copyright
   b. Collective mark
   c. Celler-Kefauver Act
   d. Reasonable person standard

33. The _____ is a United States copyright law that implements two 1996 treaties of the World Intellectual Property Organization (WIPO.) It criminalizes production and dissemination of technology, devices whether or not there is actual infringement of copyright itself. In addition, the _____ heightens the penalties for copyright infringement on the Internet.
   a. Priority right
   b. Regulatory
   c. Digital Millennium Copyright Act
   d. Copyright infringement

34. Cognition is the scientific term for 'the process of thought.' Its usage varies in different ways in accord with different disciplines: For example, in psychology and _____ science it refers to an information processing view of an individual's psychological functions. Other interpretations of the meaning of cognition link it to the development of concepts; individual minds, groups, organizations, and even larger coalitions of entities, can be modelled as 'societies' (Society of Mind), which cooperate to form concepts.

The autonomous elements of each 'society' would have the opportunity to demonstrate emergent behavior in the face of some crisis or opportunity.

   a. 180SearchAssistant
   b. Power III
   c. Cognitive
   d. 6-3-5 Brainwriting

35. _____ is an uncomfortable feeling caused by holding two contradictory ideas simultaneously. The 'ideas' or 'cognitions' in question may include attitudes and beliefs, and also the awareness of one's behavior. The theory of _____ proposes that people have a motivational drive to reduce dissonance by changing their attitudes, beliefs, and behaviors, or by justifying or rationalizing their attitudes, beliefs, and behaviors.
   a. Cognitive dissonance
   b. Perception
   c. 180SearchAssistant
   d. Power III

36. In economics, an _____ is any good or commodity, transported from one country to another country in a legitimate fashion, typically for use in trade. _____ goods or services are provided to foreign consumers by domestic producers. _____ is an important part of international trade.
   a. ADTECH
   b. Export
   c. AMAX
   d. ACNielsen

Chapter 6. Business-to-Business (B2B) Marketing

1. A _____ is a collection of symbols, experiences and associations connected with a product, a service, a person or any other artifact or entity.

   _____s have become increasingly important components of culture and the economy, now being described as 'cultural accessories and personal philosophies'.

   Some people distinguish the psychological aspect of a _____ from the experiential aspect.

   a. Brandable software
   b. Store brand
   c. Brand equity
   d. Brand

2. The _____ is a database of consumer perception of brands created and managed by BrandAsset Consulting, a division of Young ' Rubicam Brands to provide information to enable firms to improve the marketing decision-making process and to manage brands better. _____ and _____ also describe the Y'R group managing the database.

   _____ measures the value of a brand along four dimensions: 'Differentiation,' 'Relevance,' 'Esteem,' and 'Knowledge.' Differentiation and Relevance build up to 'Brand Strength.' Esteem and Knowledge are used to calculate 'Brand Stature.' _____ defines these terms as follows.

   a. Target audience
   b. Brand Asset Valuator
   c. Hoover free flights promotion
   d. Targeted advertising

3. _____ is a term commonly used to describe commerce transactions between businesses like the one between a manufacturer and a wholesaler or a wholesaler and a retailer i.e both the buyer and the seller are business entity.This is unlike business-to-consumers (B2C) which involve a business entity and end consumer, or business-to-government (B2G) which involve a business entity and government.

   The volume of B2B transactions is much higher than the volume of B2C transactions. The primary reason for this is that in a typical supply chain there will be many B2B transactions involving subcomponent or raw materials, and only one B2C transaction, specifically sale of the finished product to the end customer.

   a. Disruptive technology
   b. Customer relationship management
   c. Social marketing
   d. Business-to-business

4. _____ is defined by the American _____ Association as the activity, set of institutions, and processes for creating, communicating, delivering, and exchanging offerings that have value for customers, clients, partners, and society at large. The term developed from the original meaning which referred literally to going to market, as in shopping, or going to a market to sell goods or services.

   _____ practice tends to be seen as a creative industry, which includes advertising, distribution and selling.

   a. Marketing myopia
   b. Product naming
   c. Customer acquisition management
   d. Marketing

5. _____ describes activities of businesses serving end consumers with products and/or services.

Chapter 6. Business-to-Business (B2B) Marketing   51

An example of a B2C transaction would be a person buying a pair of shoes from a retailer. The transactions that led to the shoes being available for purchase, that is the purchase of the leather, laces, rubber, etc.

a. Demand generation
c. Societal marketing
b. Corporate capabilities package
d. Business-to-consumer

6. Electronic commerce, commonly known as _____ or eCommerce, consists of the buying and selling of products or services over electronic systems such as the Internet and other computer networks. The amount of trade conducted electronically has grown extraordinarily with wide-spread Internet usage. A wide variety of commerce is conducted in this way, spurring and drawing on innovations in electronic funds transfer, supply chain management, Internet marketing, online transaction processing, electronic data interchange (EDI), inventory management systems, and automated data collection systems.

a. ACNielsen
c. AMAX
b. E-commerce
d. ADTECH

7. A _____ is a company or individual that purchases goods or services with the intention of reselling them rather than consuming or using them. This is usually done for profit (but could be resold at a loss.) One example can be found in the industry of telecommunications, where companies buy excess amounts of transmission capacity or call time from other carriers and resell it to smaller carriers.

a. Discontinuation
c. Jobbing house
b. Reseller
d. Value-based pricing

8. _____ refer to a collection of facts usually collected as the result of experience, observation or experiment or a set of premises. This may consist of numbers, words particularly as measurements or observations of a set of variables. _____ are often viewed as a lowest level of abstraction from which information and knowledge are derived.

a. Sample size
c. Data
b. Pearson product-moment correlation coefficient
d. Mean

9. _____, also referred to as i-marketing, web marketing, online marketing is the marketing of products or services over the Internet.

The Internet has brought many unique benefits to marketing, one of which being lower costs for the distribution of information and media to a global audience. The interactive nature of _____, both in terms of providing instant response and eliciting responses, is a unique quality of the medium.

a. Internet marketing
c. ACNielsen
b. AMAX
d. ADTECH

10. A _____ is a subgroup of people or organizations sharing one or more characteristics that cause them to have similar product and/or service needs. A true _____ meets all of the following criteria: it is distinct from other segments (different segments have different needs), it is homogeneous within the segment (exhibits common needs); it responds similarly to a market stimulus, and it can be reached by a market intervention. The term is also used when consumers with identical product and/or service needs are divided up into groups so they can be charged different amounts.

a. Market segment
b. Production orientation
c. Commercial planning
d. Customer insight

11. A _____ is a list of the general tasks and responsibilities of a position. Typically, it also includes to whom the position reports, specifications such as the qualifications needed by the person in the job, salary range for the position, etc. A _____ is usually developed by conducting a job analysis, which includes examining the tasks and sequences of tasks necessary to perform the job.
    a. Job description
    b. 180SearchAssistant
    c. Power III
    d. 6-3-5 Brainwriting

12. A _____ is a process that can allow an organization to concentrate its limited resources on the greatest opportunities to increase sales and achieve a sustainable competitive advantage. A _____ should be centered around the key concept that customer satisfaction is the main goal.

    A _____ is most effective when it is an integral component of corporate strategy, defining how the organization will successfully engage customers, prospects, and competitors in the market arena.

    a. Marketing strategy
    b. Psychographic
    c. Cyberdoc
    d. Societal marketing

13. _____ refers to a business or organization attempting to acquire goods or services to accomplish the goals of the enterprise. Though there are several organizations that attempt to set standards in the _____ process, processes can vary greatly between organizations. Typically the word '_____' is not used interchangeably with the word 'procurement', since procurement typically includes Expediting, Supplier Quality, and Traffic and Logistics (T'L) in addition to _____.
    a. Supply network
    b. Drop shipping
    c. Supply chain
    d. Purchasing

14. A _____ is a type of wholesale merchant business that buys goods and bulk products from importers, other wholesalers and then sells to retailers. _____s can deal in any commodity destined for the retail market. Typical categories are food, lumber, hardware, fuel, and textiles.
    a. Jobbing house
    b. Chief privacy officer
    c. Tacit collusion
    d. Refusal to deal

15. _____ is a broad label that refers to any individuals or households that use goods and services generated within the economy. The concept of a _____ is used in different contexts, so that the usage and significance of the term may vary.

    A _____ is a person who uses any product or service.

    a. Power III
    b. 180SearchAssistant
    c. 6-3-5 Brainwriting
    d. Consumer

16. _____ is the study of the Earth and its lands, features, inhabitants, and phenomena. A literal translation would be 'to describe or write about the Earth'. The first person to use the word '_____' was Eratosthenes .

Chapter 6. Business-to-Business (B2B) Marketing

a. 6-3-5 Brainwriting
c. Geography
b. Power III
d. 180SearchAssistant

17. In economics, _____ is the desire to own something and the ability to pay for it. The term _____ signifies the ability or the willingness to buy a particular commodity at a given point of time .

a. Discretionary spending
b. Market system
c. Market dominance
d. Demand

18. _____ is a term in economics, where demand for one good or service occurs as a result of demand for another. This may occur as the former is a part of production of the second. For example, demand for coal leads to _____ for mining, as coal must be mined for coal to be consumed.

a. Derived demand
b. Power III
c. 180SearchAssistant
d. 6-3-5 Brainwriting

19. _____ is a term used to describe practice of sourcing from the global market for goods and services across geopolitical boundaries. _____ often aims to exploit global efficiencies in the delivery of a product or service. These efficiencies include low cost skilled labor, low cost raw material and other economic factors like tax breaks and low trade tariffs.

a. 6-3-5 Brainwriting
b. Global sourcing
c. Power III
d. 180SearchAssistant

20. An _____ is the manufacturing of a good or service within a category. Although _____ is a broad term for any kind of economic production, in economics and urban planning _____ is a synonym for the secondary sector, which is a type of economic activity involved in the manufacturing of raw materials into goods and products.

There are four key industrial economic sectors: the primary sector, largely raw material extraction industries such as mining and farming; the secondary sector, involving refining, construction, and manufacturing; the tertiary sector, which deals with services (such as law and medicine) and distribution of manufactured goods; and the quaternary sector, a relatively new type of knowledge _____ focusing on technological research, design and development such as computer programming, and biochemistry.

a. AMAX
b. ACNielsen
c. ADTECH
d. Industry

21. In economics, _____ describes demand that is not very sensitive to a change in price.
a. AMAX
b. ACNielsen
c. Inelastic
d. ADTECH

22. _____ is a list for goods and materials held available in stock by a business. It is also used for a list of the contents of a household and for a list for testamentary purposes of the possessions of someone who has died. In accounting _____ is considered an asset.
a. Ending Inventory
b. Inventory
c. ACNielsen
d. ADTECH

Chapter 6. Business-to-Business (B2B) Marketing

23. _____ is subcontracting a process, such as product design or manufacturing, to a third-party company. The decision to outsource is often made in the interest of lowering cost or making better use of time and energy costs, redirecting or conserving energy directed at the competencies of a particular business, or to make more efficient use of land, labor, capital, (information) technology and resources. _____ became part of the business lexicon during the 1980s.
  a. ACNielsen
  b. Outsourcing
  c. Intangible assets
  d. In-house

24. _____ is an advertisement in which a particular product specifically mentions a competitor by name for the express purpose of showing why the competitor is inferior to the product naming it.

This should not be confused with parody advertisements, where a fictional product is being advertised for the purpose of poking fun at the particular advertisement, nor should it be confused with the use of a coined brand name for the purpose of comparing the product without actually naming an actual competitor. ('Wikipedia tastes better and is less filling than the Encyclopedia Galactica.')

In the 1980s, during what has been referred to as the cola wars, soft-drink manufacturer Pepsi ran a series of advertisements where people, caught on hidden camera, in a blind taste test, chose Pepsi over rival Coca-Cola.

  a. Comparative advertising
  b. Cost per conversion
  c. Heavy-up
  d. GL-70

25. A _____ is an entity that provides services to other entities. Usually this refers to a business that provides subscription or web service to other businesses or individuals. Examples of these services include Internet access, Mobile phone operator, and web application hosting.
  a. Freebie marketing
  b. Yield management
  c. Cross-selling
  d. Service provider

26. The _____ is a 1990 United States Federal law. It was signed into law on November 8, 1990 by the president.

The law gives the Food and Drug Administration (FDA) authority to require nutrition labeling of most foods regulated by the Agency; and to require that all nutrient content claims (for example, 'high fiber', 'low fat', etc).

  a. Fair Debt Collection Practices Act
  b. Copyright infringement
  c. Nutrition Labeling and Education Act
  d. Trespass to land

27. _____ is a strategic planning method used to evaluate the Strengths, Weaknesses, Opportunities, and Threats involved in a project or in a business venture. It involves specifying the objective of the business venture or project and identifying the internal and external factors that are favorable and unfavorable to achieving that objective. The technique is credited to Albert Humphrey, who led a research project at Stanford University in the 1960s and 1970s using data from Fortune 500 companies.
  a. SWOT analysis
  b. Product differentiation
  c. Lead scoring
  d. Market environment

Chapter 6. Business-to-Business (B2B) Marketing

28. A _____, in marketing, procurement, and organizational studies, is a group of employees, family members, or members of any type of organization responsible for purchasing an item for the organization. In a business setting, major purchases typically require input from various parts of the organization, including finance, accounting, purchasing, information technology management, and senior management. Highly technical purchases, such as information systems or production equipment, also require the expertise of technical specialists.
   - a. Buying center
   - b. Commercialization
   - c. Marketing myopia
   - d. Packshot

29. A personal and cultural _____ is a relative ethic _____, an assumption upon which implementation can be extrapolated. A _____ system is a set of consistent _____s and measures that is soo not true. A principle _____ is a foundation upon which other _____s and measures of integrity are based.
   - a. Package-on-Package
   - b. Perceptual maps
   - c. Supreme Court of the United States
   - d. Value

30.

_____ is a systematic method to improve the 'value' of goods or products and services by using an examination of function. Value, as defined, is the ratio of function to cost. Value can therefore be increased by either improving the function or reducing the cost.

   - a. Productivity
   - b. 180SearchAssistant
   - c. Value engineering
   - d. Power III

31. _____ refers to 'controlling human or societal behaviour by rules or restrictions.' _____ can take many forms: legal restrictions promulgated by a government authority, self-_____, social _____, co-_____ and market _____. One can consider _____ as actions of conduct imposing sanctions (such as a fine.) This action of administrative law, or implementing regulatory law, may be contrasted with statutory or case law.
   - a. Non-conventional trademark
   - b. Rule of four
   - c. Regulation
   - d. CAN-SPAM

32. The _____ is a marketing term and refers to all of the forces outside of marketing that affect marketing management's ability to build and maintain successful relationships with target customers. The _____ consists of both the macroenvironment and the microenvironment.

The microenvironment refers to the forces that are close to the company and affect its ability to serve its customers.

   - a. Customer franchise
   - b. Business-to-consumer
   - c. Psychographic
   - d. Market environment

Chapter 7. Serving Global Markets

1. The Oxford University Press defines _____ as 'marketing on a worldwide scale reconciling or taking commercial advantage of global operational differences, similarities and opportunities in order to meet global objectives.' Oxford University Press' Glossary of Marketing Terms.

Here are three reasons for the shift from domestic to _____ as given by the authors of the textbook, _____ Management--3rd Edition by Masaaki Kotabe and Kristiaan Helsen, 2004.

One of the product categories in which global competition has been easy to track is in U.S. automotive sales.

   a. Diversity marketing
   c. Digital marketing
   b. Guerrilla Marketing
   d. Global marketing

2. _____ is defined by the American _____ Association as the activity, set of institutions, and processes for creating, communicating, delivering, and exchanging offerings that have value for customers, clients, partners, and society at large. The term developed from the original meaning which referred literally to going to market, as in shopping, or going to a market to sell goods or services.

_____ practice tends to be seen as a creative industry, which includes advertising, distribution and selling.

   a. Customer acquisition management
   c. Product naming
   b. Marketing myopia
   d. Marketing

3. A _____ is a process that can allow an organization to concentrate its limited resources on the greatest opportunities to increase sales and achieve a sustainable competitive advantage. A _____ should be centered around the key concept that customer satisfaction is the main goal.

A _____ is most effective when it is an integral component of corporate strategy, defining how the organization will successfully engage customers, prospects, and competitors in the market arena.

   a. Psychographic
   c. Marketing strategy
   b. Societal marketing
   d. Cyberdoc

4. A _____ is a plan of action designed to achieve a particular goal.

_____ is different from tactics. In military terms, tactics is concerned with the conduct of an engagement while _____ is concerned with how different engagements are linked.

   a. Power III
   c. 6-3-5 Brainwriting
   b. 180SearchAssistant
   d. Strategy

5. _____ often refers to either primary or secondary research. Secondary research involves a company using information compiled from various sources, which is about a new or existing product. The advantages of secondary research are that it is relatively cheap and easily accessible.

   a. Mystery shoppers
   c. Mystery shopping
   b. Questionnaire
   d. Market Research

Chapter 7. Serving Global Markets

6. _____ is exchange of capital, goods, and services across international borders or territories. In most countries, it represents a significant share of gross domestic product (GDP.) While _____ has been present throughout much of history , its economic, social, and political importance has been on the rise in recent centuries.
    a. ACNielsen
    b. Incoterms
    c. International trade
    d. ADTECH

7. In economics, an _____ is any good or commodity, transported from one country to another country in a legitimate fashion, typically for use in trade. _____ goods or services are provided to foreign consumers by domestic producers. _____ is an important part of international trade.
    a. ADTECH
    b. AMAX
    c. ACNielsen
    d. Export

8. _____ consists of the sale of goods or merchandise from a fixed location, such as a department store or kiosk in small or individual lots for direct consumption by the purchaser. _____ may include subordinated services, such as delivery. Purchasers may be individuals or businesses.
    a. Retailing
    b. Charity shop
    c. Thrifting
    d. Warehouse store

9. _____ is an advertisement in which a particular product specifically mentions a competitor by name for the express purpose of showing why the competitor is inferior to the product naming it.

This should not be confused with parody advertisements, where a fictional product is being advertised for the purpose of poking fun at the particular advertisement, nor should it be confused with the use of a coined brand name for the purpose of comparing the product without actually naming an actual competitor. ('Wikipedia tastes better and is less filling than the Encyclopedia Galactica.')

In the 1980s, during what has been referred to as the cola wars, soft-drink manufacturer Pepsi ran a series of advertisements where people, caught on hidden camera, in a blind taste test, chose Pepsi over rival Coca-Cola.

   a. Cost per conversion
   b. GL-70
   c. Heavy-up
   d. Comparative advertising

10. A _____ or trade mark, identified by the symbols â„¢ (not yet registered) and Â® (registered) business organization or other legal entity to identify that the products and/or services to consumers with which the _____ appears originate from a unique source of origin, and to distinguish its products or services from those of other entities. A _____ is a type of intellectual property, and typically a name, word, phrase, logo, symbol, design, image, or a combination of these elements. There is also a range of non-conventional _____s comprising marks which do not fall into these standard categories.
    a. Power III
    b. 180SearchAssistant
    c. Trademark
    d. Risk management

11. _____ is a trademark law concept permitting the owner of a famous trademark to forbid others from using that mark in a way that would lessen its uniqueness. In most cases, _____ involves an unauthorized use of another's trademark on products that do not compete with, and have little connection with, those of the trademark owner. For example, a famous trademark used by one company to refer to hair care products might be diluted if another company began using a similar mark to refer to breakfast cereals or spark plugs.

a. Trademark attorney
b. Trespass to land
c. Federal Bureau of Investigation
d. Trademark Dilution

12. An _____ is the manufacturing of a good or service within a category. Although _____ is a broad term for any kind of economic production, in economics and urban planning _____ is a synonym for the secondary sector, which is a type of economic activity involved in the manufacturing of raw materials into goods and products.

There are four key industrial economic sectors: the primary sector, largely raw material extraction industries such as mining and farming; the secondary sector, involving refining, construction, and manufacturing; the tertiary sector, which deals with services (such as law and medicine) and distribution of manufactured goods; and the quaternary sector, a relatively new type of knowledge _____ focusing on technological research, design and development such as computer programming, and biochemistry.

a. Industry
b. ACNielsen
c. AMAX
d. ADTECH

13. A _____ is the space, actual or metaphorical, in which a market operates. The term is also used in a trademark law context to denote the actual consumer environment, ie. the 'real world' in which products and services are provided and consumed.

a. 180SearchAssistant
b. Marketplace
c. 6-3-5 Brainwriting
d. Power III

14. A _____ is a collection of symbols, experiences and associations connected with a product, a service, a person or any other artifact or entity.

_____s have become increasingly important components of culture and the economy, now being described as 'cultural accessories and personal philosophies'.

Some people distinguish the psychological aspect of a _____ from the experiential aspect.

a. Brand
b. Store brand
c. Brand equity
d. Brandable software

15. The _____ is a database of consumer perception of brands created and managed by BrandAsset Consulting, a division of Young ' Rubicam Brands to provide information to enable firms to improve the marketing decision-making process and to manage brands better. _____ and _____ also describe the Y'R group managing the database.

_____ measures the value of a brand along four dimensions: 'Differentiation,' 'Relevance,' 'Esteem,' and 'Knowledge.' Differentiation and Relevance build up to 'Brand Strength.' Esteem and Knowledge are used to calculate 'Brand Stature.' _____ defines these terms as follows.

a. Targeted advertising
b. Target audience
c. Hoover free flights promotion
d. Brand Asset Valuator

Chapter 7. Serving Global Markets

16. The _____ is a marketing term and refers to all of the forces outside of marketing that affect marketing management's ability to build and maintain successful relationships with target customers. The _____ consists of both the macroenvironment and the microenvironment.

The microenvironment refers to the forces that are close to the company and affect its ability to serve its customers.

a. Customer franchise
b. Psychographic
c. Market environment
d. Business-to-consumer

17. _____ or _____ data refers to selected population characteristics as used in government, marketing or opinion research, or the _____ profiles used in such research. Note the distinction from the term 'demography' Commonly-used _____ include race, age, income, disabilities, mobility (in terms of travel time to work or number of vehicles available), educational attainment, home ownership, employment status, and even location.

a. Albert Einstein
b. AStore
c. African Americans
d. Demographic

18. In finance, the _____s between two currencies specifies how much one currency is worth in terms of the other. It is the value of a foreign nation's currency in terms of the home nation's currency. For example an _____ of 102 Japanese yen to the United States dollar means that JPY 102 is worth the same as USD 1.

a. Exchange rate
b. AMAX
c. ACNielsen
d. ADTECH

19. _____s is the social science that studies the production, distribution, and consumption of goods and services. The term _____s comes from the Ancient Greek οἰκονομία from οἶκος (oikos, 'house') + νόμος (nomos, 'custom' or 'law'), hence 'rules of the house(hold)'. Current _____ models developed out of the broader field of political economy in the late 19th century, owing to a desire to use an empirical approach more akin to the physical sciences.

a. ADTECH
b. ACNielsen
c. Industrial organization
d. Economic

20. _____ is a strategic planning method used to evaluate the Strengths, Weaknesses, Opportunities, and Threats involved in a project or in a business venture. It involves specifying the objective of the business venture or project and identifying the internal and external factors that are favorable and unfavorable to achieving that objective. The technique is credited to Albert Humphrey, who led a research project at Stanford University in the 1960s and 1970s using data from Fortune 500 companies.

a. Lead scoring
b. Market environment
c. Product differentiation
d. SWOT analysis

21. _____ is a type of risk faced by investors, corporations, and governments. It is a risk that can be understood and managed with proper aforethought and investment.

Broadly, _____ refers to the complications businesses and governments may face as a result of what are commonly referred to as political decisions--or 'any political change that alters the expected outcome and value of a given economic action by changing the probability of achieving business objectives.' .

a. Political risk
c. 6-3-5 Brainwriting
b. Power III
d. 180SearchAssistant

22. _____ is a concept that denotes the precise probability of specific eventualities. Technically, the notion of _____ is independent from the notion of value and, as such, eventualities may have both beneficial and adverse consequences. However, in general usage the convention is to focus only on potential negative impact to some characteristic of value that may arise from a future event.
   a. Risk
   c. Power III
   b. 6-3-5 Brainwriting
   d. 180SearchAssistant

23. The _____ of 1977 (15 U.S.C. §§ 78dd-1, et seq.) is a United States federal law known primarily for two of its main provisions, one that addresses accounting transparency requirements under the Securities Exchange Act of 1934 and another concerning bribery of foreign officials.
   a. Tenth Amendment
   c. Copyright
   b. Trademark dilution
   d. Foreign Corrupt Practices Act

24. _____ refers to the confirmation of certain characteristics of an object, person, or organization. This confirmation is often, but not always, provided by some form of external review, education, or assessment. One of the most common types of _____ in modern society is professional _____, where a person is certified as being able to competently complete a job or task, usually by the passing of an examination.
   a. 6-3-5 Brainwriting
   c. 180SearchAssistant
   b. Power III
   d. Certification

25. A _____ is a tax imposed on goods when they are moved across a political boundary. They are usually associated with protectionism, the economic policy of restraining trade between nations. For political reasons, _____s are usually imposed on imported goods, although they may also be imposed on exported goods.
   a. Tariff
   c. Fiscal policy
   b. Monetary policy
   d. Power III

26. In economics, '_____' can refer to any kind of predatory pricing. However, the word is now generally used only in the context of international trade law, where _____ is defined as the act of a manufacturer in one country exporting a product to another country at a price which is either below the price it charges in its home market or is below its costs of production. The term has a negative connotation, but advocates of free markets see '_____' as beneficial for consumers and believe that protectionism to prevent it would have net negative consequences.
   a. Dumping
   c. Hawkers
   b. Sample sales
   d. Gold Key Matching Service

27. _____ is a term used to describe how different aspects between economies are integrated. The basics of this theory were written by the Hungarian Economist Béla Balassa in the 1960s. As _____ increases, the barriers of trade between markets diminishes.
   a. Economic integration
   c. ACNielsen
   b. Incoterms
   d. ADTECH

28. _____ is a designated group of countries that have agreed to eliminate tariffs, quotas and preferences on most (if not all) goods and services traded between them. It can be considered the second stage of economic integration. Countries choose this kind of economic integration form if their economical structures are complementary.

Chapter 7. Serving Global Markets

a. 6-3-5 Brainwriting
b. Free trade area
c. Power III
d. 180SearchAssistant

29. The _____ is an international organization designed to supervise and liberalize international trade. The _____ came into being on 1 January 1995, and is the successor to the General Agreement on Tariffs and Trade (GATT), which was created in 1947, and continued to operate for almost five decades as a de facto international organization.

The _____ deals with the rules of trade between nations at a near-global level; it is responsible for negotiating and implementing new trade agreements, and is in charge of policing member countries' adherence to all the _____ agreements, signed by the majority of the world's trading nations and ratified in their parliaments.

a. World Trade Organization
b. BSI Group
c. Merchandise Mart
d. Population Reference Bureau

30. _____ is a term commonly used to describe commerce transactions between businesses like the one between a manufacturer and a wholesaler or a wholesaler and a retailer i.e both the buyer and the seller are business entity.This is unlike business-to-consumers (B2C) which involve a business entity and end consumer, or business-to-government (B2G) which involve a business entity and government.

The volume of B2B transactions is much higher than the volume of B2C transactions. The primary reason for this is that in a typical supply chain there will be many B2B transactions involving subcomponent or raw materials, and only one B2C transaction, specifically sale of the finished product to the end customer.

a. Customer relationship management
b. Social marketing
c. Disruptive technology
d. Business-to-business

31. A _____ is a customs union with common policies on product regulation, and freedom of movement of the factors of production (capital and labour) and of enterprise. The goal is that the movement of capital, labour, goods, and services between the members is as easy as within them. This is the fourth stage of economic integration.

a. Customs union
b. Common market
c. Competitive
d. Monetary union

32. _____ is an authority or agency in a country responsible for collecting and safeguarding _____ duties and for controlling the flow of goods including animals, personal effects and hazardous items in and out of a country. Depending on local legislation and regulations, the import or export of some goods may be restricted or forbidden, and the _____ agency enforces these rules. The _____ agency may be different from the immigration authority, which monitors persons who leave or enter the country, checking for appropriate documentation, apprehending people wanted by international arrest warrants, and impeding the entry of others deemed dangerous to the country.

a. Madrid system for the international registration of marks
b. Specific Performance
c. Registered trademark symbol
d. Customs

33. A _____ is a free trade area with a common external tariff. The participant countries set up common external trade policy, but in some cases they use different import quotas. Common competition policy is also helpful to avoid competition deficiency.

a. Safeguard
b. Countervailing duties
c. Zone pricing
d. Customs union

34. Electronic commerce, commonly known as _____ or eCommerce, consists of the buying and selling of products or services over electronic systems such as the Internet and other computer networks. The amount of trade conducted electronically has grown extraordinarily with wide-spread Internet usage. A wide variety of commerce is conducted in this way, spurring and drawing on innovations in electronic funds transfer, supply chain management, Internet marketing, online transaction processing, electronic data interchange (EDI), inventory management systems, and automated data collection systems.
   a. AMAX
   b. E-commerce
   c. ACNielsen
   d. ADTECH

35. _____ is subcontracting a process, such as product design or manufacturing, to a third-party company. The decision to outsource is often made in the interest of lowering cost or making better use of time and energy costs, redirecting or conserving energy directed at the competencies of a particular business, or to make more efficient use of land, labor, capital, (information) technology and resources. _____ became part of the business lexicon during the 1980s.
   a. ACNielsen
   b. Intangible assets
   c. In-house
   d. Outsourcing

36. _____ in its literal sense is the process of transformation of local or regional phenomena into global ones. It can be described as a process by which the people of the world are unified into a single society and function together.

This process is a combination of economic, technological, sociocultural and political forces.

   a. 6-3-5 Brainwriting
   b. 180SearchAssistant
   c. Globalization
   d. Power III

37. A _____ is a subgroup of people or organizations sharing one or more characteristics that cause them to have similar product and/or service needs. A true _____ meets all of the following criteria: it is distinct from other segments (different segments have different needs), it is homogeneous within the segment (exhibits common needs); it responds similarly to a market stimulus, and it can be reached by a market intervention. The term is also used when consumers with identical product and/or service needs are divided up into groups so they can be charged different amounts.
   a. Production orientation
   b. Commercial planning
   c. Customer insight
   d. Market segment

38. _____ is a broad label that refers to any individuals or households that use goods and services generated within the economy. The concept of a _____ is used in different contexts, so that the usage and significance of the term may vary.

A _____ is a person who uses any product or service.

   a. Power III
   b. 180SearchAssistant
   c. 6-3-5 Brainwriting
   d. Consumer

39. _____ are final goods specifically intended for the mass market. For instance, _____ do not include investment assets, like precious antiques, even though these antiques are final goods.

Chapter 7. Serving Global Markets

Manufactured goods are goods that have been processed by way of machinery.

a. Consumer Goods
b. Durable good
c. Power III
d. Free good

40. _____ is one of the four Ps of the marketing mix. The other three aspects are product, promotion, and place. It is also a key variable in microeconomic price allocation theory.
a. Relationship based pricing
b. Price
c. Competitor indexing
d. Pricing

41. The most important feature of a contract is that one party makes an _____ for an arrangement that another accepts. This can be called a 'concurrence of wills' or 'ad idem' (meeting of the minds) of two or more parties. The concept is somewhat contested.
a. ACNielsen
b. ADTECH
c. AMAX
d. Offer

42. The verb _____ or grant _____ means to give permission. The noun _____ refers to that permission as well as to the document memorializing that permission. _____ may be granted by a party to another party as an element of an agreement between those parties.
a. 180SearchAssistant
b. Power III
c. 6-3-5 Brainwriting
d. License

43. Foreign _____ in its classic form is defined as a company from one country making a physical investment into building a factory in another country. It is the establishment of an enterprise by a foreigner. Its definition can be extended to include investments made to acquire lasting interest in enterprises operating outside of the economy of the investor.
a. Fountain Fresh International
b. Direct investment
c. VideoJug
d. Brash Brands

44. A _____ or transnational corporation is a corporation or enterprise that manages production or delivers services in more than one country. It can also be referred to as an international corporation.

The first modern MNC is generally thought to be the British East India Company, established in 1600.

a. Checkoff
b. HD share
c. Hechsher
d. Multinational corporation

45. _____ is a form of intellectual property which gives the creator of an original work exclusive rights for a certain time period in relation to that work, including its publication, distribution and adaptation; after which time the work is said to enter the public domain. _____ applies to any expressible form of an idea or information that is substantive and discrete. Some jurisdictions also recognize 'moral rights' of the creator of a work, such as the right to be credited for the work.
a. Reasonable person standard
b. Celler-Kefauver Act
c. Copyright
d. Collective mark

46. The _____ is a United States copyright law that implements two 1996 treaties of the World Intellectual Property Organization (WIPO.) It criminalizes production and dissemination of technology, devices whether or not there is actual infringement of copyright itself. In addition, the _____ heightens the penalties for copyright infringement on the Internet.
- a. Regulatory
- b. Copyright infringement
- c. Priority right
- d. Digital Millennium Copyright Act

47. _____ is exchanging goods or services that are paid for, in whole or part, with other goods or services.

There are five main variants of _____:

- Barter: Exchange of goods or services directly for other goods or services without the use of money as means of purchase or payment.
- Switch trading: Practice in which one company sells to another its obligation to make a purchase in a given country.
- Counter purchase: Sale of goods and services to a country by a company that promises to make a future purchase of a specific product from the country.
- Buyback: occurs when a firm builds a plant in a country - or supplies technology, equipment, training, or other services to the country and agrees to take a certain percentage of the plant's output as partial payment for the contract.
- Offset: Agreement that a company will offset a hard - currency purchase of an unspecified product from that nation in the future. Agreement by one nation to buy a product from another, subject to the purchase of some or all of the components and raw materials from the buyer of the finished product, or the assembly of such product in the buyer nation.

- a. Countertrade
- b. RFM
- c. Merchant
- d. Retail loss prevention

Chapter 8. Marketing Research, Decision Support Systems, and Sales Forecasting

1. _____ is defined by the American _____ Association as the activity, set of institutions, and processes for creating, communicating, delivering, and exchanging offerings that have value for customers, clients, partners, and society at large. The term developed from the original meaning which referred literally to going to market, as in shopping, or going to a market to sell goods or services.

_____ practice tends to be seen as a creative industry, which includes advertising, distribution and selling.

   a. Product naming
   b. Marketing myopia
   c. Customer acquisition management
   d. Marketing

2. Consumer market research is a form of applied sociology that concentrates on understanding the behaviours, whims and preferences, of consumers in a market-based economy, and aims to understand the effects and comparative success of marketing campaigns. The field of consumer _____ as a statistical science was pioneered by Arthur Nielsen with the founding of the ACNielsen Company in 1923.

Thus _____ is the systematic and objective identification, collection, analysis, and dissemination of information for the purpose of assisting management in decision making related to the identification and solution of problems and opportunities in marketing.

   a. Marketing research process
   b. Focus group
   c. Logit analysis
   d. Marketing research

3. _____ is a strategic planning method used to evaluate the Strengths, Weaknesses, Opportunities, and Threats involved in a project or in a business venture. It involves specifying the objective of the business venture or project and identifying the internal and external factors that are favorable and unfavorable to achieving that objective. The technique is credited to Albert Humphrey, who led a research project at Stanford University in the 1960s and 1970s using data from Fortune 500 companies.
   a. SWOT analysis
   b. Market environment
   c. Lead scoring
   d. Product differentiation

4. _____ constitute a class of computer-based information systems including knowledge-based systems that support decision-making activities.

_____ are a specific class of computerized information system that supports business and organizational decision-making activities. A properly-designed _____ is an interactive software-based system intended to help decision makers compile useful information from raw data, documents, personal knowledge, and/or business models to identify and solve problems and make decisions.

   a. Power III
   b. 6-3-5 Brainwriting
   c. 180SearchAssistant
   d. Decision support systems

5. _____ is an information system that helps with decision-making in the formation of a marketing plan. The reason for using an MKDSS is because it helps to support the software vendors' planning strategy for marketing products; it can help to identify advantageous levels of pricing, advertising spending, and advertising copy for the firm's products (Arinze, 1990.) This helps determines the firms marketing mix for product software.

Chapter 8. Marketing Research, Decision Support Systems, and Sales Forecasting

a. 6-3-5 Brainwriting
b. Power III
c. 180SearchAssistant
d. Marketing decision support systems

6. _____ is an advertisement in which a particular product specifically mentions a competitor by name for the express purpose of showing why the competitor is inferior to the product naming it.

This should not be confused with parody advertisements, where a fictional product is being advertised for the purpose of poking fun at the particular advertisement, nor should it be confused with the use of a coined brand name for the purpose of comparing the product without actually naming an actual competitor. ('Wikipedia tastes better and is less filling than the Encyclopedia Galactica.')

In the 1980s, during what has been referred to as the cola wars, soft-drink manufacturer Pepsi ran a series of advertisements where people, caught on hidden camera, in a blind taste test, chose Pepsi over rival Coca-Cola.

a. Cost per conversion
b. Comparative advertising
c. Heavy-up
d. GL-70

7. A supply chain is the system of organizations, people, technology, activities, information and resources involved in moving a product or service from _____ to customer. Supply chain activities transform natural resources, raw materials and components into a finished product that is delivered to the end customer. In sophisticated supply chain systems, used products may re-enter the supply chain at any point where residual value is recyclable.
a. Supplier
b. Product line extension
c. Rebate
d. Bringin' Home the Oil

8. _____, a business term, is a measure of how products and services supplied by a company meet or surpass customer expectation. It is seen as a key performance indicator within business and is part of the four perspectives of a Balanced Scorecard.

In a competitive marketplace where businesses compete for customers, _____ is seen as a key differentiator and increasingly has become a key element of business strategy.

a. Supplier diversity
b. Psychological pricing
c. Customer satisfaction
d. Customer base

9. _____ often refers to either primary or secondary research. Secondary research involves a company using information compiled from various sources, which is about a new or existing product. The advantages of secondary research are that it is relatively cheap and easily accessible.
a. Market Research
b. Questionnaire
c. Mystery shopping
d. Mystery shoppers

10. _____ is a type of research conducted because a problem has not been clearly defined. _____ helps determine the best research design, data collection method and selection of subjects. Given its fundamental nature, _____ often concludes that a perceived problem does not actually exist.
a. ACNielsen
b. Intent scale translation
c. Exploratory research
d. IDDEA

Chapter 8. Marketing Research, Decision Support Systems, and Sales Forecasting

11. _____ is a term commonly used to describe commerce transactions between businesses like the one between a manufacturer and a wholesaler or a wholesaler and a retailer i.e both the buyer and the seller are business entity.This is unlike business-to-consumers (B2C) which involve a business entity and end consumer, or business-to-government (B2G) which involve a business entity and government.

The volume of B2B transactions is much higher than the volume of B2C transactions. The primary reason for this is that in a typical supply chain there will be many B2B transactions involving subcomponent or raw materials, and only one B2C transaction, specifically sale of the finished product to the end customer.

a. Social marketing
c. Disruptive technology
b. Customer relationship management
d. Business-to-business

12. In economics, business, retail, and accounting, a _____ is the value of money that has been used up to produce something, and hence is not available for use anymore. In economics, a _____ is an alternative that is given up as a result of a decision. In business, the _____ may be one of acquisition, in which case the amount of money expended to acquire it is counted as _____.

a. Cost
c. Variable cost
b. Transaction cost
d. Fixed costs

13. _____ refer to a collection of facts usually collected as the result of experience, observation or experiment or a set of premises. This may consist of numbers, words particularly as measurements or observations of a set of variables. _____ are often viewed as a lowest level of abstraction from which information and knowledge are derived.

a. Data
c. Pearson product-moment correlation coefficient
b. Sample size
d. Mean

14. _____ is a term used to describe a process of preparing and collecting data - for example as part of a process improvement or similar project.

_____ usually takes place early on in an improvement project, and is often formalised through a _____ Plan which often contains the following activity.

1. Pre collection activity - Agree goals, target data, definitions, methods
2. Collection - _____
3. Present Findings - usually involves some form of sorting analysis and/or presentation.

A formal _____ process is necessary as it ensures that data gathered is both defined and accurate and that subsequent decisions based on arguments embodied in the findings are valid . The process provides both a baseline from which to measure from and in certain cases a target on what to improve. Types of _____ 1-By mail questionnaires 2-By personal interview

- Six sigma
- Sampling (statistics)

Chapter 8. Marketing Research, Decision Support Systems, and Sales Forecasting

a. Power III
b. 6-3-5 Brainwriting
c. 180SearchAssistant
d. Data collection

15. A _____ is the price one pays as remuneration for services, especially the honorarium paid to a doctor, lawyer, consultant, or other member of a learned profession. _____s usually allow for overhead, wages, costs, and markup.

Traditionally, professionals in Great Britain received a _____ in contradistinction to a payment, salary, or wage, and would often use guineas rather than pounds as units of account.

a. Price shading
b. Fee
c. Transfer pricing
d. Price war

16. _____ is a term for unprocessed data, it is also known as primary data. It is a relative term _____ can be input to a computer program or used in manual analysis procedures such as gathering statistics from a survey.

a. Chief marketing officer
b. Shoppers Food ' Pharmacy
c. Product manager
d. Raw data

17. A number of different _____s are indicated below.

- Randomized controlled trial
    - Double-blind randomized trial
    - Single-blind randomized trial
    - Non-blind trial
- Nonrandomized trial (quasi-experiment)
    - Interrupted time series design (measures on a sample or a series of samples from the same population are obtained several times before and after a manipulated event or a naturally occurring event) - considered a type of quasi-experiment
- Cohort study
    - Prospective cohort
    - Retrospective cohort
    - Time series study
- Case-control study
    - Nested case-control study
- Cross-sectional study
    - Community survey (a type of cross-sectional study)

When choosing a _____, many factors must be taken into account. Different types of studies are subject to different types of bias. For example, recall bias is likely to occur in cross-sectional or case-control studies where subjects are asked to recall exposure to risk factors.

a. Study design
b. 180SearchAssistant
c. Longitudinal studies
d. Power III

18. Combining Existing _____ Sources with New Primary Data Sources

Chapter 8. Marketing Research, Decision Support Systems, and Sales Forecasting

Imagine that we could get hold of a good collection of surveys taken in earlier years, such as detailed studies about changes going on in this phase and hopefully additional studies in the years to come. Analyzing this data base over time could give us a good picture of what changes actually have taken place in the orientation of the population and of the extent to which new technical concepts did have an impact on subgroups of the population. Furthermore, data archives can help to prepare studies on change over time by monitoring what questions have been asked in earlier years and alerting principal investigators to important questions which should be repeated in planned research projects.

a. Power III
c. 180SearchAssistant
b. 6-3-5 Brainwriting
d. Secondary data

19. A _____, broadcast market, media region, designated market area (DMA), Television Market Area (FCC term) or simply market is a region where the population can receive the same (or similar) television and radio station offerings, and may also include other types of media including newspapers and Internet content. They can coincide with metropolitan areas, though rural regions with few significant population centers can also be designated as markets. Conversely, very large metropolitan areas can sometimes be subdivided into multiple segments.

a. Power III
c. 180SearchAssistant
b. 6-3-5 Brainwriting
d. Media Market

20. A _____ is an optical machine-readable representation of data. Originally, _____s represented data in the widths (lines) and the spacings of parallel lines and may be referred to as linear or 1D (1 dimensional) barcodes or symbologies. But they also come in patterns of squares, dots, hexagons and other geometric patterns within images termed 2D (2 dimensional) matrix codes or symbologies.

a. 6-3-5 Brainwriting
c. Power III
b. 180SearchAssistant
d. Bar code

21. _____ is that part of statistical practice concerned with the selection of individual observations intended to yield some knowledge about a population of concern, especially for the purposes of statistical inference. Each observation measures one or more properties (weight, location, etc.) of an observable entity enumerated to distinguish objects or individuals.

a. Sampling
c. AStore
b. Richard Buckminster 'Bucky' Fuller
d. Sports Marketing Group

22. _____ is a broad label that refers to any individuals or households that use goods and services generated within the economy. The concept of a _____ is used in different contexts, so that the usage and significance of the term may vary.

A _____ is a person who uses any product or service.

a. 180SearchAssistant
c. Power III
b. 6-3-5 Brainwriting
d. Consumer

23. _____ are final goods specifically intended for the mass market. For instance, _____ do not include investment assets, like precious antiques, even though these antiques are final goods.

Chapter 8. Marketing Research, Decision Support Systems, and Sales Forecasting

Manufactured goods are goods that have been processed by way of machinery.

a. Free good
c. Power III
b. Durable good
d. Consumer Goods

24. _____ is one of the four Ps of the marketing mix. The other three aspects are product, promotion, and place. It is also a key variable in microeconomic price allocation theory.
   a. Price
   c. Pricing
   b. Relationship based pricing
   d. Competitor indexing

25. _____ is a form of communication that typically attempts to persuade potential customers to purchase or to consume more of a particular brand of product or service. 'While now central to the contemporary global economy and the reproduction of global production networks, it is only quite recently that _____ has been more than a marginal influence on patterns of sales and production. The formation of modern _____ was intimately bound up with the emergence of new forms of monopoly capitalism around the end of the 19th and beginning of the 20th century as one element in corporate strategies to create, organize and where possible control markets, especially for mass produced consumer goods.
   a. ACNielsen
   c. ADTECH
   b. AMAX
   d. Advertising

26. _____ is anything that is intended to save time, energy or frustration. A _____ store at a petrol station, for example, sells items that have nothing to do with gasoline/petrol, but it saves the consumer from having to go to a grocery store. '_____' is a very relative term and its meaning tends to change over time.
   a. MaxDiff
   c. Demographic profile
   b. Marketing buzz
   d. Convenience

27. _____ is a way of expressing knowledge or belief that an event will occur or has occurred. In mathematics the concept has been given an exact meaning in _____ theory, that is used extensively in such areas of study as mathematics, statistics, finance, gambling, science, and philosophy to draw conclusions about the likelihood of potential events and the underlying mechanics of complex systems.
   a. Linear regression
   c. Data
   b. Heteroskedastic
   d. Probability

28. A sample is a subject chosen from a population for investigation. A _____ is one chosen by a method involving an unpredictable component. Random sampling can also refer to taking a number of independent observations from the same probability distribution, without involving any real population.
   a. 180SearchAssistant
   c. Selection bias
   b. Power III
   d. Random sample

29. The _____ is a 1990 United States Federal law. It was signed into law on November 8, 1990 by the president.

The law gives the Food and Drug Administration (FDA) authority to require nutrition labeling of most foods regulated by the Agency; and to require that all nutrient content claims (for example, 'high fiber', 'low fat', etc).

Chapter 8. Marketing Research, Decision Support Systems, and Sales Forecasting 71

a. Trespass to land
b. Copyright infringement
c. Nutrition Labeling and Education Act
d. Fair Debt Collection Practices Act

30. _____ is a method of direct marketing in which a salesperson solicits to prospective customers to buy products or services, either over the phone or through a subsequent face to face or Web conferencing appointment scheduled during the call.

_____ can also include recorded sales pitches programmed to be played over the phone via automatic dialing. _____ has come under fire in recent years, being viewed as an annoyance by many.

a. Telemarketing
b. Directory Harvest Attack
c. Phishing
d. Joe job

31. A _____ is a tool used to measure the viewing habits of TV and cable audiences.

The _____ is a 'box', about the size of a paperback book. The box is hooked up to each television set and is accompanied by a remote control unit.

a. Power III
b. People meter
c. 6-3-5 Brainwriting
d. 180SearchAssistant

32. A _____ is an entity that provides services to other entities. Usually this refers to a business that provides subscription or web service to other businesses or individuals. Examples of these services include Internet access, Mobile phone operator, and web application hosting.
a. Service provider
b. Cross-selling
c. Freebie marketing
d. Yield management

33. A _____ is a form of qualitative research in which a group of people are asked about their attitude towards a product, service, concept, advertisement, idea, or packaging. Questions are asked in an interactive group setting where participants are free to talk with other group members.

Ernest Dichter originated the idea of having a 'group therapy' for products and this process is what became known as a _____.

a. Marketing research process
b. Cross tabulation
c. Focus group
d. Logit analysis

34. Electronic commerce, commonly known as _____ or eCommerce, consists of the buying and selling of products or services over electronic systems such as the Internet and other computer networks. The amount of trade conducted electronically has grown extraordinarily with wide-spread Internet usage. A wide variety of commerce is conducted in this way, spurring and drawing on innovations in electronic funds transfer, supply chain management, Internet marketing, online transaction processing, electronic data interchange (EDI), inventory management systems, and automated data collection systems.
a. ADTECH
b. AMAX
c. ACNielsen
d. E-commerce

Chapter 8. Marketing Research, Decision Support Systems, and Sales Forecasting

35. _____ are used to collect quantitative information about items in a population. Surveys of human populations and institutions are common in political polling and government, health, social science and marketing research. A survey may focus on opinions or factual information depending on its purpose, and many surveys involve administering questions to individuals.

   a. Statistical surveys
   b. BeyondROI
   c. Gross Margin Return on Inventory Investment
   d. Convergent

36. _____s is the social science that studies the production, distribution, and consumption of goods and services. The term _____s comes from the Ancient Greek οἰκονομῖα from οἶκος (oikos, 'house') + νόμος (nomos, 'custom' or 'law'), hence 'rules of the house(hold)'. Current _____ models developed out of the broader field of political economy in the late 19th century, owing to a desire to use an empirical approach more akin to the physical sciences.

   a. ADTECH
   b. Industrial organization
   c. Economic
   d. ACNielsen

37. _____ is the process of extracting hidden patterns from data. As more data is gathered, with the amount of data doubling every three years, _____ is becoming an increasingly important tool to transform this data into information. It is commonly used in a wide range of profiling practices, such as marketing, surveillance, fraud detection and scientific discovery.

   a. Data mining
   b. Structure mining
   c. 180SearchAssistant
   d. Power III

38. A _____ is a collection of symbols, experiences and associations connected with a product, a service, a person or any other artifact or entity.

_____s have become increasingly important components of culture and the economy, now being described as 'cultural accessories and personal philosophies'.

Some people distinguish the psychological aspect of a _____ from the experiential aspect.

   a. Brandable software
   b. Brand
   c. Store brand
   d. Brand equity

39. The _____ is a database of consumer perception of brands created and managed by BrandAsset Consulting, a division of Young ' Rubicam Brands to provide information to enable firms to improve the marketing decision-making process and to manage brands better. _____ and _____ also describe the Y'R group managing the database.

_____ measures the value of a brand along four dimensions: 'Differentiation,' 'Relevance,' 'Esteem,' and 'Knowledge.' Differentiation and Relevance build up to 'Brand Strength.' Esteem and Knowledge are used to calculate 'Brand Stature.' _____ defines these terms as follows.

   a. Hoover free flights promotion
   b. Target audience
   c. Targeted advertising
   d. Brand Asset Valuator

Chapter 8. Marketing Research, Decision Support Systems, and Sales Forecasting

40. A _____ or trade mark, identified by the symbols ™ (not yet registered) and ® (registered) business organization or other legal entity to identify that the products and/or services to consumers with which the _____ appears originate from a unique source of origin, and to distinguish its products or services from those of other entities. A _____ is a type of intellectual property, and typically a name, word, phrase, logo, symbol, design, image, or a combination of these elements. There is also a range of non-conventional _____s comprising marks which do not fall into these standard categories.
   a. Trademark
   b. 180SearchAssistant
   c. Risk management
   d. Power III

41. Competitiveness is a comparative concept of the ability and performance of a firm, sub-sector or country to sell and supply goods and/or services in a given market. Although widely used in economics and business management, the usefulness of the concept, particularly in the context of national competitiveness, is vigorously disputed by economists, such as Paul Krugman .

    The term may also be applied to markets, where it is used to refer to the extent to which the market structure may be regarded as perfectly _____.

   a. Free trade zone
   b. Competitive
   c. Geographical pricing
   d. Customs union

42. _____ is the process of estimation in unknown situations. Prediction is a similar, but more general term. Both can refer to estimation of time series, cross-sectional or longitudinal data.
   a. 180SearchAssistant
   b. 6-3-5 Brainwriting
   c. Power III
   d. Forecasting

43. A _____ attribute is one that exists in a range of magnitudes, and can therefore be measured. Measurements of any particular _____ property are expressed as a specific quantity, referred to as a unit, multiplied by a number. Examples of physical quantities are distance, mass, and time.
   a. BeyondROI
   b. Lifestyle city
   c. Dolly Dimples
   d. Quantitative

44. In statistics, _____ is a technique that can be applied to time series data, either to produce smoothed data for presentation, or to make forecasts. The time series data themselves are a sequence of observations. The observed phenomenon may be an essentially random process, or it may be an orderly, but noisy, process.
   a. ACNielsen
   b. AMAX
   c. ADTECH
   d. Exponential smoothing

45. In statistics and image processing, to smooth a data set is to create an approximating function that attempts to capture important patterns in the data, while leaving out noise or other fine-scale structures/rapid phenomena. Many different algorithms are used in _____. One of the most common algorithms is the 'moving average', often used to try to capture important trends in repeated statistical surveys.
   a. Power III
   b. 180SearchAssistant
   c. 6-3-5 Brainwriting
   d. Smoothing

Chapter 8. Marketing Research, Decision Support Systems, and Sales Forecasting

46. A _____, in the field of business and marketing, is a geographic region or demographic group used to gauge the viability of a product or service in the mass market prior to a wide scale roll-out. The criteria used to judge the acceptability of a _____ region or group include:

1. a population that is demographically similar to the proposed target market; and
2. relative isolation from densely populated media markets so that advertising to the test audience can be efficient and economical.

The _____ ideally aims to duplicate 'everything' - promotion and distribution as well as `product' - on a smaller scale. The technique replicates, typically in one area, what is planned to occur in a national launch; and the results are very carefully monitored, so that they can be extrapolated to projected national results. The `area' may be any one of the following:

- Television area
- Test town
- Residential neighborhood
- Test site

A number of decisions have to be taken about any _____:

- Which _____?
- What is to be tested?
- How long a test?
- What are the success criteria?

The simple go or no-go decision, together with the related reduction of risk, is normally the main justification for the expense of _____s. At the same time, however, such _____s can be used to test specific elements of a new product's marketing mix; possibly the version of the product itself, the promotional message and media spend, the distribution channels and the price.

a. 180SearchAssistant
b. Power III
c. Preadolescence
d. Test market

Chapter 9. Market Segmentation, Targeting, and Positioning

1. A _____ is a subgroup of people or organizations sharing one or more characteristics that cause them to have similar product and/or service needs. A true _____ meets all of the following criteria: it is distinct from other segments (different segments have different needs), it is homogeneous within the segment (exhibits common needs); it responds similarly to a market stimulus, and it can be reached by a market intervention. The term is also used when consumers with identical product and/or service needs are divided up into groups so they can be charged different amounts.

    a. Commercial planning
    b. Customer insight
    c. Production orientation
    d. Market segment

2. A _____ is a collection of symbols, experiences and associations connected with a product, a service, a person or any other artifact or entity.

    _____s have become increasingly important components of culture and the economy, now being described as 'cultural accessories and personal philosophies'.

    Some people distinguish the psychological aspect of a _____ from the experiential aspect.

    a. Brand equity
    b. Brand
    c. Store brand
    d. Brandable software

3. The _____ is a database of consumer perception of brands created and managed by BrandAsset Consulting, a division of Young ' Rubicam Brands to provide information to enable firms to improve the marketing decision-making process and to manage brands better. _____ and _____ also describe the Y'R group managing the database.

    _____ measures the value of a brand along four dimensions: 'Differentiation,' 'Relevance,' 'Esteem,' and 'Knowledge.' Differentiation and Relevance build up to 'Brand Strength.' Esteem and Knowledge are used to calculate 'Brand Stature.' _____ defines these terms as follows.

    a. Hoover free flights promotion
    b. Target audience
    c. Targeted advertising
    d. Brand Asset Valuator

4. _____ is a broad label that refers to any individuals or households that use goods and services generated within the economy. The concept of a _____ is used in different contexts, so that the usage and significance of the term may vary.

    A _____ is a person who uses any product or service.

    a. 180SearchAssistant
    b. Power III
    c. 6-3-5 Brainwriting
    d. Consumer

5. _____ are final goods specifically intended for the mass market. For instance, _____ do not include investment assets, like precious antiques, even though these antiques are final goods.

    Manufactured goods are goods that have been processed by way of machinery.

    a. Power III
    b. Durable good
    c. Consumer Goods
    d. Free good

Chapter 9. Market Segmentation, Targeting, and Positioning

6. _____ is one of the four Ps of the marketing mix. The other three aspects are product, promotion, and place. It is also a key variable in microeconomic price allocation theory.
   a. Competitor indexing
   b. Price
   c. Pricing
   d. Relationship based pricing

7. _____ is a strategic planning method used to evaluate the Strengths, Weaknesses, Opportunities, and Threats involved in a project or in a business venture. It involves specifying the objective of the business venture or project and identifying the internal and external factors that are favorable and unfavorable to achieving that objective. The technique is credited to Albert Humphrey, who led a research project at Stanford University in the 1960s and 1970s using data from Fortune 500 companies.
   a. SWOT analysis
   b. Product differentiation
   c. Market environment
   d. Lead scoring

8. _____ is defined by the American _____ Association as the activity, set of institutions, and processes for creating, communicating, delivering, and exchanging offerings that have value for customers, clients, partners, and society at large. The term developed from the original meaning which referred literally to going to market, as in shopping, or going to a market to sell goods or services.

   _____ practice tends to be seen as a creative industry, which includes advertising, distribution and selling.

   a. Marketing myopia
   b. Marketing
   c. Product naming
   d. Customer acquisition management

9. A _____ is a written document that details the necessary actions to achieve one or more marketing objectives. It can be for a product or service, a brand, or a product line. _____s cover between one and five years.
   a. Marketing plan
   b. Marketing strategy
   c. Disruptive technology
   d. Prosumer

10. _____ is a business term meaning the market segment to which a particular good or service is marketed. It is mainly defined by age, gender, geography, socio-economic grouping, technographic, or any other combination of demographics. It is generally studied and mapped by an organization through lists and reports containing demographic information that may have an effect on the marketing of key products or services.
    a. Distribution
    b. Category Development Index
    c. Brando
    d. Market specialization

11. _____ is the study of when, why, how, where and what people do or do not buy products. It blends elements from psychology, sociology, social psychology, anthropology and economics. It attempts to understand the buyer decision making process, both individually and in groups. It studies characteristics of individual consumers such as demographics and behavioural variables in an attempt to understand people's wants. It also tries to assess influences on the consumer from groups such as family, friends, reference groups, and society in general.
    a. Consumer behavior
    b. Communal marketing
    c. Consumer confidence
    d. Multidimensional scaling

12. An _____ is the manufacturing of a good or service within a category. Although _____ is a broad term for any kind of economic production, in economics and urban planning _____ is a synonym for the secondary sector, which is a type of economic activity involved in the manufacturing of raw materials into goods and products.

Chapter 9. Market Segmentation, Targeting, and Positioning 77

There are four key industrial economic sectors: the primary sector, largely raw material extraction industries such as mining and farming; the secondary sector, involving refining, construction, and manufacturing; the tertiary sector, which deals with services (such as law and medicine) and distribution of manufactured goods; and the quaternary sector, a relatively new type of knowledge _____ focusing on technological research, design and development such as computer programming, and biochemistry.

a. ACNielsen
b. ADTECH
c. Industry
d. AMAX

13. _____ is the study of the Earth and its lands, features, inhabitants, and phenomena. A literal translation would be 'to describe or write about the Earth'. The first person to use the word '_____' was Eratosthenes .

a. 180SearchAssistant
b. Power III
c. Geography
d. 6-3-5 Brainwriting

14. A _____ or trade mark, identified by the symbols â"¢ (not yet registered) and Â® (registered) business organization or other legal entity to identify that the products and/or services to consumers with which the _____ appears originate from a unique source of origin, and to distinguish its products or services from those of other entities. A _____ is a type of intellectual property, and typically a name, word, phrase, logo, symbol, design, image, or a combination of these elements. There is also a range of non-conventional _____s comprising marks which do not fall into these standard categories.

a. Trademark
b. 180SearchAssistant
c. Risk management
d. Power III

15. In the United States, the Office of Management and Budget (OMB) has produced a formal definition of metropolitan areas. These are referred to as '_____s' (_____s) and 'Combined Statistical Areas.' An earlier version of the _____ was the 'Standard _____' (SMetropolitan statistical area.) _____s are composed of counties and for some county equivalents.

a. Power III
b. 180SearchAssistant
c. Race and ethnicity in the United States Census
d. Metropolitan statistical area

16. United States _____ , as defined by the Census Bureau and the Office of Management and Budget, are urban areas in the United States based around a core city or town with a population of 10,000 to 49,999. The micropolitan area designation was created in 2003. Like the better-known metropolitan area, a micropolitan area is a geographic entity used for statistical purposes based on counties and county-equivalents .

a. Micropolitan statistical areas
b. 6-3-5 Brainwriting
c. 180SearchAssistant
d. Power III

17. _____ or _____ data refers to selected population characteristics as used in government, marketing or opinion research, or the _____ profiles used in such research. Note the distinction from the term 'demography' Commonly-used _____ include race, age, income, disabilities, mobility (in terms of travel time to work or number of vehicles available), educational attainment, home ownership, employment status, and even location.

a. AStore
b. African Americans
c. Albert Einstein
d. Demographic

18. A _____ captures, stores, analyzes, manages, and presents data that is linked to location.

Chapter 9. Market Segmentation, Targeting, and Positioning

In the strictest sense, the term describes any information system that integrates, stores, edits, analyzes, shares, and displays geographic information. In a more generic sense, _____ applications are tools that allow users to create interactive queries (user created searches), analyze spatial information, edit data, maps, and present the results of all these operations.

a. Power III
b. 180SearchAssistant
c. 6-3-5 Brainwriting
d. Geographic information system

19. A _____ is a type of wholesale merchant business that buys goods and bulk products from importers, other wholesalers and then sells to retailers. _____s can deal in any commodity destined for the retail market. Typical categories are food, lumber, hardware, fuel, and textiles.

a. Tacit collusion
b. Chief privacy officer
c. Refusal to deal
d. Jobbing house

20. _____ is a term used to describe a person who was born during the demographic Post-World War II baby boom. Many analysts now believe that two distinct cultural generations were born during this baby boom; the older generation is often called the Baby Boom Generation and the younger generation is often called Generation Jones. The term '_____' is sometimes used in a cultural context, and sometimes used to describe someone who was born during the post-WWII baby boom.

a. Generation X
b. Greatest Generation
c. AStore
d. Baby boomer

21. A _____ or digger group is a sociological group that does not constitute a politically dominant voting majority of the total population of a given society. A sociological _____ is not necessarily a numerical _____ -- it may include any group that is subnormal with respect to a dominant group in terms of social status, education, employment, wealth and political power. To avoid confusion, some writers prefer the terms 'subordinate group' and 'dominant group' rather than '_____' and 'majority', respectively.

a. Minority
b. Reference group
c. Power III
d. Mociology

22. _____ is a term commonly used to describe commerce transactions between businesses like the one between a manufacturer and a wholesaler or a wholesaler and a retailer i.e both the buyer and the seller are business entity.This is unlike business-to-consumers (B2C) which involve a business entity and end consumer, or business-to-government (B2G) which involve a business entity and government.

The volume of B2B transactions is much higher than the volume of B2C transactions. The primary reason for this is that in a typical supply chain there will be many B2B transactions involving subcomponent or raw materials, and only one B2C transaction, specifically sale of the finished product to the end customer.

a. Social marketing
b. Customer relationship management
c. Disruptive technology
d. Business-to-business

23. _____ refer to a collection of facts usually collected as the result of experience, observation or experiment or a set of premises. This may consist of numbers, words particularly as measurements or observations of a set of variables. _____ are often viewed as a lowest level of abstraction from which information and knowledge are derived.

Chapter 9. Market Segmentation, Targeting, and Positioning

a. Pearson product-moment correlation coefficient
b. Mean
c. Sample size
d. Data

24. _____ is a term used to describe a process of preparing and collecting data - for example as part of a process improvement or similar project.

_____ usually takes place early on in an improvement project, and is often formalised through a _____ Plan which often contains the following activity.

1. Pre collection activity - Agree goals, target data, definitions, methods
2. Collection - _____
3. Present Findings - usually involves some form of sorting analysis and/or presentation.

A formal _____ process is necessary as it ensures that data gathered is both defined and accurate and that subsequent decisions based on arguments embodied in the findings are valid. The process provides both a baseline from which to measure from and in certain cases a target on what to improve. Types of _____ 1-By mail questionnaires 2-By personal interview

- Six sigma
- Sampling (statistics)

a. 180SearchAssistant
b. Power III
c. 6-3-5 Brainwriting
d. Data collection

25. In the field of marketing, demographics, opinion research, and social research in general, _____ variables are any attributes relating to personality, values, attitudes, interests, or lifestyles. They are also called IAO variables. They can be contrasted with demographic variables (such as age and gender), behavioral variables (such as usage rate or loyalty), and bizographic variables (such as industry, seniority and functional area.)

a. Lifetime value
b. Business-to-business
c. Marketing myopia
d. Psychographic

26. _____ was originally coined by Austrian psychologist Alfred Adler in 1929. The current broader sense of the word dates from 1961.

In sociology, a _____ is the way a person lives.

a. Lifestyle
b. 6-3-5 Brainwriting
c. Power III
d. 180SearchAssistant

27. _____ is an advertisement in which a particular product specifically mentions a competitor by name for the express purpose of showing why the competitor is inferior to the product naming it.

This should not be confused with parody advertisements, where a fictional product is being advertised for the purpose of poking fun at the particular advertisement, nor should it be confused with the use of a coined brand name for the purpose of comparing the product without actually naming an actual competitor. ('Wikipedia tastes better and is less filling than the Encyclopedia Galactica.')

In the 1980s, during what has been referred to as the cola wars, soft-drink manufacturer Pepsi ran a series of advertisements where people, caught on hidden camera, in a blind taste test, chose Pepsi over rival Coca-Cola.

a. Heavy-up
b. Cost per conversion
c. Comparative advertising
d. GL-70

28. A _____ is an entity that provides services to other entities. Usually this refers to a business that provides subscription or web service to other businesses or individuals. Examples of these services include Internet access, Mobile phone operator, and web application hosting.

a. Yield management
b. Cross-selling
c. Service provider
d. Freebie marketing

29. _____, in marketing, consists of a consumer's commitment to repurchase the brand and can be demonstrated by repeated buying of a product or service or other positive behaviors such as word of mouth advocacy. True _____ implies that the consumer is willing, at least on occasion, to put aside their own desires in the interest of the brand. _____ has been proclaimed by some to be the ultimate goal of marketing.

a. Brand implementation
b. Trade Symbols
c. Brand awareness
d. Brand loyalty

30. _____ is a retailing concept in which the total range of products sold by a retailer is broken down into discrete groups of similar or related products; these groups are known as product categories. Examples of grocery categories may be: tinned fish, washing detergent, toothpastes, etc.Each category is then run like a 'mini business' (Business Unit) in its own right, with its own set of turnover and/or profitability targets and strategies. An important facet of _____ is the shift in relationship between retailer and supplier : instead of the traditional adversarial relationship, the relationship moves to one of collaboration, exchange of information and data and joint business building.The focus of all negotiations is centered around the effects of the turnover of the total category, not just the sales on the individual products therein.

a. Category management
b. Brochure
c. Market segment
d. Societal marketing

31. _____ is the process of estimation in unknown situations. Prediction is a similar, but more general term. Both can refer to estimation of time series, cross-sectional or longitudinal data.

a. 180SearchAssistant
b. 6-3-5 Brainwriting
c. Power III
d. Forecasting

32. _____, in strategic management and marketing, is the percentage or proportion of the total available market or market segment that is being serviced by a company. It can be expressed as a company's sales revenue (from that market) divided by the total sales revenue available in that market. It can also be expressed as a company's unit sales volume (in a market) divided by the total volume of units sold in that market.

a. Demand generation
c. Customer relationship management
b. Cyberdoc
d. Market share

33. _____ is the practice of tailoring products, brands (microbrands), and promotions to meet the needs and wants of microsegments within a market. It is a type of market customization that deals with pricing of customer/product combinations at the store or individual level.

Standard pricing policy ignores the differences in customer segments of specific stores within a regional chain of stores.

a. Chief privacy officer
c. Discontinuation
b. Soft sell
d. Micromarketing

34. In marketing, _____ has come to mean the process by which marketers try to create an image or identity in the minds of their target market for its product, brand, or organization. It is the 'relative competitive comparison' their product occupies in a given market as perceived by the target market.

Re-_____ involves changing the identity of a product, relative to the identity of competing products, in the collective minds of the target market.

a. Containerization
c. GE matrix
b. Positioning
d. Moratorium

Chapter 10. Relationship Marketing, Customer Relationship Management (CRM)

1. _____ is defined by the American _____ Association as the activity, set of institutions, and processes for creating, communicating, delivering, and exchanging offerings that have value for customers, clients, partners, and society at large. The term developed from the original meaning which referred literally to going to market, as in shopping, or going to a market to sell goods or services.

_____ practice tends to be seen as a creative industry, which includes advertising, distribution and selling.

    a. Customer acquisition management   b. Product naming
    c. Marketing myopia   d. Marketing

2. _____ is a form of marketing developed from direct response marketing campaigns conducted in the 1970's and 1980's which emphasizes customer retention and satisfaction, rather than a dominant focus on 'point of sale' transactions.

_____ differs from other forms of marketing in that it recognizes the long term value to the firm of keeping customers, as opposed to direct or 'Intrusion' marketing, which focuses upon acquisition of new clients by targeting majority demographics based upon prospective client lists.

_____ refers to long-term and mutually beneficial arrangement wherein both buyer and seller focus on value enhancement through the certain of more satisfying exchange. This approach attempts to transcend the simple purchase exchange process with customer to make more meaningful and richer contact by providing a more holistic, personalized purchase, and use orn consumption experience to create stronger ties.

    a. Guerrilla Marketing   b. Global marketing
    c. Relationship marketing   d. Diversity marketing

3. In economics, an _____ is any good or commodity, transported from one country to another country in a legitimate fashion, typically for use in trade. _____ goods or services are provided to foreign consumers by domestic producers. _____ is an important part of international trade.

    a. AMAX   b. ADTECH
    c. ACNielsen   d. Export

4. In economics, an externality or spillover of an economic transaction is an impact on a party that is not directly involved in the transaction. In such a case, prices do not reflect the full costs or benefits in production or consumption of a product or service. A positive impact is called an _____ benefit, while a negative impact is called an _____ cost.

    a. External   b. AMAX
    c. ADTECH   d. ACNielsen

5. _____ is a technical term used in management science popularized by Joseph M. Juran

He defined an internal and external customers as anyone affected by the product or by the process used to produce the product, in the context of quality management. _____s may play the role as supplier, processer, and customer in the sequence of product development.

He claimed that the organization must understand and identify both internal and external customers and their needs.

Chapter 10. Relationship Marketing, Customer Relationship Management (CRM)

a. ACNielsen
c. Internal customer
b. AMAX
d. ADTECH

6. _____ is an ongoing process that occurs strictly within a company or organization whereby the functional process aligns, motivates and empowers employees at all management levels to consistently deliver a satisfying customer experience. According to Burkitt and Zealley, 'the challenge for _____ is not only to get the right messages across, but to embed them in such a way that they both change and reinforce employee behaviour'.

a. ACNielsen
c. AMAX
b. ADTECH
d. Internal marketing

7. _____ is a method of direct marketing in which a salesperson solicits to prospective customers to buy products or services, either over the phone or through a subsequent face to face or Web conferencing appointment scheduled during the call.

_____ can also include recorded sales pitches programmed to be played over the phone via automatic dialing. _____ has come under fire in recent years, being viewed as an annoyance by many.

a. Directory Harvest Attack
c. Joe job
b. Phishing
d. Telemarketing

8. _____ refer to a collection of facts usually collected as the result of experience, observation or experiment or a set of premises. This may consist of numbers, words particularly as measurements or observations of a set of variables. _____ are often viewed as a lowest level of abstraction from which information and knowledge are derived.

a. Mean
c. Data
b. Sample size
d. Pearson product-moment correlation coefficient

9. In statistics, an _____ is a term in a statistical model added when the effect of two or more variables is not simply additive. Such a term reflects that the effect of one variable depends on the values of one or more other variables.

Thus, for a response Y and two variables x_1 and x_2 an additive model would be:

$$Y = ax_1 + bx_2 + \text{error}$$

In contrast to this,

$$Y = ax_1 + bx_2 + c(x_1 \times x_2) + \text{error},$$

is an example of a model with an _____ between variables x_1 and x_2 ('error' refers to the random variable whose value by which y differs from the expected value of y.)

a. AMAX
c. ADTECH
b. ACNielsen
d. Interaction

Chapter 10. Relationship Marketing, Customer Relationship Management (CRM)

10. A _____ is a type of business entity in which partners (owners) share with each other the profits or losses of the business undertaking in which all have invested. _____s are often favored over corporations for taxation purposes, as the _____ structure does not generally incur a tax on profits before it is distributed to the partners (i.e. there is no dividend tax levied.) However, depending on the _____ structure and the jurisdiction in which it operates, owners of a _____ may be exposed to greater personal liability than they would as shareholders of a corporation.
    a. Fair Debt Collection Practices Act
    b. Brand piracy
    c. Partnership
    d. Competition law

11. A _____ or trade mark, identified by the symbols ™ (not yet registered) and ® (registered) business organization or other legal entity to identify that the products and/or services to consumers with which the _____ appears originate from a unique source of origin, and to distinguish its products or services from those of other entities. A _____ is a type of intellectual property, and typically a name, word, phrase, logo, symbol, design, image, or a combination of these elements. There is also a range of non-conventional _____s comprising marks which do not fall into these standard categories.
    a. Trademark
    b. 180SearchAssistant
    c. Risk management
    d. Power III

12. _____ is a trademark law concept permitting the owner of a famous trademark to forbid others from using that mark in a way that would lessen its uniqueness. In most cases, _____ involves an unauthorized use of another's trademark on products that do not compete with, and have little connection with, those of the trademark owner. For example, a famous trademark used by one company to refer to hair care products might be diluted if another company began using a similar mark to refer to breakfast cereals or spark plugs.
    a. Federal Bureau of Investigation
    b. Trademark attorney
    c. Trespass to land
    d. Trademark Dilution

13. _____, a business term, is a measure of how products and services supplied by a company meet or surpass customer expectation. It is seen as a key performance indicator within business and is part of the four perspectives of a Balanced Scorecard.

In a competitive marketplace where businesses compete for customers, _____ is seen as a key differentiator and increasingly has become a key element of business strategy.

    a. Customer base
    b. Customer satisfaction
    c. Psychological pricing
    d. Supplier diversity

14. _____ describes the situation when output from (or information about the result of) an event or phenomenon in the past will influence the same event/phenomenon in the present or future. When an event is part of a chain of cause-and-effect that forms a circuit or loop, then the event is said to 'feed back' into itself.

_____ is also a synonym for:

- _____ Signal; the information about the initial event that is the basis for subsequent modification of the event.
- _____ Loop; the causal path that leads from the initial generation of the _____ signal to the subsequent modification of the event.

Chapter 10. Relationship Marketing, Customer Relationship Management (CRM)

_____ is a mechanism, process or signal that is looped back to control a system within itself. Such a loop is called a _____ loop.

a. 180SearchAssistant
c. Power III
b. 6-3-5 Brainwriting
d. Feedback

15. _____ is the activity that the selling organization undertakes to reduce customer account defections. The success of this activity is when the customer account places an additional order before a 12-month period has expired. Note that ideally these orders will need to contribute similar financial amounts to the previous 12 months.
    a. Customer base
    b. First-mover advantage
    c. Customer centricity
    d. Customer retention

16. _____s is the social science that studies the production, distribution, and consumption of goods and services. The term _____s comes from the Ancient Greek oá¼°κονομῖα from oá¼¶κος (oikos, 'house') + vÏŒμος (nomos, 'custom' or 'law'), hence 'rules of the house(hold)'. Current _____ models developed out of the broader field of political economy in the late 19th century, owing to a desire to use an empirical approach more akin to the physical sciences.
    a. ACNielsen
    b. ADTECH
    c. Industrial organization
    d. Economic

17. In marketing generally and in retailing more specifically, a _____, rewards card, points card, advantage card visually similar to a credit card or debit card, that identifies the card holder as a member in a loyalty program. _____s are a system of the loyalty business model. In the United Kingdom it is typically called a _____, in Canada a rewards card or a points card, and in the United States either a discount card, a club card or a rewards card.
    a. 6-3-5 Brainwriting
    b. Loyalty card
    c. 180SearchAssistant
    d. Power III

18. A _____ is a collection of symbols, experiences and associations connected with a product, a service, a person or any other artifact or entity.

_____s have become increasingly important components of culture and the economy, now being described as 'cultural accessories and personal philosophies'.

Some people distinguish the psychological aspect of a _____ from the experiential aspect.

a. Brand
b. Brandable software
c. Brand equity
d. Store brand

19. The _____ is a database of consumer perception of brands created and managed by BrandAsset Consulting, a division of Young ' Rubicam Brands to provide information to enable firms to improve the marketing decision-making process and to manage brands better. _____ and _____ also describe the Y'R group managing the database.

_____ measures the value of a brand along four dimensions: 'Differentiation,' 'Relevance,' 'Esteem,' and 'Knowledge.' Differentiation and Relevance build up to 'Brand Strength.' Esteem and Knowledge are used to calculate 'Brand Stature.' _____ defines these terms as follows.

a. Target audience
b. Targeted advertising
c. Hoover free flights promotion
d. Brand Asset Valuator

20. A _____ is a structured collection of records or data that is stored in a computer system. The structure is achieved by organizing the data according to a _____ model. The model in most common use today is the relational model.

a. 6-3-5 Brainwriting
b. 180SearchAssistant
c. Power III
d. Database

21. _____ is a form of direct marketing using databases of customers or potential customers to generate personalized communications in order to promote a product or service for marketing purposes. The method of communication can be any addressable medium, as in direct marketing.

The distinction between direct and _____ stems primarily from the attention paid to the analysis of data.

a. Power III
b. Direct Marketing Associations
c. Direct marketing
d. Database marketing

22. The _____ is a 1990 United States Federal law. It was signed into law on November 8, 1990 by the president.

The law gives the Food and Drug Administration (FDA) authority to require nutrition labeling of most foods regulated by the Agency; and to require that all nutrient content claims (for example, 'high fiber', 'low fat', etc).

a. Nutrition Labeling and Education Act
b. Trespass to land
c. Fair Debt Collection Practices Act
d. Copyright infringement

23. _____ refers to marketing strategies applied directly to a specific consumer.

Having the knowledge on the consumer preferences, there are suggested personalized products and promotions to each consumer.

The _____ is based in four main steps in order to fulfill its goals: Those stages are identify, differentiate, interact, and customize.

a. AMAX
b. One-to-one marketing
c. ACNielsen
d. ADTECH

24. _____ is an advertisement in which a particular product specifically mentions a competitor by name for the express purpose of showing why the competitor is inferior to the product naming it.

This should not be confused with parody advertisements, where a fictional product is being advertised for the purpose of poking fun at the particular advertisement, nor should it be confused with the use of a coined brand name for the purpose of comparing the product without actually naming an actual competitor. ('Wikipedia tastes better and is less filling than the Encyclopedia Galactica.')

Chapter 10. Relationship Marketing, Customer Relationship Management (CRM)   87

In the 1980s, during what has been referred to as the cola wars, soft-drink manufacturer Pepsi ran a series of advertisements where people, caught on hidden camera, in a blind taste test, chose Pepsi over rival Coca-Cola.

a. Cost per conversion
b. GL-70
c. Heavy-up
d. Comparative advertising

25. A _____ is an entity that provides services to other entities. Usually this refers to a business that provides subscription or web service to other businesses or individuals. Examples of these services include Internet access, Mobile phone operator, and web application hosting.
a. Freebie marketing
b. Cross-selling
c. Yield management
d. Service provider

26. _____ consists of the processes a company uses to track and organize its contacts with its current and prospective customers. _____ software is used to support these processes; information about customers and customer interactions can be entered, stored and accessed by employees in different company departments. Typical _____ goals are to improve services provided to customers, and to use customer contact information for targeted marketing.
a. Product bundling
b. Demand generation
c. Commercialization
d. Customer relationship management

27. A _____ is a process that can allow an organization to concentrate its limited resources on the greatest opportunities to increase sales and achieve a sustainable competitive advantage. A _____ should be centered around the key concept that customer satisfaction is the main goal.

A _____ is most effective when it is an integral component of corporate strategy, defining how the organization will successfully engage customers, prospects, and competitors in the market arena.

a. Psychographic
b. Cyberdoc
c. Societal marketing
d. Marketing strategy

28. Customer _____ consists of the processes a company uses to track and organize its contacts with its current and prospective customers. CRelationship management software is used to support these processes; information about customers and customer interactions can be entered, stored and accessed by employees in different company departments. Typical CRelationship management goals are to improve services provided to customers, and to use customer contact information for targeted marketing.
a. Product bundling
b. Relationship management
c. Green marketing
d. Marketing

29. _____ and viral advertising refer to marketing techniques that use pre-existing social networks to produce increases in brand awareness or to achieve other marketing objectives (such as product sales) through self-replicating viral processes, analogous to the spread of pathological and computer viruses. It can be word-of-mouth delivered or enhanced by the network effects of the Internet. Viral promotions may take the form of video clips, interactive Flash games, advergames, ebooks, brandable software, images, or even text messages.

a. New Media Marketing
b. 180SearchAssistant
c. Power III
d. Viral marketing

30. _____ is a broad label that refers to any individuals or households that use goods and services generated within the economy. The concept of a _____ is used in different contexts, so that the usage and significance of the term may vary.

A _____ is a person who uses any product or service.

a. Power III
b. 6-3-5 Brainwriting
c. 180SearchAssistant
d. Consumer

31. _____ is the study of when, why, how, where and what people do or do not buy products. It blends elements from psychology, sociology, social psychology, anthropology and economics. It attempts to understand the buyer decision making process, both individually and in groups. It studies characteristics of individual consumers such as demographics and behavioural variables in an attempt to understand people's wants. It also tries to assess influences on the consumer from groups such as family, friends, reference groups, and society in general.

a. Consumer behavior
b. Communal marketing
c. Multidimensional scaling
d. Consumer confidence

32. _____ is a term commonly used to describe commerce transactions between businesses like the one between a manufacturer and a wholesaler or a wholesaler and a retailer i.e both the buyer and the seller are business entity. This is unlike business-to-consumers (B2C) which involve a business entity and end consumer, or business-to-government (B2G) which involve a business entity and government.

The volume of B2B transactions is much higher than the volume of B2C transactions. The primary reason for this is that in a typical supply chain there will be many B2B transactions involving subcomponent or raw materials, and only one B2C transaction, specifically sale of the finished product to the end customer.

a. Customer relationship management
b. Social marketing
c. Business-to-business
d. Disruptive technology

33. _____ refers to the structured transmission of data between organizations by electronic means. It is used to transfer electronic documents from one computer system to another (ie) from one trading partner to another trading partner. It is more than mere E-mail; for instance, organizations might replace bills of lading and even checks with appropriate _____ messages.

a. ACNielsen
b. AMAX
c. Electronic data interchange
d. ADTECH

Chapter 10. Relationship Marketing, Customer Relationship Management (CRM)

34. _____ is difficult to define. For example, in 1952, Alfred Kroeber and Clyde Kluckhohn compiled a list of 164 definitions of '_____' in _____: A Critical Review of Concepts and Definitions. However, the word '_____' is most commonly used in three basic senses:

- excellence of taste in the fine arts and humanities
- an integrated pattern of human knowledge, belief, and behavior that depends upon the capacity for symbolic thought and social learning
- the set of shared attitudes, values, goals, and practices that characterizes an institution, organization or group.

When the concept first emerged in eighteenth- and nineteenth-century Europe, it connoted a process of cultivation or improvement, as in agriculture or horticulture. In the nineteenth century, it came to refer first to the betterment or refinement of the individual, especially through education, and then to the fulfillment of national aspirations or ideals.

a. AStore
b. African Americans
c. Albert Einstein
d. Culture

35. _____ is a list for goods and materials held available in stock by a business. It is also used for a list of the contents of a household and for a list for testamentary purposes of the possessions of someone who has died. In accounting _____ is considered an asset.

a. ADTECH
b. ACNielsen
c. Ending Inventory
d. Inventory

36. _____ refers to the methods, practices and operations conducted to promote and sustain certain categories of commercial activity. The term is understood to have different specific meanings depending on the context. Merchandise is a sale goods at a store

In marketing, one of the definitions of _____ is the practice in which the brand or image from one product or service is used to sell another.

a. Word of mouth
b. Marketing communication
c. New Media Strategies
d. Merchandising

37. _____ is a family of business models in which the buyer of a product provides certain information to a supplier of that product and the supplier takes full responsibility for maintaining an agreed inventory of the material, usually at the buyer's consumption location (usually a store.) A third party logistics provider can also be involved to make sure that the buyer have the required level of inventory by adjusting the demand and supply gaps.

As a symbiotic relationship, _____ makes it less likely that a business will unintentionally become out of stock of a good and reduces inventory in the supply chain.

a. Reverse auction
b. Customer driven supply chain
c. Merchandise management system
d. Vendor Managed Inventory

Chapter 10. Relationship Marketing, Customer Relationship Management (CRM)

38. _____ is a recursive process where two or more people or organizations work together toward an intersection of common goals -- for example, an intellectual endeavor that is creative in nature--by sharing knowledge, learning and building consensus. _____ does not require leadership and can sometimes bring better results through decentralization and egalitarianism. In particular, teams that work collaboratively can obtain greater resources, recognition and reward when facing competition for finite resources._____ is also present in opposing goals exhibiting the notion of adversarial _____, though this notion is atypical of the annotation that people have given towards their understanding of _____.
 a. 180SearchAssistant
 b. 6-3-5 Brainwriting
 c. Power III
 d. Collaboration

39. _____ is the process of estimation in unknown situations. Prediction is a similar, but more general term. Both can refer to estimation of time series, cross-sectional or longitudinal data.
 a. 180SearchAssistant
 b. Forecasting
 c. Power III
 d. 6-3-5 Brainwriting

40. _____ in organizations and public policy is both the organizational process of creating and maintaining a plan; and the psychological process of thinking about the activities required to create a desired goal on some scale. As such, it is a fundamental property of intelligent behavior. This thought process is essential to the creation and refinement of a plan, or integration of it with other plans, that is, it combines forecasting of developments with the preparation of scenarios of how to react to them.
 a. Planning
 b. 180SearchAssistant
 c. 6-3-5 Brainwriting
 d. Power III

41. A _____ or logistics network is the system of organizations, people, technology, activities, information and resources involved in moving a product or service from supplier to customer. _____ activities transform natural resources, raw materials and components into a finished product that is delivered to the end customer. In sophisticated _____ systems, used products may re-enter the _____ at any point where residual value is recyclable.
 a. Supply chain
 b. Purchasing
 c. Supply chain network
 d. Demand chain management

42. A personal and cultural _____ is a relative ethic _____, an assumption upon which implementation can be extrapolated. A _____ system is a set of consistent _____s and measures that is soo not true. A principle _____ is a foundation upon which other _____s and measures of integrity are based.
 a. Supreme Court of the United States
 b. Perceptual maps
 c. Package-on-Package
 d. Value

43. The _____ is a concept from business management that was first described and popularized by Michael Porter in his 1985 best-seller, Competitive Advantage: Creating and Sustaining Superior Performance.

A _____ is a chain of activities. Products pass through all activities of the chain in order and at each activity the product gains some value.

 a. Value chain
 b. Mass marketing
 c. Business-to-business
 d. Relationship management

Chapter 10. Relationship Marketing, Customer Relationship Management (CRM)

44. Human beings are also considered to be _____ because they have the ability to change raw materials into valuable _____. The term Human _____ can also be defined as the skills, energies, talents, abilities and knowledge that are used for the production of goods or the rendering of services. While taking into account human beings as _____, the following things have to be kept in mind:

- The size of the population
- The capabilities of the individuals in that population

Many _____ cannot be consumed in their original form. They have to be processed in order to change them into more usable commodities.

a. Power III
c. 6-3-5 Brainwriting
b. 180SearchAssistant
d. Resources

45. In marketing, customer _____, lifetime customer value (LCV), or _____ (LTV) and a new concept of 'customer life cycle management' is the present value of the future cash flows attributed to the customer relationship. Use of customer _____ as a marketing metric tends to place greater emphasis on customer service and long-term customer satisfaction, rather than on maximizing short-term sales.

Customer _____ has intuitive appeal as a marketing concept, because in theory it represents exactly how much each customer is worth in monetary terms, and therefore exactly how much a marketing department should be willing to spend to acquire each customer.

a. Sweepstakes
c. Brand infiltration
b. Value chain
d. Lifetime value

Chapter 11. Product and Service Strategies

1. _____ is an advertisement in which a particular product specifically mentions a competitor by name for the express purpose of showing why the competitor is inferior to the product naming it.

This should not be confused with parody advertisements, where a fictional product is being advertised for the purpose of poking fun at the particular advertisement, nor should it be confused with the use of a coined brand name for the purpose of comparing the product without actually naming an actual competitor. ('Wikipedia tastes better and is less filling than the Encyclopedia Galactica.')

In the 1980s, during what has been referred to as the cola wars, soft-drink manufacturer Pepsi ran a series of advertisements where people, caught on hidden camera, in a blind taste test, chose Pepsi over rival Coca-Cola.

   a. Heavy-up
   c. GL-70
   b. Comparative advertising
   d. Cost per conversion

2. _____ is defined by the American _____ Association as the activity, set of institutions, and processes for creating, communicating, delivering, and exchanging offerings that have value for customers, clients, partners, and society at large. The term developed from the original meaning which referred literally to going to market, as in shopping, or going to a market to sell goods or services.

_____ practice tends to be seen as a creative industry, which includes advertising, distribution and selling.

   a. Marketing
   c. Product naming
   b. Marketing myopia
   d. Customer acquisition management

3. The _____ is generally accepted as the use and specification of the four p's describing the strategic position of a product in the marketplace. One version of the origins of the _____ starts in 1948 when James Culliton said that a marketing decision should be a result of something similar to a recipe. This version continued in 1953 when Neil Borden, in his American Marketing Association presidential address, took the recipe idea one step further and coined the term 'Marketing-Mix'.
   a. 180SearchAssistant
   c. 6-3-5 Brainwriting
   b. Power III
   d. Marketing mix

4. The _____ is a 1990 United States Federal law. It was signed into law on November 8, 1990 by the president.

The law gives the Food and Drug Administration (FDA) authority to require nutrition labeling of most foods regulated by the Agency; and to require that all nutrient content claims (for example, 'high fiber', 'low fat', etc).

   a. Fair Debt Collection Practices Act
   c. Copyright infringement
   b. Trespass to land
   d. Nutrition Labeling and Education Act

5. The _____ is one of the three economic sectors, the others being the secondary sector and the primary sector The general definition of the Tertiary sector is producing a service instead of just a end product, in the case of the secondary sector. Sometimes an additional sector, the 'quaternary sector', is defined for the sharing of information
   a. Tertiary sector of economy
   c. Power III
   b. 6-3-5 Brainwriting
   d. 180SearchAssistant

Chapter 11. Product and Service Strategies

6. _____ is a broad label that refers to any individuals or households that use goods and services generated within the economy. The concept of a _____ is used in different contexts, so that the usage and significance of the term may vary.

A _____ is a person who uses any product or service.

   a. 6-3-5 Brainwriting
   b. 180SearchAssistant
   c. Power III
   d. Consumer

7. _____ are final goods specifically intended for the mass market. For instance, _____ do not include investment assets, like precious antiques, even though these antiques are final goods.

Manufactured goods are goods that have been processed by way of machinery.

   a. Free good
   b. Consumer Goods
   c. Durable good
   d. Power III

8. _____ is one of the four Ps of the marketing mix. The other three aspects are product, promotion, and place. It is also a key variable in microeconomic price allocation theory.
   a. Competitor indexing
   b. Price
   c. Relationship based pricing
   d. Pricing

9. _____ is a term commonly used to describe commerce transactions between businesses like the one between a manufacturer and a wholesaler or a wholesaler and a retailer i.e both the buyer and the seller are business entity.This is unlike business-to-consumers (B2C) which involve a business entity and end consumer, or business-to-government (B2G) which involve a business entity and government.

The volume of B2B transactions is much higher than the volume of B2C transactions. The primary reason for this is that in a typical supply chain there will be many B2B transactions involving subcomponent or raw materials, and only one B2C transaction, specifically sale of the finished product to the end customer.

   a. Social marketing
   b. Customer relationship management
   c. Disruptive technology
   d. Business-to-business

10. _____ is anything that is intended to save time, energy or frustration. A _____ store at a petrol station, for example, sells items that have nothing to do with gasoline/petrol, but it saves the consumer from having to go to a grocery store. '_____' is a very relative term and its meaning tends to change over time.
   a. Marketing buzz
   b. Demographic profile
   c. MaxDiff
   d. Convenience

11. Electronic commerce, commonly known as _____ or eCommerce, consists of the buying and selling of products or services over electronic systems such as the Internet and other computer networks. The amount of trade conducted electronically has grown extraordinarily with wide-spread Internet usage. A wide variety of commerce is conducted in this way, spurring and drawing on innovations in electronic funds transfer, supply chain management, Internet marketing, online transaction processing, electronic data interchange (EDI), inventory management systems, and automated data collection systems.

Chapter 11. Product and Service Strategies

a. ACNielsen
b. E-commerce
c. ADTECH
d. AMAX

12. An _____ is an unplanned or otherwise spontaneous purchase. One who tends to make such purchases is referred to as an impulse purchaser or impulse buyer.

Marketers and retailers tend to exploit these impulses which are tied to the basic want for instant gratification.

a. ADTECH
b. AMAX
c. Impulse purchase
d. ACNielsen

13. _____ is the examining of goods or services from retailers with the intent to purchase at that time. _____ is an activity of selection and/or purchase. In some contexts it is considered a leisure activity as well as an economic one.

a. Khodebshchik
b. Hawkers
c. Discount store
d. Shopping

14. A _____ is a collection of symbols, experiences and associations connected with a product, a service, a person or any other artifact or entity.

_____s have become increasingly important components of culture and the economy, now being described as 'cultural accessories and personal philosophies'.

Some people distinguish the psychological aspect of a _____ from the experiential aspect.

a. Brand equity
b. Brand
c. Store brand
d. Brandable software

15. The _____ is a database of consumer perception of brands created and managed by BrandAsset Consulting, a division of Young ' Rubicam Brands to provide information to enable firms to improve the marketing decision-making process and to manage brands better. _____ and _____ also describe the Y'R group managing the database.

_____ measures the value of a brand along four dimensions: 'Differentiation,' 'Relevance,' 'Esteem,' and 'Knowledge.' Differentiation and Relevance build up to 'Brand Strength.' Esteem and Knowledge are used to calculate 'Brand Stature.' _____ defines these terms as follows.

a. Targeted advertising
b. Target audience
c. Hoover free flights promotion
d. Brand Asset Valuator

16. A _____ is a written document that details the necessary actions to achieve one or more marketing objectives. It can be for a product or service, a brand, or a product line. _____s cover between one and five years.

a. Prosumer
b. Marketing strategy
c. Marketing plan
d. Disruptive technology

Chapter 11. Product and Service Strategies

17. A _____ or trade mark, identified by the symbols ā„¢ (not yet registered) and Â® (registered) business organization or other legal entity to identify that the products and/or services to consumers with which the _____ appears originate from a unique source of origin, and to distinguish its products or services from those of other entities. A _____ is a type of intellectual property, and typically a name, word, phrase, logo, symbol, design, image, or a combination of these elements. There is also a range of non-conventional _____s comprising marks which do not fall into these standard categories.
    a. 180SearchAssistant
    b. Trademark
    c. Risk management
    d. Power III

18. A _____ is something that is acted upon or used by or by human labour or industry, for use as a building material to create some product or structure. Often the term is used to denote material that came from nature and is in an unprocessed or minimally processed state. Iron ore, logs, and crude oil, would be examples.
    a. 6-3-5 Brainwriting
    b. Power III
    c. 180SearchAssistant
    d. Raw material

19. _____ is the process of comparing the cost, cycle time, productivity, or quality of a specific process or method to another that is widely considered to be an industry standard or best practice. The result is often a business case for making changes in order to make improvements. The term _____ was first used by cobblers to measure ones feet for shoes.
    a. Strategic group
    b. Business strategy
    c. Switching cost
    d. Benchmarking

20. A _____ is a plan of action designed to achieve a particular goal.

    _____ is different from tactics. In military terms, tactics is concerned with the conduct of an engagement while _____ is concerned with how different engagements are linked.

    a. Power III
    b. Strategy
    c. 6-3-5 Brainwriting
    d. 180SearchAssistant

21. _____ is a business management strategy aimed at embedding awareness of quality in all organizational processes. _____ has been widely used in manufacturing, education, call centers, government, and service industries, as well as NASA space and science programs.

When used together as a phrase, the three words in this expression have the following meanings:

- Total: Involving the entire organization, supply chain, and/or product life cycle
- Quality: With its usual definitions, with all its complexities
- Management: The system of managing with steps like Plan, Organize, Control, Lead, Staff, provisioning and organizing.

As defined by the International Organization for Standardization (ISO):

> '_____ is a management approach for an organization, centered on quality, based on the participation of all its members and aiming at long-term success through customer satisfaction, and benefits to all members of the organization and to society.' ISO 8402:1994

Chapter 11. Product and Service Strategies

One major aim is to reduce variation from every process so that greater consistency of effort is obtained. (Royse, D., Thyer, B., Padgett D., ' Logan T., 2006)

In Japan, _____ comprises four process steps, namely:

1. Kaizen - Focuses on 'Continuous Process Improvement', to make processes visible, repeatable and measurable.
2. Atarimae Hinshitsu - The idea that 'things will work as they are supposed to' .
3. Kansei - Examining the way the user applies the product leads to improvement in the product itself.
4. Miryokuteki Hinshitsu - The idea that 'things should have an aesthetic quality' (for example, a pen will write in a way that is pleasing to the writer.)

_____ requires that the company maintain this quality standard in all aspects of its business. This requires ensuring that things are done right the first time and that defects and waste are eliminated from operations.

a. Power III
b. Total quality management
c. 6-3-5 Brainwriting
d. 180SearchAssistant

22. _____ is a method of direct marketing in which a salesperson solicits to prospective customers to buy products or services, either over the phone or through a subsequent face to face or Web conferencing appointment scheduled during the call.

_____ can also include recorded sales pitches programmed to be played over the phone via automatic dialing. _____ has come under fire in recent years, being viewed as an annoyance by many.

a. Joe job
b. Telemarketing
c. Directory Harvest Attack
d. Phishing

23. _____ is a strategic planning method used to evaluate the Strengths, Weaknesses, Opportunities, and Threats involved in a project or in a business venture. It involves specifying the objective of the business venture or project and identifying the internal and external factors that are favorable and unfavorable to achieving that objective. The technique is credited to Albert Humphrey, who led a research project at Stanford University in the 1960s and 1970s using data from Fortune 500 companies.

a. Lead scoring
b. Product differentiation
c. Market environment
d. SWOT analysis

24. _____ is the study of when, why, how, where and what people do or do not buy products. It blends elements from psychology, sociology,social psychology, anthropology and economics. It attempts to understand the buyer decision making process, both individually and in groups. It studies characteristics of individual consumers such as demographics and behavioural variables in an attempt to understand people's wants. It also tries to assess influences on the consumer from groups such as family, friends, reference groups, and society in general.

a. Multidimensional scaling
b. Communal marketing
c. Consumer confidence
d. Consumer behavior

Chapter 11. Product and Service Strategies

25. There are many important decisions about product and service development and marketing. In the process of product development and marketing we should focus on strategic decisions about product attributes, product branding, product packaging, product labeling and product support services. But product strategy also calls for building a _____.
   a. Technology acceptance model
   b. Pinstorm
   c. Macromarketing
   d. Product line

26. A product _____ is the use of an established product's brand name for a new item in the same product category. _____s occur when a company introduces additional items in the same product category under the same brand name such as new flavors, forms, colors, added ingredients, package sizes.Examples includei) Zen LXI, Zen VXIii) Surf, Surf Excel, Surf Excel Blueiii) Splendour, Splendour Plusiv) Coke, Diet Coke, Vanilla Cokev) Clinic All Clear, Clinic Plus

- brand
- brand management
- marketing
- product management
- Product lining

   a. Brand Development Index
   b. Targeted advertising
   c. Line extension
   d. Perishability

27. _____ Management is the succession of strategies used by management as a product goes through its _____. The conditions in which a product is sold changes over time and must be managed as it moves through its succession of stages.

The _____ goes through many phases, involves many professional disciplines, and requires many skills, tools and processes.

   a. Product life cycle
   b. Supplier diversity
   c. Customer satisfaction
   d. Chain stores

28. A _____ is an entity that provides services to other entities. Usually this refers to a business that provides subscription or web service to other businesses or individuals. Examples of these services include Internet access, Mobile phone operator, and web application hosting.
   a. Yield management
   b. Cross-selling
   c. Freebie marketing
   d. Service provider

29. An _____ is the manufacturing of a good or service within a category. Although _____ is a broad term for any kind of economic production, in economics and urban planning _____ is a synonym for the secondary sector, which is a type of economic activity involved in the manufacturing of raw materials into goods and products.

There are four key industrial economic sectors: the primary sector, largely raw material extraction industries such as mining and farming; the secondary sector, involving refining, construction, and manufacturing; the tertiary sector, which deals with services (such as law and medicine) and distribution of manufactured goods; and the quaternary sector, a relatively new type of knowledge _____ focusing on technological research, design and development such as computer programming, and biochemistry.

a. AMAX
b. ACNielsen
c. Industry
d. ADTECH

30. In business and engineering, new _____ is the term used to describe the complete process of bringing a new product or service to market. There are two parallel paths involved in the Nproduct development process: one involves the idea generation, product design, and detail engineering; the other involves market research and marketing analysis. Companies typically see new _____ as the first stage in generating and commercializing new products within the overall strategic process of product life cycle management used to maintain or grow their market share.
   a. Product development
   b. Specification tree
   c. New product screening
   d. New product development

Chapter 12. Category and Brand Management, Product Identification

1. A _____ is a collection of symbols, experiences and associations connected with a product, a service, a person or any other artifact or entity.

_____s have become increasingly important components of culture and the economy, now being described as 'cultural accessories and personal philosophies'.

Some people distinguish the psychological aspect of a _____ from the experiential aspect.

   a. Brandable software
   c. Brand
   b. Store brand
   d. Brand equity

2. The _____ is a database of consumer perception of brands created and managed by BrandAsset Consulting, a division of Young ' Rubicam Brands to provide information to enable firms to improve the marketing decision-making process and to manage brands better. _____ and _____ also describe the Y'R group managing the database.

_____ measures the value of a brand along four dimensions: 'Differentiation,' 'Relevance,' 'Esteem,' and 'Knowledge.' Differentiation and Relevance build up to 'Brand Strength.' Esteem and Knowledge are used to calculate 'Brand Stature.' _____ defines these terms as follows.

   a. Target audience
   c. Hoover free flights promotion
   b. Targeted advertising
   d. Brand Asset Valuator

3. _____ is a retailing concept in which the total range of products sold by a retailer is broken down into discrete groups of similar or related products; these groups are known as product categories. Examples of grocery categories may be: tinned fish, washing detergent, toothpastes, etc. Each category is then run like a 'mini business' (Business Unit) in its own right, with its own set of turnover and/or profitability targets and strategies. An important facet of _____ is the shift in relationship between retailer and supplier : instead of the traditional adversarial relationship, the relationship moves to one of collaboration, exchange of information and data and joint business building. The focus of all negotiations is centered around the effects of the turnover of the total category, not just the sales on the individual products therein.
   a. Brochure
   c. Category management
   b. Market segment
   d. Societal marketing

4. Merchandising refers to the methods, practices and operations conducted to promote and sustain certain categories of commercial activity. The term is understood to have different specific meanings depending on the context. _____ is a sale goods at a store

In marketing, one of the definitions of merchandising is the practice in which the brand or image from one product or service is used to sell another.

   a. Merchandising
   c. Merchandise
   b. Sales promotion
   d. New Media Strategies

5. Competitiveness is a comparative concept of the ability and performance of a firm, sub-sector or country to sell and supply goods and/or services in a given market. Although widely used in economics and business management, the usefulness of the concept, particularly in the context of national competitiveness, is vigorously disputed by economists, such as Paul Krugman .

The term may also be applied to markets, where it is used to refer to the extent to which the market structure may be regarded as perfectly _____.

    a. Competitive
    c. Free trade zone
    b. Geographical pricing
    d. Customs union

6. _____ is, in very basic words, a position a firm occupies against its competitors.

According to Michael Porter, the three methods for creating a sustainable _____ are through:

1. Cost leadership - Cost advantage occurs when a firm delivers the same services as its competitors but at a lower cost;

2.

    a. Power III
    c. 180SearchAssistant
    b. 6-3-5 Brainwriting
    d. Competitive advantage

7. _____ is a broad label that refers to any individuals or households that use goods and services generated within the economy. The concept of a _____ is used in different contexts, so that the usage and significance of the term may vary.

A _____ is a person who uses any product or service.

    a. 180SearchAssistant
    c. Consumer
    b. 6-3-5 Brainwriting
    d. Power III

8. _____ are final goods specifically intended for the mass market. For instance, _____ do not include investment assets, like precious antiques, even though these antiques are final goods.

Manufactured goods are goods that have been processed by way of machinery.

    a. Consumer Goods
    c. Free good
    b. Power III
    d. Durable good

9. _____ is one of the four Ps of the marketing mix. The other three aspects are product, promotion, and place. It is also a key variable in microeconomic price allocation theory.
    a. Competitor indexing
    c. Relationship based pricing
    b. Price
    d. Pricing

10. A brand which is widely known in the marketplace acquires _____. When _____ builds up to a point where a brand enjoys a critical mass of positive sentiment in the marketplace, it is said to have achieved brand franchise. One goal in _____ is the identification of a brand without the name of the company present.

a. Brand recognition
b. Trade Symbols
c. Trademark distinctiveness
d. Brand blunder

11. _____ generally refers to a list of all planned expenses and revenues. It is a plan for saving and spending. A _____ is an important concept in microeconomics, which uses a _____ line to illustrate the trade-offs between two or more goods.
   a. 6-3-5 Brainwriting
   b. Power III
   c. 180SearchAssistant
   d. Budget

12. A _____ product is an imitation which infringes upon a production monopoly held by either a state or corporation. Goods are produced with the intent to bypass this monopoly and thus take advantage of the established worth of the previous product. The word _____ frequently describes both the forgeries of currency and documents, as well as the imitations of clothing, software, pharmaceuticals, watches, electronics, and company logos and brands.
   a. Power III
   b. 6-3-5 Brainwriting
   c. 180SearchAssistant
   d. Counterfeit

13. The brand name of a product that is distributed nationally under a brand name owned by the producer or distributor, as opposed to local brands (products distributed only in some areas of the country), and private label brands (products that carry the brand of the retailer rather than the producer.)

   _____s must compete with local and private brands._____s are produced by ,widely distuted by, and carry the name of the manufacturer.

   - Local brands may appeal to those consumers who favor small, local producers over large national or global producers, and may be willing to pay a premium to 'buy local'

   - The private label producer can offer lower prices because they avoid the cost of marketing and advertising to create and protect the brand. In North America, large retailers such as Loblaws, Walgreen and Wal-Mart all offer private label products.

   a. Market intelligence
   b. National brand
   c. Specialty catalogs
   d. Line extension

14. _____ is when a large distribution channel member (usually a retailer), buys from a manufacturer in bulk and puts its own name on the product. This strategy is only practical when the retailer does very high levels of volume. The advantages to the retailer are:

   - more freedom and flexibility in pricing
   - more control over product attributes and quality
   - higher margins (or lower selling price)
   - eliminates much of the manufacturer's promotional costs

Chapter 12. Category and Brand Management, Product Identification

The advantages to the manufacturer are:

- reduced promotional costs
- stability of sales volume (at least while the contract is operative)

- Kumar, Nirmalya; Steenkamp, Jan-Benedict E.M., Private Label Strategy - How to Meet the Store Brand Challenge. Harvard Business Press 2007

- private label
- brand management
- brand
- product management
- marketing

a. Rural market
c. Promotion
b. Private branding
d. Customization

15. _____ refers to the marketing effects or outcomes that accrue to a product with its brand name compared with those that would accrue if the same product did not have the brand name . And, at the root of these marketing effects is consumers' knowledge. In other words, consumers' knowledge about a brand makes manufacturers/advertisers respond differently or adopt appropriately adapt measures for the marketing of the brand .
   a. Brand image
   c. Brand aversion
   b. Product extension
   d. Brand equity

16. A _____ or trade mark, identified by the symbols â„¢ (not yet registered) and Â® (registered) business organization or other legal entity to identify that the products and/or services to consumers with which the _____ appears originate from a unique source of origin, and to distinguish its products or services from those of other entities. A _____ is a type of intellectual property, and typically a name, word, phrase, logo, symbol, design, image, or a combination of these elements. There is also a range of non-conventional _____s comprising marks which do not fall into these standard categories.
   a. 180SearchAssistant
   c. Trademark
   b. Power III
   d. Risk management

17. _____ is a trademark law concept permitting the owner of a famous trademark to forbid others from using that mark in a way that would lessen its uniqueness. In most cases, _____ involves an unauthorized use of another's trademark on products that do not compete with, and have little connection with, those of the trademark owner. For example, a famous trademark used by one company to refer to hair care products might be diluted if another company began using a similar mark to refer to breakfast cereals or spark plugs.
   a. Trademark attorney
   c. Trespass to land
   b. Federal Bureau of Investigation
   d. Trademark Dilution

18. _____ is a legal term of art that generally refers to characteristics of the visual appearance of a product or its packaging (or even the design of a building) that signify the source of the product to consumers. _____ is a form of intellectual property. In the U.S., like trademarks, a product's _____ is legally protected by the Lanham Act, the federal statute which regulates trademarks and _____.
   a. Geographical indication
   b. Gripe site
   c. Trade dress
   d. Wheeler-Lea Act

19. The _____ is a US law that applies to labels on many consumer products. It requires the label to state:

   - The identity of the product;
   - The name and place of business of the manufacturer, packer, or distributor; and
   - The net quantity of contents.

The contents statement must include both metric and U.S. customary units.

Passed under Lyndon B. Johnson in 1966, the law first took effect on July 1, 1967. The metric labeling requirement was added in 1992 and took effect on February 14, 1994.

   a. 6-3-5 Brainwriting
   b. Fair Packaging and Labeling Act
   c. Power III
   d. 180SearchAssistant

20. The _____ is a 1990 United States Federal law. It was signed into law on November 8, 1990 by the president.

The law gives the Food and Drug Administration (FDA) authority to require nutrition labeling of most foods regulated by the Agency; and to require that all nutrient content claims (for example, 'high fiber', 'low fat', etc).

   a. Trespass to land
   b. Fair Debt Collection Practices Act
   c. Nutrition Labeling and Education Act
   d. Copyright infringement

21. _____ or brand stretching is a marketing strategy in which a firm marketing a product with a well-developed image uses the same brand name in a different product category. Organizations use this strategy to increase and leverage brand equity (definition: the net worth and long-term sustainability just from the renowned name.) An example of a _____ is Jello-gelatin creating Jello pudding pops.
   a. Brand extension
   b. Web 2.0
   c. Brand awareness
   d. Brand orientation

Chapter 12. Category and Brand Management, Product Identification

22. A product _____ is the use of an established product's brand name for a new item in the same product category. _____s occur when a company introduces additional items in the same product category under the same brand name such as new flavors, forms, colors, added ingredients, package sizes.Examples includei) Zen LXI, Zen VXIii) Surf, Surf Excel, Surf Excel Blueiii) Splendour, Splendour Plusiv) Coke, Diet Coke, Vanilla Cokev) Clinic All Clear, Clinic Plus

- brand
- brand management
- marketing
- product management
- Product lining

a. Brand Development Index
b. Targeted advertising
c. Perishability
d. Line extension

23. _____ is the process of creating and managing contracts between the owner of a brand and a company or individual who wants to use the brand in association with a product, for an agreed period of time, within an agreed territory. Licensing is used by brand owners to extend a trademark or character onto products of a completely different nature.

_____ a is well-established business, both in the area of patents and trademarks.

a. Brand licensing
b. Brand culture
c. Brand loyalty
d. Brand strength analysis

24. The verb _____ or grant _____ means to give permission. The noun _____ refers to that permission as well as to the document memorializing that permission. _____ may be granted by a party to another party as an element of an agreement between those parties.
a. 180SearchAssistant
b. License
c. Power III
d. 6-3-5 Brainwriting

25. _____ in organizations and public policy is both the organizational process of creating and maintaining a plan; and the psychological process of thinking about the activities required to create a desired goal on some scale. As such, it is a fundamental property of intelligent behavior. This thought process is essential to the creation and refinement of a plan, or integration of it with other plans, that is, it combines forecasting of developments with the preparation of scenarios of how to react to them.
a. Planning
b. Power III
c. 6-3-5 Brainwriting
d. 180SearchAssistant

26. _____ Management is the succession of strategies used by management as a product goes through its _____. The conditions in which a product is sold changes over time and must be managed as it moves through its succession of stages.

The _____ goes through many phases, involves many professional disciplines, and requires many skills, tools and processes.

Chapter 12. Category and Brand Management, Product Identification

a. Chain stores
b. Customer satisfaction
c. Supplier diversity
d. Product life cycle

27. _____ is the ongoing process of identifying and articulating market requirements that define a product's feature set.
a. Brand parity
b. Market intelligence
c. Targeted advertising
d. Product planning

28. _____ is an advertisement in which a particular product specifically mentions a competitor by name for the express purpose of showing why the competitor is inferior to the product naming it.

This should not be confused with parody advertisements, where a fictional product is being advertised for the purpose of poking fun at the particular advertisement, nor should it be confused with the use of a coined brand name for the purpose of comparing the product without actually naming an actual competitor. ('Wikipedia tastes better and is less filling than the Encyclopedia Galactica.')

In the 1980s, during what has been referred to as the cola wars, soft-drink manufacturer Pepsi ran a series of advertisements where people, caught on hidden camera, in a blind taste test, chose Pepsi over rival Coca-Cola.

a. Heavy-up
b. Comparative advertising
c. GL-70
d. Cost per conversion

29. In marketing and strategy, _____ refers to a reduction in the sales volume, sales revenue, or market share of one product as a result of the introduction of a new product by the same producer.

For example, if Coca Cola were to introduce a similar product (say, Diet Coke or Cherry Coke), this new product could take some of the sales away from the original Coke. _____ is a key consideration in product portfolio analysis.

a. Marketing
b. Business-to-consumer
c. Cannibalization
d. Co-marketing

30. A _____ strategy targets non-buying customers in currently targeted segments. It also targets new customers in new segments. (Winer)

A marketing manager has to think about the following questions before implementing a _____ strategy: Is it profitable? Will it require the introduction of new or modified products? Is the customer and channel well enough researched and understood?

The marketing manager uses these four groups to give more focus to the market segment decision: existing customers, competitor customers, non-buying in current segments, new segments.

a. Perceptual mapping
b. Kano model
c. Market development
d. Commercial planning

31. A _____ is a subgroup of people or organizations sharing one or more characteristics that cause them to have similar product and/or service needs. A true _____ meets all of the following criteria: it is distinct from other segments (different segments have different needs), it is homogeneous within the segment (exhibits common needs); it responds similarly to a market stimulus, and it can be reached by a market intervention. The term is also used when consumers with identical product and/or service needs are divided up into groups so they can be charged different amounts.
- a. Commercial planning
- b. Customer insight
- c. Production orientation
- d. Market segment

32. In marketing, _____ has come to mean the process by which marketers try to create an image or identity in the minds of their target market for its product, brand, or organization. It is the 'relative competitive comparison' their product occupies in a given market as perceived by the target market.

Re-_____ involves changing the identity of a product, relative to the identity of competing products, in the collective minds of the target market.

- a. GE matrix
- b. Moratorium
- c. Containerization
- d. Positioning

33. In business and engineering, new _____ is the term used to describe the complete process of bringing a new product or service to market. There are two parallel paths involved in the Nproduct development process: one involves the idea generation, product design, and detail engineering; the other involves market research and marketing analysis. Companies typically see new _____ as the first stage in generating and commercializing new products within the overall strategic process of product life cycle management used to maintain or grow their market share.
- a. Product development
- b. Specification tree
- c. New product screening
- d. New product development

34. A _____ is a plan of action designed to achieve a particular goal.

_____ is different from tactics. In military terms, tactics is concerned with the conduct of an engagement while _____ is concerned with how different engagements are linked.

- a. 6-3-5 Brainwriting
- b. Power III
- c. Strategy
- d. 180SearchAssistant

35. _____ is the process by which a new idea or new product is accepted by the market. The rate of _____ is the speed that the new idea spreads from one consumer to the next. Adoption is similar to _____ except that it deals with the psychological processes an individual goes through, rather than an aggregate market process.
- a. Perceptual maps
- b. Diffusion
- c. Market development
- d. Kano model

36. In probability theory, a branch of mathematics, a _____ is a solution to a stochastic differential equation. It is a continuous-time Markov process with continuous sample paths.

A sample path of a _____ mimics the trajectory of a molecule, which is embedded in a flowing fluid and at the same time subjected to random displacements due to collisions with other molecules, i.e. Brownian motion.

Chapter 12. Category and Brand Management, Product Identification

a. 180SearchAssistant
c. Power III
b. 6-3-5 Brainwriting
d. Diffusion process

37. _____ is the study of when, why, how, where and what people do or do not buy products. It blends elements from psychology, sociology, social psychology, anthropology and economics. It attempts to understand the buyer decision making process, both individually and in groups. It studies characteristics of individual consumers such as demographics and behavioural variables in an attempt to understand people's wants. It also tries to assess influences on the consumer from groups such as family, friends, reference groups, and society in general.
a. Consumer behavior
c. Consumer confidence
b. Multidimensional scaling
d. Communal marketing

38. A _____ researches, selects, develops, and places a company's products.

A _____ considers numerous factors such as target demographic, the products offered by the competition, and how well the product fits in with the company's business model. Generally, a _____ manages one or more tangible products.

a. Promotional mix
c. Pick and pack
b. Power III
d. Product manager

39. _____ refer to a collection of facts usually collected as the result of experience, observation or experiment or a set of premises. This may consist of numbers, words particularly as measurements or observations of a set of variables. _____ are often viewed as a lowest level of abstraction from which information and knowledge are derived.
a. Sample size
c. Pearson product-moment correlation coefficient
b. Mean
d. Data

40. _____ is the set of tasks, knowledge, and techniques required to identify business needs and determine solutions to business problems. Solutions often include a systems development component, but may also consist of process improvement or organizational change. The person who carries out this task is called a business analyst or _____.
a. Fast moving consumer goods
c. Business analysis
b. Marketing management
d. Door-to-door

41. _____ is the process of using quantitative methods and qualitative methods to evaluate consumer response to a product idea prior to the introduction of a product to the market. It can also be used to generate communication designed to alter consumer attitudes toward existing products. These methods involve the evaluation by consumers of product concepts having certain rational benefits, such as 'a detergent that removes stains but is gentle on fabrics,' or non-rational benefits, such as 'a shampoo that lets you be yourself.' Such methods are commonly referred to as _____ and have been performed using field surveys, personal interviews and focus groups, in combination with various quantitative methods, to generate and evaluate product concepts.
a. Logit analysis
c. Market analysis
b. Cross tabulation
d. Concept testing

42. The _____, abbreviated _____ is a mathematically based algorithm for scheduling a set of project activities. It is an important tool for effective project management.

Chapter 12. Category and Brand Management, Product Identification

It was developed in the 1950s by the US Navy when trying to better organize the building of submarines and later, especially, when building nuclear submarines.

a. 180SearchAssistant
b. Power III
c. 6-3-5 Brainwriting
d. Critical path method

43. _____ is systematic determination of merit, worth, and significance of something or someone using criteria against a set of standards. _____ often is used to characterize and appraise subjects of interest in a wide range of human enterprises, including the arts, criminal justice, foundations and non-profit organizations, government, health care, and other human services.

Depending on the topic of interest, there are professional groups which look to the quality and rigor of the _____ process.

a. Evaluation
b. ADTECH
c. ACNielsen
d. AMAX

44. The _____, is a model for project management designed to analyze and represent the tasks involved in completing a given project.

_____ is a method to analyze the involved tasks in completing a given project, especially the time needed to complete each task, and identifying the minimum time needed to complete the total project.

PERT was developed primarily to simplify the planning and scheduling of large and complex projects.

a. 180SearchAssistant
b. 6-3-5 Brainwriting
c. Program evaluation and review technique
d. Power III

45. _____ is the process or cycle of introducing a new product into the market. The actual launch of a new product is the final stage of new product development, and the one where the most money will have to be spent for advertising, sales promotion, and other marketing efforts. In the case of a new consumer packaged good, costs will be at least $ 10 million, but can reach up to $ 200 million.

a. Customer Interaction Tracker
b. Sweepstakes
c. Confusion marketing
d. Commercialization

46. _____ is the area of law in which manufacturers, distributors, suppliers, retailers, and others who make products available to the public are held responsible for the injuries those products cause.

In the United States, the claims most commonly associated with _____ are negligence, strict liability, breach of warranty, and various consumer protection claims. The majority of _____ laws are determined at the state level and vary widely from state to state.

a. Mediation
b. Trespass to land
c. Product liability
d. Registered trademark symbol

47. A _____ is a type of wholesale merchant business that buys goods and bulk products from importers, other wholesalers and then sells to retailers. _____s can deal in any commodity destined for the retail market. Typical categories are food, lumber, hardware, fuel, and textiles.
   a. Refusal to deal
   b. Jobbing house
   c. Chief privacy officer
   d. Tacit collusion

Chapter 13. Marketing Channels and Supply Chain Management

1. _____ is defined by the American _____ Association as the activity, set of institutions, and processes for creating, communicating, delivering, and exchanging offerings that have value for customers, clients, partners, and society at large. The term developed from the original meaning which referred literally to going to market, as in shopping, or going to a market to sell goods or services.

_____ practice tends to be seen as a creative industry, which includes advertising, distribution and selling.

   a. Product naming
   b. Customer acquisition management
   c. Marketing myopia
   d. Marketing

2. _____ is a form of intellectual property which gives the creator of an original work exclusive rights for a certain time period in relation to that work, including its publication, distribution and adaptation; after which time the work is said to enter the public domain. _____ applies to any expressible form of an idea or information that is substantive and discrete. Some jurisdictions also recognize 'moral rights' of the creator of a work, such as the right to be credited for the work.
   a. Collective mark
   b. Celler-Kefauver Act
   c. Reasonable person standard
   d. Copyright

3. The _____ is a United States copyright law that implements two 1996 treaties of the World Intellectual Property Organization (WIPO.) It criminalizes production and dissemination of technology, devices whether or not there is actual infringement of copyright itself. In addition, the _____ heightens the penalties for copyright infringement on the Internet.
   a. Priority right
   b. Regulatory
   c. Copyright infringement
   d. Digital Millennium Copyright Act

4. _____ is one of the four elements of marketing mix. An organization or set of organizations (go-betweens) involved in the process of making a product or service available for use or consumption by a consumer or business user.

The other three parts of the marketing mix are product, pricing, and promotion.

   a. Distribution
   b. Japan Advertising Photographers' Association
   c. Better Living Through Chemistry
   d. Comparison-Shopping agent

5. A _____ is a list of the general tasks and responsibilities of a position. Typically, it also includes to whom the position reports, specifications such as the qualifications needed by the person in the job, salary range for the position, etc. A _____ is usually developed by conducting a job analysis, which includes examining the tasks and sequences of tasks necessary to perform the job.
   a. 6-3-5 Brainwriting
   b. Power III
   c. 180SearchAssistant
   d. Job description

6. _____ is the management of the flow of goods, information and other resources, including energy and people, between the point of origin and the point of consumption in order to meet the requirements of consumers (frequently, and originally, military organizations.) _____ involves the integration of information, transportation, inventory, warehousing, material-handling, and packaging. _____ is a channel of the supply chain which adds the value of time and place utility.
   a. Power III
   b. 180SearchAssistant
   c. 6-3-5 Brainwriting
   d. Logistics

Chapter 13. Marketing Channels and Supply Chain Management 111

7. A _____ is a process that can allow an organization to concentrate its limited resources on the greatest opportunities to increase sales and achieve a sustainable competitive advantage. A _____ should be centered around the key concept that customer satisfaction is the main goal.

A _____ is most effective when it is an integral component of corporate strategy, defining how the organization will successfully engage customers, prospects, and competitors in the market arena.

   a. Cyberdoc
   b. Societal marketing
   c. Psychographic
   d. Marketing strategy

8. A _____ is a plan of action designed to achieve a particular goal.

_____ is different from tactics. In military terms, tactics is concerned with the conduct of an engagement while _____ is concerned with how different engagements are linked.

   a. Strategy
   b. Power III
   c. 6-3-5 Brainwriting
   d. 180SearchAssistant

9. _____ consists of the sale of goods or merchandise from a fixed location, such as a department store or kiosk in small or individual lots for direct consumption by the purchaser. _____ may include subordinated services, such as delivery. Purchasers may be individuals or businesses.

   a. Warehouse store
   b. Retailing
   c. Charity shop
   d. Thrifting

10. _____, also referred to as i-marketing, web marketing, online marketing is the marketing of products or services over the Internet.

The Internet has brought many unique benefits to marketing, one of which being lower costs for the distribution of information and media to a global audience. The interactive nature of _____, both in terms of providing instant response and eliciting responses, is a unique quality of the medium.

   a. Internet marketing
   b. ADTECH
   c. AMAX
   d. ACNielsen

11. _____ is a broad label that refers to any individuals or households that use goods and services generated within the economy. The concept of a _____ is used in different contexts, so that the usage and significance of the term may vary.

A _____ is a person who uses any product or service.

   a. 6-3-5 Brainwriting
   b. Power III
   c. 180SearchAssistant
   d. Consumer

12. _____ are final goods specifically intended for the mass market. For instance, _____ do not include investment assets, like precious antiques, even though these antiques are final goods.

Chapter 13. Marketing Channels and Supply Chain Management

Manufactured goods are goods that have been processed by way of machinery.

a. Free good
c. Consumer Goods
b. Durable good
d. Power III

13. _____ is one of the four Ps of the marketing mix. The other three aspects are product, promotion, and place. It is also a key variable in microeconomic price allocation theory.
   a. Price
   b. Competitor indexing
   c. Relationship based pricing
   d. Pricing

14. In algebra, a _____ is a function depending on n that associates a scalar, det(A), to an n×n square matrix A. The fundamental geometric meaning of a _____ is a scale factor for measure when A is regarded as a linear transformation. _____s are important both in calculus, where they enter the substitution rule for several variables, and in multilinear algebra.

For a fixed nonnegative integer n, there is a unique _____ function for the n×n matrices over any commutative ring R. In particular, this function exists when R is the field of real or complex numbers.

a. Determinant
c. Package-on-Package
b. Motion Picture Association of America's film-rating system
d. Black Friday

15. _____ is a retail channel for the distribution of goods and services. At a basic level it may be defined as marketing and selling products, direct to consumers away from a fixed retail location. Sales are typically made through party plan, one to one demonstrations, and other personal contact arrangements.
   a. 6-3-5 Brainwriting
   b. Direct selling
   c. Power III
   d. 180SearchAssistant

16. A _____ or trade mark, identified by the symbols ™ (not yet registered) and ® (registered) business organization or other legal entity to identify that the products and/or services to consumers with which the _____ appears originate from a unique source of origin, and to distinguish its products or services from those of other entities. A _____ is a type of intellectual property, and typically a name, word, phrase, logo, symbol, design, image, or a combination of these elements. There is also a range of non-conventional _____s comprising marks which do not fall into these standard categories.
   a. 180SearchAssistant
   b. Risk management
   c. Power III
   d. Trademark

17. _____ is a term commonly used to describe commerce transactions between businesses like the one between a manufacturer and a wholesaler or a wholesaler and a retailer i.e both the buyer and the seller are business entity.This is unlike business-to-consumers (B2C) which involve a business entity and end consumer, or business-to-government (B2G) which involve a business entity and government.

The volume of B2B transactions is much higher than the volume of B2C transactions. The primary reason for this is that in a typical supply chain there will be many B2B transactions involving subcomponent or raw materials, and only one B2C transaction, specifically sale of the finished product to the end customer.

Chapter 13. Marketing Channels and Supply Chain Management

a. Business-to-business
b. Social marketing
c. Customer relationship management
d. Disruptive technology

18. Competitiveness is a comparative concept of the ability and performance of a firm, sub-sector or country to sell and supply goods and/or services in a given market. Although widely used in economics and business management, the usefulness of the concept, particularly in the context of national competitiveness, is vigorously disputed by economists, such as Paul Krugman .

The term may also be applied to markets, where it is used to refer to the extent to which the market structure may be regarded as perfectly _____.

a. Free trade zone
b. Customs union
c. Geographical pricing
d. Competitive

19. Electronic commerce, commonly known as _____ or eCommerce, consists of the buying and selling of products or services over electronic systems such as the Internet and other computer networks. The amount of trade conducted electronically has grown extraordinarily with wide-spread Internet usage. A wide variety of commerce is conducted in this way, spurring and drawing on innovations in electronic funds transfer, supply chain management, Internet marketing, online transaction processing, electronic data interchange (EDI), inventory management systems, and automated data collection systems.

a. ADTECH
b. ACNielsen
c. AMAX
d. E-commerce

20. _____ often refers to either primary or secondary research. Secondary research involves a company using information compiled from various sources, which is about a new or existing product. The advantages of secondary research are that it is relatively cheap and easily accessible.

a. Questionnaire
b. Mystery shoppers
c. Mystery shopping
d. Market Research

21. _____ is a form of communication that typically attempts to persuade potential customers to purchase or to consume more of a particular brand of product or service. 'While now central to the contemporary global economy and the reproduction of global production networks, it is only quite recently that _____ has been more than a marginal influence on patterns of sales and production. The formation of modern _____ was intimately bound up with the emergence of new forms of monopoly capitalism around the end of the 19th and beginning of the 20th century as one element in corporate strategies to create, organize and where possible control markets, especially for mass produced consumer goods.

a. ADTECH
b. AMAX
c. ACNielsen
d. Advertising

22. A _____ is defined by the International Co-operative Alliance's Statement on the Co-operative Identity as an autonomous association of persons united voluntarily to meet their common economic, social, and cultural needs and aspirations through a jointly-owned and democratically-controlled enterprise. It is a business organization owned and operated by a group of individuals for their mutual benefit. A _____ may also be defined as a business owned and controlled equally by the people who use its services or who work at it.

a. Power III
b. 6-3-5 Brainwriting
c. Cooperative
d. 180SearchAssistant

23. The _____ is an independent agency of the United States government, established in 1914 by the _____ Act. Its principal mission is the promotion of 'consumer protection' and the elimination and prevention of what regulators perceive to be harmfully 'anti-competitive' business practices, such as coercive monopoly.

The _____ Act was one of President Wilson's major acts against trusts.

a. Power III
c. 6-3-5 Brainwriting
b. 180SearchAssistant
d. Federal Trade Commission

24. The _____ of 1914 (15 U.S.C §§ 41-58, as amended) established the Federal Trade Commission (FTC), a bipartisan body of five members appointed by the President of the United States for seven year terms. This Commission was authorized to issue Cease and Desist orders to large corporations to curb unfair trade practices. This Act also gave more flexibility to the US congress for judicial matters.

a. Gripe site
c. Product liability
b. Comparative negligence
d. Federal Trade Commission Act

25. _____ refers to when a retailer or wholesaler is 'tied' to purchase from a supplier on the understanding that no other distributor will be appointed or receive supplies in a given area. When the sales outlets are owned by the supplier, _____ is because of vertical integration, where the outlets are independent _____ is illegal due to the Restrictive Trade Practices Act, however, if it is registered and approved it is allowed.

_____ can be a barrier to entry, it can be defended on the grounds that it is beneficial to consumers as it can allow after sales service to be better.

a. Exclusive dealing
c. ACNielsen
b. AMAX
d. ADTECH

26. _____ is the study of when, why, how, where and what people do or do not buy products. It blends elements from psychology, sociology, social psychology, anthropology and economics. It attempts to understand the buyer decision making process, both individually and in groups. It studies characteristics of individual consumers such as demographics and behavioural variables in an attempt to understand people's wants. It also tries to assess influences on the consumer from groups such as family, friends, reference groups, and society in general.

a. Multidimensional scaling
c. Communal marketing
b. Consumer behavior
d. Consumer confidence

27. An _____ is the manufacturing of a good or service within a category. Although _____ is a broad term for any kind of economic production, in economics and urban planning _____ is a synonym for the secondary sector, which is a type of economic activity involved in the manufacturing of raw materials into goods and products.

There are four key industrial economic sectors: the primary sector, largely raw material extraction industries such as mining and farming; the secondary sector, involving refining, construction, and manufacturing; the tertiary sector, which deals with services (such as law and medicine) and distribution of manufactured goods; and the quaternary sector, a relatively new type of knowledge _____ focusing on technological research, design and development such as computer programming, and biochemistry.

Chapter 13. Marketing Channels and Supply Chain Management

   a. ACNielsen
   c. AMAX
   b. Industry
   d. ADTECH

28. A _____ is a type of wholesale merchant business that buys goods and bulk products from importers, other wholesalers and then sells to retailers. _____s can deal in any commodity destined for the retail market. Typical categories are food, lumber, hardware, fuel, and textiles.
   a. Tacit collusion
   c. Refusal to deal
   b. Jobbing house
   d. Chief privacy officer

29. A _____ is the price one pays as remuneration for services, especially the honorarium paid to a doctor, lawyer, consultant, or other member of a learned profession. _____s usually allow for overhead, wages, costs, and markup.

Traditionally, professionals in Great Britain received a _____ in contradistinction to a payment, salary, or wage, and would often use guineas rather than pounds as units of account.

   a. Price war
   c. Fee
   b. Price shading
   d. Transfer pricing

30. _____s is the social science that studies the production, distribution, and consumption of goods and services. The term _____s comes from the Ancient Greek oá¼°κονομία from oá¼¶κος (oikos, 'house') + νόμος (nomos, 'custom' or 'law'), hence 'rules of the house(hold)'. Current _____ models developed out of the broader field of political economy in the late 19th century, owing to a desire to use an empirical approach more akin to the physical sciences.
   a. ADTECH
   c. Industrial organization
   b. Economic
   d. ACNielsen

31. The most important feature of a contract is that one party makes an _____ for an arrangement that another accepts. This can be called a 'concurrence of wills' or 'ad idem' (meeting of the minds) of two or more parties. The concept is somewhat contested.
   a. ACNielsen
   c. AMAX
   b. Offer
   d. ADTECH

32. A _____ is an optical machine-readable representation of data. Originally, _____s represented data in the widths (lines) and the spacings of parallel lines and may be referred to as linear or 1D (1 dimensional) barcodes or symbologies. But they also come in patterns of squares, dots, hexagons and other geometric patterns within images termed 2D (2 dimensional) matrix codes or symbologies.
   a. Bar code
   c. Power III
   b. 6-3-5 Brainwriting
   d. 180SearchAssistant

33. A _____ or logistics network is the system of organizations, people, technology, activities, information and resources involved in moving a product or service from supplier to customer. _____ activities transform natural resources, raw materials and components into a finished product that is delivered to the end customer. In sophisticated _____ systems, used products may re-enter the _____ at any point where residual value is recyclable.
   a. Supply chain network
   c. Supply chain
   b. Demand chain management
   d. Purchasing

Chapter 13. Marketing Channels and Supply Chain Management

34. A personal and cultural _____ is a relative ethic _____, an assumption upon which implementation can be extrapolated. A _____ system is a set of consistent _____s and measures that is soo not true. A principle _____ is a foundation upon which other _____s and measures of integrity are based.

   a. Value
   b. Supreme Court of the United States
   c. Perceptual maps
   d. Package-on-Package

35. The _____ is a concept from business management that was first described and popularized by Michael Porter in his 1985 best-seller, Competitive Advantage: Creating and Sustaining Superior Performance.

A _____ is a chain of activities. Products pass through all activities of the chain in order and at each activity the product gains some value.

   a. Value chain
   b. Mass marketing
   c. Business-to-business
   d. Relationship management

36. _____ is the use of an object (typically referred to as an RFID tag) applied to or incorporated into a product, animal, or person for the purpose of identification and tracking using radio waves. Some tags can be read from several meters away and beyond the line of sight of the reader.

Most RFID tags contain at least two parts.

   a. Power III
   b. 6-3-5 Brainwriting
   c. 180SearchAssistant
   d. Radio-frequency identification

37. _____ is an advertisement in which a particular product specifically mentions a competitor by name for the express purpose of showing why the competitor is inferior to the product naming it.

This should not be confused with parody advertisements, where a fictional product is being advertised for the purpose of poking fun at the particular advertisement, nor should it be confused with the use of a coined brand name for the purpose of comparing the product without actually naming an actual competitor. ('Wikipedia tastes better and is less filling than the Encyclopedia Galactica.')

In the 1980s, during what has been referred to as the cola wars, soft-drink manufacturer Pepsi ran a series of advertisements where people, caught on hidden camera, in a blind taste test, chose Pepsi over rival Coca-Cola.

   a. GL-70
   b. Cost per conversion
   c. Heavy-up
   d. Comparative advertising

38. _____ refers to the additional value of a commodity over the cost of commodities used to produce it from the previous stage of production. An example is the price of gasoline at the pump over the price of the oil in it. In national accounts used in macroeconomics, it refers to the contribution of the factors of production, i.e., land, labor, and capital goods, to raising the value of a product and corresponds to the incomes received by the owners of these factors. The factors of production provide 'services' which raise the unit price of a product (X) relative to the cost per unit of intermediate goods used up in the production of X. _____ is shared between the factors of production (capital, labor, also human capital), giving rise to issues of distribution.

Chapter 13. Marketing Channels and Supply Chain Management

a. Power III
b. Value added
c. Consumer spending
d. Deregulation

39. _____ refer to a collection of facts usually collected as the result of experience, observation or experiment or a set of premises. This may consist of numbers, words particularly as measurements or observations of a set of variables. _____ are often viewed as a lowest level of abstraction from which information and knowledge are derived.
    a. Pearson product-moment correlation coefficient
    b. Sample size
    c. Mean
    d. Data

40. In economics, an _____ is any good or commodity, transported from one country to another country in a legitimate fashion, typically for use in trade. _____ goods or services are provided to foreign consumers by domestic producers. _____ is an important part of international trade.
    a. AMAX
    b. ADTECH
    c. ACNielsen
    d. Export

41. _____ is a method of direct marketing in which a salesperson solicits to prospective customers to buy products or services, either over the phone or through a subsequent face to face or Web conferencing appointment scheduled during the call.

    _____ can also include recorded sales pitches programmed to be played over the phone via automatic dialing. _____ has come under fire in recent years, being viewed as an annoyance by many.

    a. Joe job
    b. Phishing
    c. Directory Harvest Attack
    d. Telemarketing

42. _____ is exchange of capital, goods, and services across international borders or territories. In most countries, it represents a significant share of gross domestic product (GDP.) While _____ has been present throughout much of history, its economic, social, and political importance has been on the rise in recent centuries.
    a. Incoterms
    b. ACNielsen
    c. ADTECH
    d. International trade

43. _____ is a measure of the strength of a brand, product, service relative to competitive offerings. There is often a geographic element to the competitive landscape. In defining _____, you must see to what extent a product, brand, or firm controls a product category in a given geographic area.
    a. Productivity
    b. Market system
    c. Discretionary spending
    d. Market dominance

44. _____ in organizations and public policy is both the organizational process of creating and maintaining a plan; and the psychological process of thinking about the activities required to create a desired goal on some scale. As such, it is a fundamental property of intelligent behavior. This thought process is essential to the creation and refinement of a plan, or integration of it with other plans, that is, it combines forecasting of developments with the preparation of scenarios of how to react to them.
    a. 180SearchAssistant
    b. Power III
    c. 6-3-5 Brainwriting
    d. Planning

45. The _____ is a 1990 United States Federal law. It was signed into law on November 8, 1990 by the president.

Chapter 13. Marketing Channels and Supply Chain Management

The law gives the Food and Drug Administration (FDA) authority to require nutrition labeling of most foods regulated by the Agency; and to require that all nutrient content claims (for example, 'high fiber', 'low fat', etc.).

a. Nutrition Labeling and Education Act
b. Fair Debt Collection Practices Act
c. Copyright infringement
d. Trespass to land

46. _____ is a list for goods and materials held available in stock by a business. It is also used for a list of the contents of a household and for a list for testamentary purposes of the possessions of someone who has died. In accounting _____ is considered an asset.

a. ACNielsen
b. ADTECH
c. Ending Inventory
d. Inventory

47. _____ operations or facilities are commonly called 'distribution centers'. '_____' is the term generally used to describe the process or the work flow associated with the picking, packing and delivery of the packed item(s) to a shipping carrier.

a. ADTECH
b. AMAX
c. ACNielsen
d. Order processing

48. A _____ is an entity that provides services to other entities. Usually this refers to a business that provides subscription or web service to other businesses or individuals. Examples of these services include Internet access, Mobile phone operator, and web application hosting.

a. Service provider
b. Cross-selling
c. Yield management
d. Freebie marketing

49. _____ is a family of business models in which the buyer of a product provides certain information to a supplier of that product and the supplier takes full responsibility for maintaining an agreed inventory of the material, usually at the buyer's consumption location (usually a store.) A third party logistics provider can also be involved to make sure that the buyer have the required level of inventory by adjusting the demand and supply gaps.

As a symbiotic relationship, _____ makes it less likely that a business will unintentionally become out of stock of a good and reduces inventory in the supply chain.

a. Merchandise management system
b. Customer driven supply chain
c. Reverse auction
d. Vendor Managed Inventory

50. _____ is a system of intermodal freight transport using standard intermodal containers that are standardised by the International Organization for Standardization (ISO.) These can be loaded and sealed intact onto container ships, railroad cars, planes, and trucks.

a. Scientific controls
b. Containerization
c. BeyondROI
d. Rebate

Chapter 14. Direct Marketing and Marketing Resellers: Retailers and Wholesalers

1. _____ consists of the sale of goods or merchandise from a fixed location, such as a department store or kiosk in small or individual lots for direct consumption by the purchaser. _____ may include subordinated services, such as delivery. Purchasers may be individuals or businesses.
   a. Charity shop
   b. Retailing
   c. Warehouse store
   d. Thrifting

2. _____ is a term commonly used to describe commerce transactions between businesses like the one between a manufacturer and a wholesaler or a wholesaler and a retailer i.e both the buyer and the seller are business entity.This is unlike business-to-consumers (B2C) which involve a business entity and end consumer, or business-to-government (B2G) which involve a business entity and government.

   The volume of B2B transactions is much higher than the volume of B2C transactions. The primary reason for this is that in a typical supply chain there will be many B2B transactions involving subcomponent or raw materials, and only one B2C transaction, specifically sale of the finished product to the end customer.

   a. Business-to-business
   b. Social marketing
   c. Customer relationship management
   d. Disruptive technology

3. _____ is a strategic planning method used to evaluate the Strengths, Weaknesses, Opportunities, and Threats involved in a project or in a business venture. It involves specifying the objective of the business venture or project and identifying the internal and external factors that are favorable and unfavorable to achieving that objective. The technique is credited to Albert Humphrey, who led a research project at Stanford University in the 1960s and 1970s using data from Fortune 500 companies.
   a. Lead scoring
   b. SWOT analysis
   c. Product differentiation
   d. Market environment

4. A _____ is a plan of action designed to achieve a particular goal.

   _____ is different from tactics. In military terms, tactics is concerned with the conduct of an engagement while _____ is concerned with how different engagements are linked.

   a. Power III
   b. 180SearchAssistant
   c. 6-3-5 Brainwriting
   d. Strategy

5. _____ is a retailing concept in which the total range of products sold by a retailer is broken down into discrete groups of similar or related products; these groups are known as product categories. Examples of grocery categories may be: tinned fish, washing detergent, toothpastes, etc.Each category is then run like a 'mini business' (Business Unit) in its own right, with its own set of turnover and/or profitability targets and strategies. An important facet of _____ is the shift in relationship between retailer and supplier : instead of the traditional adversarial relationship, the relationship moves to one of collaboration, exchange of information and data and joint business building.The focus of all negotiations is centered around the effects of the turnover of the total category, not just the sales on the individual products therein.
   a. Category management
   b. Market segment
   c. Societal marketing
   d. Brochure

6. _____ refers to the methods, practices and operations conducted to promote and sustain certain categories of commercial activity. The term is understood to have different specific meanings depending on the context. Merchandise is a sale goods at a store

Chapter 14. Direct Marketing and Marketing Resellers: Retailers and Wholesalers

In marketing, one of the definitions of _____ is the practice in which the brand or image from one product or service is used to sell another.

   a. New Media Strategies   b. Merchandising
   c. Marketing communication   d. Word of mouth

7. A _____ is a diagram of fixtures and products that illustrates how and where retail products should be displayed, usually on a store shelf in order to increase customer purchases. They may also be referred to as plano-grams, plan-o-grams, schematics (archaic) or POGs.

A _____ is often received before a product reaches a store, and is useful when a retailer wants multiple store displays to have the same look and feel.

   a. Planogram   b. Layaway
   c. Khodebshchik   d. Power centre

8. _____ is the provision of service to customers before, during and after a purchase.

According to Turban et al., '_____ is a series of activities designed to enhance the level of customer satisfaction - that is, the feeling that a product or service has met the customer expectation.'

Its importance varies by product, industry and customer.

   a. Customer service   b. COPC Inc.
   c. Facing   d. Customer experience

9. _____ is an advertisement in which a particular product specifically mentions a competitor by name for the express purpose of showing why the competitor is inferior to the product naming it.

This should not be confused with parody advertisements, where a fictional product is being advertised for the purpose of poking fun at the particular advertisement, nor should it be confused with the use of a coined brand name for the purpose of comparing the product without actually naming an actual competitor. ('Wikipedia tastes better and is less filling than the Encyclopedia Galactica.')

In the 1980s, during what has been referred to as the cola wars, soft-drink manufacturer Pepsi ran a series of advertisements where people, caught on hidden camera, in a blind taste test, chose Pepsi over rival Coca-Cola.

   a. Cost per conversion   b. Heavy-up
   c. Comparative advertising   d. GL-70

10. _____ is one of the four elements of marketing mix. An organization or set of organizations (go-betweens) involved in the process of making a product or service available for use or consumption by a consumer or business user.

The other three parts of the marketing mix are product, pricing, and promotion.

Chapter 14. Direct Marketing and Marketing Resellers: Retailers and Wholesalers

a. Better Living Through Chemistry
b. Distribution
c. Japan Advertising Photographers' Association
d. Comparison-Shopping agent

11. _____ is a lightweight markup language, originally created by John Gruber and Aaron Swartz to help maximum readability and 'publishability' of both its input and output forms. The language takes many cues from existing conventions for marking up plain text in email. _____ converts its marked-up text input to valid, well-formed XHTML and replaces left-pointing angle brackets ('<') and ampersands with their corresponding character entity references.

a. 180SearchAssistant
b. 6-3-5 Brainwriting
c. Power III
d. Markdown

12. _____ is the examining of goods or services from retailers with the intent to purchase at that time. _____ is an activity of selection and/or purchase. In some contexts it is considered a leisure activity as well as an economic one.

a. Discount store
b. Shopping
c. Hawkers
d. Khodebshchik

13. _____ is a form of communication that typically attempts to persuade potential customers to purchase or to consume more of a particular brand of product or service. 'While now central to the contemporary global economy and the reproduction of global production networks, it is only quite recently that _____ has been more than a marginal influence on patterns of sales and production. The formation of modern _____ was intimately bound up with the emergence of new forms of monopoly capitalism around the end of the 19th and beginning of the 20th century as one element in corporate strategies to create, organize and where possible control markets, especially for mass produced consumer goods.

a. AMAX
b. Advertising
c. ACNielsen
d. ADTECH

14. _____ was originally coined by Austrian psychologist Alfred Adler in 1929. The current broader sense of the word dates from 1961.

In sociology, a _____ is the way a person lives.

a. 180SearchAssistant
b. Lifestyle
c. 6-3-5 Brainwriting
d. Power III

15. A _____ is a shopping center or mixed-used commercial development that combines the traditional retail functions of a shopping mall but with leisure amenities oriented towards upscale consumers. _____s, which were first labeled as such by Memphis developers Poag and McEwen in the late 1980s and emerged as a retailing trend in the late 1990s, are sometimes labeled 'boutique malls'. They are often located in affluent suburban areas.

a. Flighting
b. Category Development Index
c. Private branding
d. Lifestyle center

16. A _____ is a collection of symbols, experiences and associations connected with a product, a service, a person or any other artifact or entity.

_____s have become increasingly important components of culture and the economy, now being described as 'cultural accessories and personal philosophies'.

Some people distinguish the psychological aspect of a _____ from the experiential aspect.

a. Brandable software
c. Brand
b. Store brand
d. Brand equity

17. The _____ is a database of consumer perception of brands created and managed by BrandAsset Consulting, a division of Young ' Rubicam Brands to provide information to enable firms to improve the marketing decision-making process and to manage brands better. _____ and _____ also describe the Y'R group managing the database.

_____ measures the value of a brand along four dimensions: 'Differentiation,' 'Relevance,' 'Esteem,' and 'Knowledge.' Differentiation and Relevance build up to 'Brand Strength.' Esteem and Knowledge are used to calculate 'Brand Stature.' _____ defines these terms as follows.

a. Hoover free flights promotion
c. Targeted advertising
b. Target audience
d. Brand Asset Valuator

18. _____ is a broad label that refers to any individuals or households that use goods and services generated within the economy. The concept of a _____ is used in different contexts, so that the usage and significance of the term may vary.

A _____ is a person who uses any product or service.

a. 6-3-5 Brainwriting
c. 180SearchAssistant
b. Power III
d. Consumer

19. _____ is the study of when, why, how, where and what people do or do not buy products. It blends elements from psychology, sociology, social psychology, anthropology and economics. It attempts to understand the buyer decision making process, both individually and in groups. It studies characteristics of individual consumers such as demographics and behavioural variables in an attempt to understand people's wants. It also tries to assess influences on the consumer from groups such as family, friends, reference groups, and society in general.

a. Communal marketing
c. Consumer confidence
b. Consumer behavior
d. Multidimensional scaling

20. An _____ is the manufacturing of a good or service within a category. Although _____ is a broad term for any kind of economic production, in economics and urban planning _____ is a synonym for the secondary sector, which is a type of economic activity involved in the manufacturing of raw materials into goods and products.

There are four key industrial economic sectors: the primary sector, largely raw material extraction industries such as mining and farming; the secondary sector, involving refining, construction, and manufacturing; the tertiary sector, which deals with services (such as law and medicine) and distribution of manufactured goods; and the quaternary sector, a relatively new type of knowledge _____ focusing on technological research, design and development such as computer programming, and biochemistry.

a. ADTECH
c. AMAX
b. Industry
d. ACNielsen

21. _____ are final goods specifically intended for the mass market. For instance, _____ do not include investment assets, like precious antiques, even though these antiques are final goods.

Chapter 14. Direct Marketing and Marketing Resellers: Retailers and Wholesalers

Manufactured goods are goods that have been processed by way of machinery.

a. Durable good
c. Free good
b. Consumer Goods
d. Power III

22. A _____ is a type of wholesale merchant business that buys goods and bulk products from importers, other wholesalers and then sells to retailers. _____s can deal in any commodity destined for the retail market. Typical categories are food, lumber, hardware, fuel, and textiles.

a. Refusal to deal
c. Jobbing house
b. Chief privacy officer
d. Tacit collusion

23. _____ is one of the four Ps of the marketing mix. The other three aspects are product, promotion, and place. It is also a key variable in microeconomic price allocation theory.

a. Price
c. Competitor indexing
b. Relationship based pricing
d. Pricing

24. _____ are retail outlets, usually corporate owned businesses, that share brands and central management, often with standardized business methods and practices, and these may include stores, restaurants, and some service-oriented businesses.

The displacement of independent businesses by chains has generated controversy in many countries, and has sparked increased collaboration among independent businesses and communities to prevent chain proliferation. Such efforts occur within national trade groups such as the American Booksellers Association, as well as community-based coalitions such as Independent Business Alliances.

a. Supplier diversity
c. Chain stores
b. Customer base
d. Product life cycle management

25. _____ is anything that is intended to save time, energy or frustration. A _____ store at a petrol station, for example, sells items that have nothing to do with gasoline/petrol, but it saves the consumer from having to go to a grocery store. '_____' is a very relative term and its meaning tends to change over time.

a. Demographic profile
c. Convenience
b. Marketing buzz
d. MaxDiff

26. _____ is the state or fact of exclusive rights and control over property, which may be an object, land/real estate, or some other kind of property (like government-granted monopolies collectively referred to as intellectual property.) It is embodied in an _____ right also referred to as title.

_____ is the key building block in the development of the capitalist socio-economic system.

a. ADTECH
c. AMAX
b. ACNielsen
d. Ownership

Chapter 14. Direct Marketing and Marketing Resellers: Retailers and Wholesalers

27. _____ is a term used in marketing and strategic management to describe a product, service, brand, or company that has such a distinct sustainable competitive advantage that competing firms find it almost impossible to operate profitably in that industry. The existence of a _____ will eliminate almost all market entities, whether real or virtual. Many existing firms will leave the industry, thereby increasing the industry's concentration ratio.
   a. 6-3-5 Brainwriting
   b. Power III
   c. 180SearchAssistant
   d. Category killer

28. Merchandising refers to the methods, practices and operations conducted to promote and sustain certain categories of commercial activity. The term is understood to have different specific meanings depending on the context. _____ is a sale goods at a store

In marketing, one of the definitions of merchandising is the practice in which the brand or image from one product or service is used to sell another.

   a. Merchandise
   b. New Media Strategies
   c. Sales promotion
   d. Merchandising

29. _____ are small stores which specialize in a specific range of merchandise and related items. Most stores have an extensive width and depth of stock in the item that they specify in and provide high levels of service and expertise. The pricing policy is generally in the medium to high range, depending on factors like the type and exclusivity of merchandise and ownership, that is, whether they are owner operated or a chain operation which has the advantage of bulk purchasing and centralized warehousing system.
   a. Catalog merchant
   b. Wardrobing
   c. Brick and mortar business
   d. Specialty stores

30. _____ is a form of intellectual property which gives the creator of an original work exclusive rights for a certain time period in relation to that work, including its publication, distribution and adaptation; after which time the work is said to enter the public domain. _____ applies to any expressible form of an idea or information that is substantive and discrete. Some jurisdictions also recognize 'moral rights' of the creator of a work, such as the right to be credited for the work.
   a. Collective mark
   b. Celler-Kefauver Act
   c. Copyright
   d. Reasonable person standard

31. The _____ is a United States copyright law that implements two 1996 treaties of the World Intellectual Property Organization (WIPO.) It criminalizes production and dissemination of technology, devices whether or not there is actual infringement of copyright itself. In addition, the _____ heightens the penalties for copyright infringement on the Internet.
   a. Copyright infringement
   b. Regulatory
   c. Priority right
   d. Digital Millennium Copyright Act

32. The _____ is a 1990 United States Federal law. It was signed into law on November 8, 1990 by the president.

The law gives the Food and Drug Administration (FDA) authority to require nutrition labeling of most foods regulated by the Agency; and to require that all nutrient content claims (for example, 'high fiber', 'low fat', etc).

   a. Copyright infringement
   b. Trespass to land
   c. Fair Debt Collection Practices Act
   d. Nutrition Labeling and Education Act

Chapter 14. Direct Marketing and Marketing Resellers: Retailers and Wholesalers 125

33. A _____ is a retail establishment which specializes in selling a wide range of products without a single predominant merchandise line. _____s usually sell products including apparel, furniture, appliances, electronics, and additionally select other lines of products such as paint, hardware, toiletries, cosmetics, photographic equipment, jewelery, toys, and sporting goods. Certain _____s are further classified as discount _____s.
   a. 180SearchAssistant
   b. Power III
   c. 6-3-5 Brainwriting
   d. Department store

34. _____ is a market coverage strategy in which a firm decides to ignore market segment differences and go after the whole market with one offer.it is type of marketing (or attempting to sell through persuasion) of a product to a wide audience. The idea is to broadcast a message that will reach the largest number of people possible. Traditionally _____ has focused on radio, television and newspapers as the medium used to reach this broad audience.
   a. Marketspace
   b. Cyberdoc
   c. Mass marketing
   d. Business-to-consumer

35. A _____ is a commercial building for storage of goods. _____s are used by manufacturers, importers, exporters, wholesalers, transport businesses, customs, etc. They are usually large plain buildings in industrial areas of cities and towns.
   a. 6-3-5 Brainwriting
   b. Warehouse
   c. Power III
   d. 180SearchAssistant

36. A _____ is a retail store, usually selling a wide variety of merchandise, in which customers pay annual membership fees in order to shop. The clubs are able to keep prices low due to the no-frills format of the stores. In addition, customers are required to buy large, wholesale quantities of the store's products, which makes these clubs attractive to both bargain hunters and small business owners.
   a. Self service
   b. Warehouse club
   c. Consignment
   d. Power centre

37. Electronic commerce, commonly known as _____ or eCommerce, consists of the buying and selling of products or services over electronic systems such as the Internet and other computer networks. The amount of trade conducted electronically has grown extraordinarily with wide-spread Internet usage. A wide variety of commerce is conducted in this way, spurring and drawing on innovations in electronic funds transfer, supply chain management, Internet marketing, online transaction processing, electronic data interchange (EDI), inventory management systems, and automated data collection systems.
   a. E-commerce
   b. ACNielsen
   c. AMAX
   d. ADTECH

38. In commerce, a _____ is a superstore which combines a supermarket and a department store. The result is a very large retail facility which carries an enormous range of products under one roof, including full lines of groceries and general merchandise. In theory, _____s allow customers to satisfy all their routine weekly shopping needs in one trip.
   a. Power III
   b. 6-3-5 Brainwriting
   c. 180SearchAssistant
   d. Hypermarket

39. In economics, _____ is a measure of the relative satisfaction from consumption of various goods and services. Given this measure, one may speak meaningfully of increasing or decreasing _____, and thereby explain economic behavior in terms of attempts to increase one's _____. For illustrative purposes, changes in _____ are sometimes expressed in units called utils.

126 *Chapter 14. Direct Marketing and Marketing Resellers: Retailers and Wholesalers*

a. ACNielsen	b. ADTECH
c. AMAX	d. Utility

40. A _____ or trade mark, identified by the symbols â„¢ (not yet registered) and Â® (registered) business organization or other legal entity to identify that the products and/or services to consumers with which the _____ appears originate from a unique source of origin, and to distinguish its products or services from those of other entities. A _____ is a type of intellectual property, and typically a name, word, phrase, logo, symbol, design, image, or a combination of these elements. There is also a range of non-conventional _____s comprising marks which do not fall into these standard categories.

a. 180SearchAssistant	b. Power III
c. Risk management	d. Trademark

41. _____ is a trademark law concept permitting the owner of a famous trademark to forbid others from using that mark in a way that would lessen its uniqueness. In most cases, _____ involves an unauthorized use of another's trademark on products that do not compete with, and have little connection with, those of the trademark owner. For example, a famous trademark used by one company to refer to hair care products might be diluted if another company began using a similar mark to refer to breakfast cereals or spark plugs.

a. Trespass to land	b. Federal Bureau of Investigation
c. Trademark Dilution	d. Trademark attorney

42. _____ is a branch of philosophy which seeks to address questions about morality, such as how a moral outcome can be achieved in a specific situation (applied _____), how moral values should be determined (normative _____), what moral values people actually abide by (descriptive _____), what the fundamental semantic, ontological, and epistemic nature of _____ or morality is (meta-_____), and how moral capacity or moral agency develops and what its nature is (moral psychology.)

Socrates was one of the first Greek philosophers to encourage both scholars and the common citizen to turn their attention from the outside world to the condition of man. In this view, Knowledge having a bearing on human life was placed highest, all other knowledge being secondary.

a. AMAX	b. ACNielsen
c. Ethics	d. ADTECH

43. _____ is defined by the American _____ Association as the activity, set of institutions, and processes for creating, communicating, delivering, and exchanging offerings that have value for customers, clients, partners, and society at large. The term developed from the original meaning which referred literally to going to market, as in shopping, or going to a market to sell goods or services.

_____ practice tends to be seen as a creative industry, which includes advertising, distribution and selling.

a. Marketing myopia	b. Product naming
c. Customer acquisition management	d. Marketing

Chapter 14. Direct Marketing and Marketing Resellers: Retailers and Wholesalers

44. _____ is a concept that denotes the precise probability of specific eventualities. Technically, the notion of _____ is independent from the notion of value and, as such, eventualities may have both beneficial and adverse consequences. However, in general usage the convention is to focus only on potential negative impact to some characteristic of value that may arise from a future event.
   a. Power III
   b. Risk
   c. 6-3-5 Brainwriting
   d. 180SearchAssistant

45. When opened in 1930, the _____ or the Mart, located in Chicago, Illinois, was the largest building in the world with 4,000,000 square feet (372,000 m^2) of floor space. Previously owned by the Marshall Field family, the Mart centralized Chicago's wholesale goods business by consolidating vendors and trade under a single roof. Massive in its construction, and serving as a monument to early 20th century merchandising and architecture, the art deco landmark anchors the daytime skyline at the junction of the Chicago River branches.
   a. John F. Kennedy International Airport
   b. BSI Group
   c. Merchandise mart
   d. Population Reference Bureau

46. _____s function as professionals who deal with trade, dealing in commodities that they do not produce themselves, in order to produce profit.

   _____s can be of two types:

   1. A wholesale _____ operates in the chain between producer and retail _____. Some wholesale _____s only organize the movement of goods rather than move the goods themselves.
   2. A retail _____ or retailer, sells commodities to consumers (including businesses.) A shop owner is a retail _____.

   A _____ class characterizes many pre-modern societies. Its status can range from high (even achieving titles like that of _____ prince or nabob) to low, such as in Chinese culture, due to the soiling capabilities of profiting from 'mere' trade, rather than from the labor of others reflected in agricultural produce, craftsmanship, and tribute.

   In the United States, '_____' is defined (under the Uniform Commercial Code) as any person while engaged in a business or profession or a seller who deals regularly in the type of goods sold.

   a. Retail loss prevention
   b. RFM
   c. Trade credit
   d. Merchant

47. A _____ is a party that mediates between a buyer and a seller. A _____ who also acts as a seller or as a buyer becomes a principal party to the deal. Distinguish agent: one who acts on behalf of a principal.
   a. Power III
   b. Spokesperson
   c. 180SearchAssistant
   d. Broker

Chapter 14. Direct Marketing and Marketing Resellers: Retailers and Wholesalers

48. _____ wholesale represents a type of operation within the wholesale sector. Its main features are summarized best by the following definitions:

- _____ is a form of trade in which goods are sold from a wholesale warehouse operated either on a self-service basis, or on the basis of samples (with the customer selecting from specimen articles using a manual or computerized ordering system but not serving himself) or a combination of the two. Customers (retailers, professional users, caterers, institutional buyers, etc.) settle the invoice on the spot and in cash, and carry the goods away themselves.

- Though wholesalers buy primarily from manufacturers and sell mostly to retailers, industrial users and other wholesalers, they also perform many value added functions. The wholesaler, an intermediary, is used based on principles of specialisation and division of labour as well as contractual efficiency. (OECD -Organisation for Economic Cooperation and Development.)

a. Self branding
c. Cash and carry
b. Containerization
d. Davie Brown Index

49. _____ often refers to either primary or secondary research. Secondary research involves a company using information compiled from various sources, which is about a new or existing product. The advantages of secondary research are that it is relatively cheap and easily accessible.

a. Market Research
c. Mystery shoppers
b. Mystery shopping
d. Questionnaire

50. In economics, an _____ is any good or commodity, transported from one country to another country in a legitimate fashion, typically for use in trade. _____ goods or services are provided to foreign consumers by domestic producers. _____ is an important part of international trade.

a. ADTECH
c. Export
b. AMAX
d. ACNielsen

51. Advertising mail junk mail is the delivery of advertising material to recipients of postal mail. The delivery of advertising mail forms a large and growing service for many postal services, and _____ marketing forms a significant portion of the direct marketing industry. Some organizations attempt to help people opt-out of receiving advertising mail, in many cases motivated by a concern over its negative environmental impact.

a. Phishing
c. Directory Harvest Attack
b. Telemarketing
d. Direct mail

52. _____ is a sub-discipline and type of marketing. There are two main definitional characteristics which distinguish it from other types of marketing. The first is that it attempts to send its messages directly to consumers, without the use of intervening media.

a. Direct marketing
c. Database marketing
b. Power III
d. Direct Marketing Associations

53. _____ are long-format television commercials, typically five minutes or longer.. _____ are also known as paid programming (or teleshopping in Europe.) Originally, they were a phenomenon that started in the United States where they were typically shown overnight (usually 2:00 a.m. to 6:00 a.m.)

Chapter 14. Direct Marketing and Marketing Resellers: Retailers and Wholesalers 129

a. ACNielsen
c. ADTECH
b. AMAX
d. Infomercials

54. _____ is a method of direct marketing in which a salesperson solicits to prospective customers to buy products or services, either over the phone or through a subsequent face to face or Web conferencing appointment scheduled during the call.

_____ can also include recorded sales pitches programmed to be played over the phone via automatic dialing. _____ has come under fire in recent years, being viewed as an annoyance by many.

a. Phishing
c. Directory Harvest Attack
b. Joe job
d. Telemarketing

Chapter 15. Integrated Marketing Communications

1. _____ , according to The American Marketing Association, is 'a planning process designed to assure that all brand contacts received by a customer or prospect for a product, service, or organization are relevant to that person and consistent over time.' (Marketing Power Dictionary)

_____ is a term used to describe a holistic approach to marketing. It aims to ensure consistency of message and the complementary use of media. The concept includes online and offline marketing channels.

   a. AMAX
   b. ADTECH
   c. Integrated marketing communications
   d. ACNielsen

2. _____ is defined by the American _____ Association as the activity, set of institutions, and processes for creating, communicating, delivering, and exchanging offerings that have value for customers, clients, partners, and society at large. The term developed from the original meaning which referred literally to going to market, as in shopping, or going to a market to sell goods or services.

_____ practice tends to be seen as a creative industry, which includes advertising, distribution and selling.

   a. Marketing
   b. Marketing myopia
   c. Customer acquisition management
   d. Product naming

3. _____ refers to messages and related media used to communicate with a market. Those who practice advertising, branding, direct marketing, graphic design, marketing, packaging, promotion, publicity, sponsorship, public relations, sales, sales promotion and online marketing are termed marketing communicators, _____ managers, or more briefly as marcom managers.
   a. Merchandise
   b. Marketing communication
   c. Sales promotion
   d. Merchandising

4. _____ involves disseminating information about a product, product line, brand, or company. It is one of the four key aspects of the marketing mix. (The other three elements are product marketing, pricing, and distribution). P>_____ is generally sub-divided into two parts:

   - Above the line _____: Promotion in the media (e.g. TV, radio, newspapers, Internet and Mobile Phones) in which the advertiser pays an advertising agency to place the ad
   - Below the line _____: All other _____. Much of this is intended to be subtle enough for the consumer to be unaware that _____ is taking place. E.g. sponsorship, product placement, endorsements, sales _____, merchandising, direct mail, personal selling, public relations, trade shows

   a. Davie Brown Index
   b. Promotion
   c. Cashmere Agency
   d. Bottling lines

5. _____ is a strategic planning method used to evaluate the Strengths, Weaknesses, Opportunities, and Threats involved in a project or in a business venture. It involves specifying the objective of the business venture or project and identifying the internal and external factors that are favorable and unfavorable to achieving that objective. The technique is credited to Albert Humphrey, who led a research project at Stanford University in the 1960s and 1970s using data from Fortune 500 companies.

Chapter 15. Integrated Marketing Communications 131

a. Lead scoring
c. Product differentiation
b. Market environment
d. SWOT analysis

6. _____ is a term commonly used to describe commerce transactions between businesses like the one between a manufacturer and a wholesaler or a wholesaler and a retailer i.e both the buyer and the seller are business entity.This is unlike business-to-consumers (B2C) which involve a business entity and end consumer, or business-to-government (B2G) which involve a business entity and government.

The volume of B2B transactions is much higher than the volume of B2C transactions. The primary reason for this is that in a typical supply chain there will be many B2B transactions involving subcomponent or raw materials, and only one B2C transaction, specifically sale of the finished product to the end customer.

a. Social marketing
c. Business-to-business
b. Customer relationship management
d. Disruptive technology

7. _____ is a form of intellectual property which gives the creator of an original work exclusive rights for a certain time period in relation to that work, including its publication, distribution and adaptation; after which time the work is said to enter the public domain. _____ applies to any expressible form of an idea or information that is substantive and discrete. Some jurisdictions also recognize 'moral rights' of the creator of a work, such as the right to be credited for the work.

a. Celler-Kefauver Act
c. Reasonable person standard
b. Collective mark
d. Copyright

8. The _____ is a United States copyright law that implements two 1996 treaties of the World Intellectual Property Organization (WIPO.) It criminalizes production and dissemination of technology, devices whether or not there is actual infringement of copyright itself. In addition, the _____ heightens the penalties for copyright infringement on the Internet.

a. Copyright infringement
c. Regulatory
b. Priority right
d. Digital Millennium Copyright Act

9. _____ is a form of communication that typically attempts to persuade potential customers to purchase or to consume more of a particular brand of product or service. 'While now central to the contemporary global economy and the reproduction of global production networks, it is only quite recently that _____ has been more than a marginal influence on patterns of sales and production. The formation of modern _____ was intimately bound up with the emergence of new forms of monopoly capitalism around the end of the 19th and beginning of the 20th century as one element in corporate strategies to create, organize and where possible control markets, especially for mass produced consumer goods.

a. ACNielsen
c. AMAX
b. ADTECH
d. Advertising

10. A _____ is a process that can allow an organization to concentrate its limited resources on the greatest opportunities to increase sales and achieve a sustainable competitive advantage. A _____ should be centered around the key concept that customer satisfaction is the main goal.

A _____ is most effective when it is an integral component of corporate strategy, defining how the organization will successfully engage customers, prospects, and competitors in the market arena.

a. Cyberdoc
b. Psychographic
c. Marketing strategy
d. Societal marketing

11. _____ is that part of statistical practice concerned with the selection of individual observations intended to yield some knowledge about a population of concern, especially for the purposes of statistical inference. Each observation measures one or more properties (weight, location, etc.) of an observable entity enumerated to distinguish objects or individuals.
   a. Richard Buckminster 'Bucky' Fuller
   b. Sports Marketing Group
   c. AStore
   d. Sampling

12. A _____ is a plan of action designed to achieve a particular goal.

_____ is different from tactics. In military terms, tactics is concerned with the conduct of an engagement while _____ is concerned with how different engagements are linked.
   a. 6-3-5 Brainwriting
   b. 180SearchAssistant
   c. Power III
   d. Strategy

13. A _____ is a type of wholesale merchant business that buys goods and bulk products from importers, other wholesalers and then sells to retailers. _____s can deal in any commodity destined for the retail market. Typical categories are food, lumber, hardware, fuel, and textiles.
   a. Tacit collusion
   b. Chief privacy officer
   c. Refusal to deal
   d. Jobbing house

14. A _____ or trade mark, identified by the symbols ™ (not yet registered) and ® (registered) business organization or other legal entity to identify that the products and/or services to consumers with which the _____ appears originate from a unique source of origin, and to distinguish its products or services from those of other entities. A _____ is a type of intellectual property, and typically a name, word, phrase, logo, symbol, design, image, or a combination of these elements. There is also a range of non-conventional _____s comprising marks which do not fall into these standard categories.
   a. Risk management
   b. Power III
   c. 180SearchAssistant
   d. Trademark

15. _____ is a trademark law concept permitting the owner of a famous trademark to forbid others from using that mark in a way that would lessen its uniqueness. In most cases, _____ involves an unauthorized use of another's trademark on products that do not compete with, and have little connection with, those of the trademark owner. For example, a famous trademark used by one company to refer to hair care products might be diluted if another company began using a similar mark to refer to breakfast cereals or spark plugs.
   a. Trademark attorney
   b. Federal Bureau of Investigation
   c. Trespass to land
   d. Trademark Dilution

Chapter 15. Integrated Marketing Communications   133

16. _____ is the reverse of encoding, which is the process of transforming information from one format into another. Information about _____ can be found in the following:

- Digital-to-analog converter, the use of analog circuit for _____ operations
- Code, a rule for converting a piece of information into another form or representation
- Code (cryptography), a method used to transform a message into an obscured form
- _____
- _____ methods, methods in communication theory for _____ codewords sent over a noisy channel
- Digital signal processing, the study of signals in a digital representation and the processing methods of these signals
- Word _____, the use of phonics to decipher print patterns and translate them into the sounds of language
- deCODE genetics

a. Power III
b. 180SearchAssistant
c. 6-3-5 Brainwriting
d. Decoding

17. _____ describes the situation when output from (or information about the result of) an event or phenomenon in the past will influence the same event/phenomenon in the present or future. When an event is part of a chain of cause-and-effect that forms a circuit or loop, then the event is said to 'feed back' into itself.

_____ is also a synonym for:

- _____ Signal; the information about the initial event that is the basis for subsequent modification of the event.
- _____ Loop; the causal path that leads from the initial generation of the _____ signal to the subsequent modification of the event.

_____ is a mechanism, process or signal that is looped back to control a system within itself. Such a loop is called a _____ loop.

a. 6-3-5 Brainwriting
b. Power III
c. 180SearchAssistant
d. Feedback

18. In economics, _____ is the desire to own something and the ability to pay for it. The term _____ signifies the ability or the willingness to buy a particular commodity at a given point of time .

a. Market system
b. Market dominance
c. Discretionary spending
d. Demand

19. In marketing, _____ is the process of distinguishing the differences of a product or offering from others, to make it more attractive to a particular target market. This involves differentiating it from competitors' products as well as one's own product offerings.

Differentiation is a source of competitive advantage.

a. Marketing myopia
b. Packshot
c. Corporate image
d. Product differentiation

20. There are four main aspects of a _____. These are:

1 Advertising- Any paid presentation and promotion of ideas, goods, or services by an identified sponsor. Examples: Print ads, radio, television, billboard, direct mail, brochures and catalogs, signs, in-store displays, posters, motion pictures, Web pages, banner ads, and emails.

a. Product manager
b. Power III
c. Pick and pack
d. Promotional mix

21. _____ is a form of advertisement, where branded goods or services are placed in a context usually devoid of ads, such as movies, the story line of television shows Broadcasting ' Cable reported, 'Two thirds of advertisers employ 'branded entertainment'--_____--with the vast majority of that (80%) in commercial TV programming.' The story, based on a survey by the Association of National Advertisers, added, 'Reasons for using in-show plugs varied from 'stronger emotional connection' to better dovetailing with relevant content, to targetting a specific group.'

_____ became common in the 1980s, but can be traced back to the nineteenth century in publishing.

a. 6-3-5 Brainwriting
b. Product placement
c. Power III
d. 180SearchAssistant

22. _____ is one of the four aspects of promotional mix. (The other three parts of the promotional mix are advertising, personal selling, and publicity/public relations.) Media and non-media marketing communication are employed for a pre-determined, limited time to increase consumer demand, stimulate market demand or improve product availability.

a. New Media Strategies
b. Marketing communication
c. Sales promotion
d. Merchandise

23. _____ is a sub-discipline and type of marketing. There are two main definitional characteristics which distinguish it from other types of marketing. The first is that it attempts to send its messages directly to consumers, without the use of intervening media.

a. Direct Marketing Associations
b. Power III
c. Database marketing
d. Direct marketing

24. _____ is the practice of managing the flow of information between an organization and its publics. _____ - often referred to as _____ - gains an organization or individual exposure to their audiences using topics of public interest and news items that do not require direct payment. Because _____ places exposure in credible third-party outlets, it offers a third-party legitimacy that advertising does not have.

a. Power III
b. Symbolic analysis
c. Public relations
d. Graphic communication

25. _____ is the deliberate attempt to manage the public's perception of a subject. The subjects of _____ include people (for example, politicians and performing artists), goods and services, organizations of all kinds, and works of art or entertainment.

Chapter 15. Integrated Marketing Communications

From a marketing perspective, _____ is one component of promotion.

a. Pearson's chi-square
c. Brando
b. Little value placed on potential benefits
d. Publicity

26. The _____ is generally accepted as the use and specification of the four p's describing the strategic position of a product in the marketplace. One version of the origins of the _____ starts in 1948 when James Culliton said that a marketing decision should be a result of something similar to a recipe. This version continued in 1953 when Neil Borden, in his American Marketing Association presidential address, took the recipe idea one step further and coined the term 'Marketing-Mix'.

a. Marketing mix
c. Power III
b. 6-3-5 Brainwriting
d. 180SearchAssistant

27. A _____ is a subgroup of people or organizations sharing one or more characteristics that cause them to have similar product and/or service needs. A true _____ meets all of the following criteria: it is distinct from other segments (different segments have different needs), it is homogeneous within the segment (exhibits common needs); it responds similarly to a market stimulus, and it can be reached by a market intervention. The term is also used when consumers with identical product and/or service needs are divided up into groups so they can be charged different amounts.

a. Commercial planning
c. Market segment
b. Customer insight
d. Production orientation

28. _____ is a marketing campaign that takes place around an event but does not involve payment of a sponsorship fee to the event. For most events of any significance, one brand will pay to become the exclusive and official sponsor of the event in a particular category or categories, and this exclusivity creates a problem for one or more other brands. Those other brands then find ways to promote themselves in connection with the same event, without paying the sponsorship fee and without breaking any laws.

a. AMAX
c. Ambush marketing
b. ACNielsen
d. ADTECH

29. _____ is a method of direct marketing in which a salesperson solicits to prospective customers to buy products or services, either over the phone or through a subsequent face to face or Web conferencing appointment scheduled during the call.

_____ can also include recorded sales pitches programmed to be played over the phone via automatic dialing. _____ has come under fire in recent years, being viewed as an annoyance by many.

a. Phishing
c. Telemarketing
b. Joe job
d. Directory Harvest Attack

30. Advertising mail junk mail is the delivery of advertising material to recipients of postal mail. The delivery of advertising mail forms a large and growing service for many postal services, and _____ marketing forms a significant portion of the direct marketing industry. Some organizations attempt to help people opt-out of receiving advertising mail, in many cases motivated by a concern over its negative environmental impact.

Chapter 15. Integrated Marketing Communications

a. Direct mail
b. Phishing
c. Directory Harvest Attack
d. Telemarketing

31. A _____ is a statement or claim that a particular event will occur in the future in more certain terms than a forecast. The etymology of this word is Latin . In regards to predicting the future Howard H. Stevenson Says, ' _____ is at least two things: Important and hard.' Important, because we have to act, and hard because we have to realize the future we want, and what is the best way to get there.

a. Power III
b. 180SearchAssistant
c. 6-3-5 Brainwriting
d. Prediction

32. A _____ is a collection of symbols, experiences and associations connected with a product, a service, a person or any other artifact or entity.

_____s have become increasingly important components of culture and the economy, now being described as 'cultural accessories and personal philosophies'.

Some people distinguish the psychological aspect of a _____ from the experiential aspect.

a. Brand equity
b. Store brand
c. Brandable software
d. Brand

33. The _____ is a database of consumer perception of brands created and managed by BrandAsset Consulting, a division of Young ' Rubicam Brands to provide information to enable firms to improve the marketing decision-making process and to manage brands better. _____ and _____ also describe the Y'R group managing the database.

_____ measures the value of a brand along four dimensions: 'Differentiation,' 'Relevance,' 'Esteem,' and 'Knowledge.' Differentiation and Relevance build up to 'Brand Strength.' Esteem and Knowledge are used to calculate 'Brand Stature.' _____ defines these terms as follows.

a. Brand Asset Valuator
b. Target audience
c. Hoover free flights promotion
d. Targeted advertising

34. _____ commonly refers to the electronic retailing / _____ channels industry, which includes such billion dollar companies as Home shoppingN, QVC, eBay, ShopNBC, Buy.com, and Amazon.com. _____ allows consumers to shop for goods while in the privacy of their own home, as opposed to traditional shopping, which requires you to visit brick and mortar stores and shopping malls.

The _____ / electronic retailing industry was created in 1977 when small market radio talk show host Bob Circosta was asked to sell avocado-green-colored can openers live on the air by station owner Bud Paxson when an advertiser traded 112 units of product instead of paying his advertising bill.

a. 6-3-5 Brainwriting
b. Power III
c. 180SearchAssistant
d. Home shopping

Chapter 15. Integrated Marketing Communications

35. _____ are long-format television commercials, typically five minutes or longer.. _____ are also known as paid programming (or teleshopping in Europe.) Originally, they were a phenomenon that started in the United States where they were typically shown overnight (usually 2:00 a.m. to 6:00 a.m.)
   a. Infomercials
   b. AMAX
   c. ACNielsen
   d. ADTECH

36. _____ is the examining of goods or services from retailers with the intent to purchase at that time. _____ is an activity of selection and/or purchase. In some contexts it is considered a leisure activity as well as an economic one.
   a. Discount store
   b. Hawkers
   c. Khodebshchik
   d. Shopping

37. In the Mediterranean Basin and the Near East, a _____ is a small, separated garden pavilion open on some or all sides. _____s were common in Persia, India, Pakistan, and in the Ottoman Empire from the 13th century onward. Today, there are many _____s in and around the Topkapı Palace in Istanbul, and they are still a relatively common sight in Greece.
   a. 6-3-5 Brainwriting
   b. 180SearchAssistant
   c. Power III
   d. Kiosk

38. Consumer market research is a form of applied sociology that concentrates on understanding the behaviours, whims and preferences, of consumers in a market-based economy, and aims to understand the effects and comparative success of marketing campaigns. The field of consumer _____ as a statistical science was pioneered by Arthur Nielsen with the founding of the ACNielsen Company in 1923.

Thus _____ is the systematic and objective identification, collection, analysis, and dissemination of information for the purpose of assisting management in decision making related to the identification and solution of problems and opportunities in marketing.

   a. Logit analysis
   b. Focus group
   c. Marketing research process
   d. Marketing research

39. _____ refers to marketing strategies applied directly to a specific consumer.

Having the knowledge on the consumer preferences, there are suggested personalized products and promotions to each consumer.

The _____ is based in four main steps in order to fulfill its goals: Those stages are identify, differentiate, interact, and customize.

   a. ADTECH
   b. AMAX
   c. ACNielsen
   d. One-to-one marketing

40. _____ is a form of marketing developed from direct response marketing campaigns conducted in the 1970's and 1980's which emphasizes customer retention and satisfaction, rather than a dominant focus on 'point of sale' transactions.

Chapter 15. Integrated Marketing Communications

_____ differs from other forms of marketing in that it recognizes the long term value to the firm of keeping customers, as opposed to direct or 'Intrusion' marketing, which focuses upon acquisition of new clients by targeting majority demographics based upon prospective client lists.

_____ refers to long-term and mutually beneficial arrangement wherein both buyer and seller focus on value enhancement through the certain of more satisfying exchange. This approach attempts to transcend the simple purchase exchange process with customer to make more meaningful and richer contact by providing a more holistic, personalized purchase, and use orn consumption experience to create stronger ties.

a. Diversity marketing
b. Relationship marketing
c. Global marketing
d. Guerrilla Marketing

41. _____ Management is the succession of strategies used by management as a product goes through its _____. The conditions in which a product is sold changes over time and must be managed as it moves through its succession of stages.

The _____ goes through many phases, involves many professional disciplines, and requires many skills, tools and processes.

a. Customer satisfaction
b. Chain stores
c. Supplier diversity
d. Product life cycle

42. _____ generally refers to a list of all planned expenses and revenues. It is a plan for saving and spending. A _____ is an important concept in microeconomics, which uses a _____ line to illustrate the trade-offs between two or more goods.

a. 180SearchAssistant
b. Power III
c. 6-3-5 Brainwriting
d. Budget

43. _____ is a rivalry between individuals, groups, nations for territory, a niche, or allocation of resources. It arises whenever two or more parties strive for a goal which cannot be shared. _____ occurs naturally between living organisms which co-exist in the same environment.

a. Price fixing
b. Price competition
c. Competition
d. Non-price competition

44. Electronic commerce, commonly known as _____ or eCommerce, consists of the buying and selling of products or services over electronic systems such as the Internet and other computer networks. The amount of trade conducted electronically has grown extraordinarily with wide-spread Internet usage. A wide variety of commerce is conducted in this way, spurring and drawing on innovations in electronic funds transfer, supply chain management, Internet marketing, online transaction processing, electronic data interchange (EDI), inventory management systems, and automated data collection systems.

a. AMAX
b. ADTECH
c. E-commerce
d. ACNielsen

Chapter 15. Integrated Marketing Communications

45. _____ is systematic determination of merit, worth, and significance of something or someone using criteria against a set of standards. _____ often is used to characterize and appraise subjects of interest in a wide range of human enterprises, including the arts, criminal justice, foundations and non-profit organizations, government, health care, and other human services.

Depending on the topic of interest, there are professional groups which look to the quality and rigor of the _____ process.

a. ADTECH
c. AMAX
b. ACNielsen
d. Evaluation

46. _____, also referred to as i-marketing, web marketing, online marketing is the marketing of products or services over the Internet.

The Internet has brought many unique benefits to marketing, one of which being lower costs for the distribution of information and media to a global audience. The interactive nature of _____, both in terms of providing instant response and eliciting responses, is a unique quality of the medium.

a. ACNielsen
c. ADTECH
b. AMAX
d. Internet marketing

47. _____ is a broad label that refers to any individuals or households that use goods and services generated within the economy. The concept of a _____ is used in different contexts, so that the usage and significance of the term may vary.

A _____ is a person who uses any product or service.

a. Power III
c. 6-3-5 Brainwriting
b. Consumer
d. 180SearchAssistant

48. _____ are final goods specifically intended for the mass market. For instance, _____ do not include investment assets, like precious antiques, even though these antiques are final goods.

Manufactured goods are goods that have been processed by way of machinery.

a. Durable good
c. Power III
b. Free good
d. Consumer Goods

49. _____ is one of the four Ps of the marketing mix. The other three aspects are product, promotion, and place. It is also a key variable in microeconomic price allocation theory.

a. Relationship based pricing
c. Price
b. Pricing
d. Competitor indexing

50. _____ is a way of measuring the success of an online advertising campaign. A CTR is obtained by dividing the number of users who clicked on an ad on a web page by the number of times the ad was delivered (impressions.) For example, if a banner ad was delivered 100 times (impressions delivered) and one person clicked on it (clicks recorded), then the resulting CTR would be 1 percent.

a. Display advertising
b. JICIMS
c. Web analytics
d. Click-through rate

51. In economics, business, retail, and accounting, a _____ is the value of money that has been used up to produce something, and hence is not available for use anymore. In economics, a _____ is an alternative that is given up as a result of a decision. In business, the _____ may be one of acquisition, in which case the amount of money expended to acquire it is counted as _____.

a. Transaction cost
b. Cost
c. Fixed costs
d. Variable cost

52. _____, often abbreviated to _____, is a phrase often used in online advertising and marketing related to web traffic. It is used for measuring the worth and cost of a specific e-marketing campaign. This technique is applied with web banners, text links, e-mail spam, and opt-in e-mail advertising, although opt-in e-mail advertising is more commonly charged on a cost per action (CPA) basis.

a. Cost per impression
b. Cost per time
c. Frequency capping
d. Cost per mille

53. _____ is difficult to define. For example, in 1952, Alfred Kroeber and Clyde Kluckhohn compiled a list of 164 definitions of '_____' in _____: A Critical Review of Concepts and Definitions. However, the word '_____' is most commonly used in three basic senses:

- excellence of taste in the fine arts and humanities
- an integrated pattern of human knowledge, belief, and behavior that depends upon the capacity for symbolic thought and social learning
- the set of shared attitudes, values, goals, and practices that characterizes an institution, organization or group.

When the concept first emerged in eighteenth- and nineteenth-century Europe, it connoted a process of cultivation or improvement, as in agriculture or horticulture. In the nineteenth century, it came to refer first to the betterment or refinement of the individual, especially through education, and then to the fulfillment of national aspirations or ideals.

a. AStore
b. Albert Einstein
c. Culture
d. African Americans

54. An _____ is the manufacturing of a good or service within a category. Although _____ is a broad term for any kind of economic production, in economics and urban planning _____ is a synonym for the secondary sector, which is a type of economic activity involved in the manufacturing of raw materials into goods and products.

Chapter 15. Integrated Marketing Communications

There are four key industrial economic sectors: the primary sector, largely raw material extraction industries such as mining and farming; the secondary sector, involving refining, construction, and manufacturing; the tertiary sector, which deals with services (such as law and medicine) and distribution of manufactured goods; and the quaternary sector, a relatively new type of knowledge _____ focusing on technological research, design and development such as computer programming, and biochemistry.

a. ADTECH
b. ACNielsen
c. AMAX
d. Industry

55. A personal and cultural _____ is a relative ethic _____, an assumption upon which implementation can be extrapolated. A _____ system is a set of consistent _____s and measures that is soo not true. A principle _____ is a foundation upon which other _____s and measures of integrity are based.

a. Package-on-Package
b. Perceptual maps
c. Supreme Court of the United States
d. Value

56. _____ is the set of tasks, knowledge, and techniques required to identify business needs and determine solutions to business problems. Solutions often include a systems development component, but may also consist of process improvement or organizational change. The person who carries out this task is called a business analyst or _____.

a. Fast moving consumer goods
b. Marketing management
c. Door-to-door
d. Business analysis

57. A _____ or community service announcement (CSA) is a non-commercial advertisement broadcast on radio or television, ostensibly for the public interest. _____s are intended to modify public attitudes by raising awareness about specific issues.

The most common topics of _____s are health and safety.

a. Power III
b. 180SearchAssistant
c. 6-3-5 Brainwriting
d. Public service announcement

58. _____ is an advertisement in which a particular product specifically mentions a competitor by name for the express purpose of showing why the competitor is inferior to the product naming it.

This should not be confused with parody advertisements, where a fictional product is being advertised for the purpose of poking fun at the particular advertisement, nor should it be confused with the use of a coined brand name for the purpose of comparing the product without actually naming an actual competitor. ('Wikipedia tastes better and is less filling than the Encyclopedia Galactica.')

In the 1980s, during what has been referred to as the cola wars, soft-drink manufacturer Pepsi ran a series of advertisements where people, caught on hidden camera, in a blind taste test, chose Pepsi over rival Coca-Cola.

a. Cost per conversion
b. Heavy-up
c. GL-70
d. Comparative advertising

Chapter 16. Advertising and Public Relations

1. _____ is a form of communication that typically attempts to persuade potential customers to purchase or to consume more of a particular brand of product or service. 'While now central to the contemporary global economy and the reproduction of global production networks, it is only quite recently that _____ has been more than a marginal influence on patterns of sales and production. The formation of modern _____ was intimately bound up with the emergence of new forms of monopoly capitalism around the end of the 19th and beginning of the 20th century as one element in corporate strategies to create, organize and where possible control markets, especially for mass produced consumer goods.
   a. Advertising
   b. ACNielsen
   c. ADTECH
   d. AMAX

2. _____ is a broad label that refers to any individuals or households that use goods and services generated within the economy. The concept of a _____ is used in different contexts, so that the usage and significance of the term may vary.

   A _____ is a person who uses any product or service.

   a. Power III
   b. 6-3-5 Brainwriting
   c. 180SearchAssistant
   d. Consumer

3. _____ are final goods specifically intended for the mass market. For instance, _____ do not include investment assets, like precious antiques, even though these antiques are final goods.

   Manufactured goods are goods that have been processed by way of machinery.

   a. Durable good
   b. Power III
   c. Free good
   d. Consumer Goods

4. _____ is one of the four Ps of the marketing mix. The other three aspects are product, promotion, and place. It is also a key variable in microeconomic price allocation theory.
   a. Price
   b. Pricing
   c. Relationship based pricing
   d. Competitor indexing

5. A _____ or trade mark, identified by the symbols ™ (not yet registered) and ® (registered) business organization or other legal entity to identify that the products and/or services to consumers with which the _____ appears originate from a unique source of origin, and to distinguish its products or services from those of other entities. A _____ is a type of intellectual property, and typically a name, word, phrase, logo, symbol, design, image, or a combination of these elements. There is also a range of non-conventional _____s comprising marks which do not fall into these standard categories.
   a. 180SearchAssistant
   b. Power III
   c. Risk management
   d. Trademark

6. In grammar, the _____ is the form of an adjective or adverb which denotes the degree or grade by which a person, thing and is used in this context with a subordinating conjunction, such as than, as...as, etc.

   The structure of a _____ in English consists normally of the positive form of the adjective or adverb, plus the suffix -er e.g. 'he is taller than his father is', or 'the village is less picturesque than the town nearby'.

a. 180SearchAssistant
c. Power III
b. 6-3-5 Brainwriting
d. Comparative

7. _____ is an advertisement in which a particular product specifically mentions a competitor by name for the express purpose of showing why the competitor is inferior to the product naming it.

This should not be confused with parody advertisements, where a fictional product is being advertised for the purpose of poking fun at the particular advertisement, nor should it be confused with the use of a coined brand name for the purpose of comparing the product without actually naming an actual competitor. ('Wikipedia tastes better and is less filling than the Encyclopedia Galactica.')

In the 1980s, during what has been referred to as the cola wars, soft-drink manufacturer Pepsi ran a series of advertisements where people, caught on hidden camera, in a blind taste test, chose Pepsi over rival Coca-Cola.

a. Cost per conversion
c. Heavy-up
b. Comparative advertising
d. GL-70

8. _____ is when advertising is carried out in an informative manner Also, _____ tends to help generate a good reputation.

In some circumstances a business might be required to run _____ as part of resolving a law suit. Tobacco companies are one of the more notable examples of this.

a. ACNielsen
c. Out-of-home advertising
b. Informative advertising
d. ADTECH

9. _____ is a form of social influence. It is the process of guiding people toward the adoption of an idea, attitude, or action by rational and symbolic (though not always logical) means. It is strategy of problem-solving relying on 'appeals' rather than coercion.

a. Persuasion
c. 6-3-5 Brainwriting
b. Power III
d. 180SearchAssistant

10. A _____ is defined by the International Co-operative Alliance's Statement on the Co-operative Identity as an autonomous association of persons united voluntarily to meet their common economic, social, and cultural needs and aspirations through a jointly-owned and democratically-controlled enterprise. It is a business organization owned and operated by a group of individuals for their mutual benefit. A _____ may also be defined as a business owned and controlled equally by the people who use its services or who work at it.

a. Power III
c. Cooperative
b. 6-3-5 Brainwriting
d. 180SearchAssistant

11. The verb _____ or grant _____ means to give permission. The noun _____ refers to that permission as well as to the document memorializing that permission. _____ may be granted by a party to another party as an element of an agreement between those parties.

a. 180SearchAssistant
c. 6-3-5 Brainwriting
b. Power III
d. License

Chapter 16. Advertising and Public Relations

12. _____ , according to The American Marketing Association, is 'a planning process designed to assure that all brand contacts received by a customer or prospect for a product, service, or organization are relevant to that person and consistent over time.' (Marketing Power Dictionary)

_____ is a term used to describe a holistic approach to marketing. It aims to ensure consistency of message and the complementary use of media. The concept includes online and offline marketing channels.

a. ACNielsen
b. ADTECH
c. AMAX
d. Integrated marketing communications

13. _____ uses online or offline interactive media to communicate with consumers and to promote products, brands, services, and public service announcements, corporate or political groups.

In the inaugural issue of the Journal of _____ , editors Li and Leckenby (2000) defined _____ as the 'paid and unpaid presentation and promotion of products, services and ideas by an identified sponsor through mediated means involving mutual action between consumers and producers.' This is most commonly performed through the Internet as a medium.

It is these mutual actions or interactions that enhance what _____ is trying to achieve.

a. Enterprise Search Marketing
b. Internet currency
c. Audience Screening
d. Interactive advertising

14. _____ is defined by the American _____ Association as the activity, set of institutions, and processes for creating, communicating, delivering, and exchanging offerings that have value for customers, clients, partners, and society at large. The term developed from the original meaning which referred literally to going to market, as in shopping, or going to a market to sell goods or services.

_____ practice tends to be seen as a creative industry, which includes advertising, distribution and selling.

a. Product naming
b. Marketing myopia
c. Customer acquisition management
d. Marketing

15. _____ refers to messages and related media used to communicate with a market. Those who practice advertising, branding, direct marketing, graphic design, marketing, packaging, promotion, publicity, sponsorship, public relations, sales, sales promotion and online marketing are termed marketing communicators, _____ managers, or more briefly as marcom managers.

a. Sales promotion
b. Merchandise
c. Marketing communication
d. Merchandising

16. An _____ is a series of advertisement messages that share a single idea and theme which make up an integrated marketing communication (IMC.) _____s appear in different media across a specific time frame.

The critical part of making an _____ is determining a campaign theme, as it sets the tone for the individual advertisements and other forms of marketing communications that will be used.

a. Advertising campaign
b. ADTECH
c. ACNielsen
d. AMAX

17. _____ is the use of sexual or erotic imagery in advertising to draw interest to a particular product, for purpose of sale. A feature of _____ is that the imagery used, such as that of a pretty woman, typically has no connection to the product being advertised. The purpose of the imagery is to attract attention of the potential customer or user.
   a. 180SearchAssistant
   b. Sex in advertising
   c. Power III
   d. 6-3-5 Brainwriting

18. An _____ is an advertisement written in the form of an objective opinion editorial, and presented in a printed publication--usually designed to look like a legitimate and independent news story.

_____s differ from traditional advertisements in that they are designed to look like the articles that appear in the publication.

   a. ACNielsen
   b. ADTECH
   c. Informative advertising
   d. Advertorial

19. A _____ or banner ad is a form of advertising on the World Wide Web. This form of online advertising entails embedding an advertisement into a web page. It is intended to attract traffic to a website by linking to the website of the advertiser.
   a. Disintermediation
   b. Consumer privacy
   c. Web banner
   d. Spamvertising

20. _____ is the study of when, why, how, where and what people do or do not buy products. It blends elements from psychology, sociology, social psychology, anthropology and economics. It attempts to understand the buyer decision making process, both individually and in groups. It studies characteristics of individual consumers such as demographics and behavioural variables in an attempt to understand people's wants. It also tries to assess influences on the consumer from groups such as family, friends, reference groups, and society in general.
   a. Communal marketing
   b. Consumer confidence
   c. Consumer behavior
   d. Multidimensional scaling

21. On the World Wide Web, _____s are web pages that are displayed before an expected content page, often to display advertisements or confirm the user's age.

Some people take issue with this form of online advertising. Less controversial uses of _____ pages include introducing another page or site before directing the user to proceed; or alerting the user that the next page requires a login, or has some other requirement which the user should know about before proceeding.

   a. AMAX
   b. ACNielsen
   c. ADTECH
   d. Interstitial

22. A _____ is an entity that provides services to other entities. Usually this refers to a business that provides subscription or web service to other businesses or individuals. Examples of these services include Internet access, Mobile phone operator, and web application hosting.

a. Freebie marketing
b. Cross-selling
c. Yield management
d. Service provider

23. A _____ is a collection of symbols, experiences and associations connected with a product, a service, a person or any other artifact or entity.

_____s have become increasingly important components of culture and the economy, now being described as 'cultural accessories and personal philosophies'.

Some people distinguish the psychological aspect of a _____ from the experiential aspect.

a. Brandable software
b. Brand equity
c. Store brand
d. Brand

24. The _____ is a database of consumer perception of brands created and managed by BrandAsset Consulting, a division of Young ' Rubicam Brands to provide information to enable firms to improve the marketing decision-making process and to manage brands better. _____ and _____ also describe the Y'R group managing the database.

_____ measures the value of a brand along four dimensions: 'Differentiation,' 'Relevance,' 'Esteem,' and 'Knowledge.' Differentiation and Relevance build up to 'Brand Strength.' Esteem and Knowledge are used to calculate 'Brand Stature.' _____ defines these terms as follows.

a. Hoover free flights promotion
b. Brand Asset Valuator
c. Targeted advertising
d. Target audience

25. _____ is a method of direct marketing in which a salesperson solicits to prospective customers to buy products or services, either over the phone or through a subsequent face to face or Web conferencing appointment scheduled during the call.

_____ can also include recorded sales pitches programmed to be played over the phone via automatic dialing. _____ has come under fire in recent years, being viewed as an annoyance by many.

a. Joe job
b. Telemarketing
c. Directory Harvest Attack
d. Phishing

26. _____ is a form of intellectual property which gives the creator of an original work exclusive rights for a certain time period in relation to that work, including its publication, distribution and adaptation; after which time the work is said to enter the public domain. _____ applies to any expressible form of an idea or information that is substantive and discrete. Some jurisdictions also recognize 'moral rights' of the creator of a work, such as the right to be credited for the work.

a. Collective mark
b. Celler-Kefauver Act
c. Reasonable person standard
d. Copyright

27. The _____ is a United States copyright law that implements two 1996 treaties of the World Intellectual Property Organization (WIPO.) It criminalizes production and dissemination of technology, devices whether or not there is actual infringement of copyright itself. In addition, the _____ heightens the penalties for copyright infringement on the Internet.

Chapter 16. Advertising and Public Relations

a. Priority right
b. Regulatory
c. Copyright infringement
d. Digital Millennium Copyright Act

28. A _____ is a large outdoor advertising structure (a billing board), typically found in high traffic areas such as alongside busy roads. _____s present large advertisements to passing pedestrians and drivers. Typically showing large, ostensibly witty slogans, and distinctive visuals, _____s are highly visible in the top designated market areas.
   a. 180SearchAssistant
   b. Billboard
   c. 6-3-5 Brainwriting
   d. Power III

29. _____ is a term commonly used to describe commerce transactions between businesses like the one between a manufacturer and a wholesaler or a wholesaler and a retailer i.e both the buyer and the seller are business entity. This is unlike business-to-consumers (B2C) which involve a business entity and end consumer, or business-to-government (B2G) which involve a business entity and government.

The volume of B2B transactions is much higher than the volume of B2C transactions. The primary reason for this is that in a typical supply chain there will be many B2B transactions involving subcomponent or raw materials, and only one B2C transaction, specifically sale of the finished product to the end customer.

   a. Social marketing
   b. Disruptive technology
   c. Customer relationship management
   d. Business-to-business

30. Advertising mail junk mail is the delivery of advertising material to recipients of postal mail. The delivery of advertising mail forms a large and growing service for many postal services, and _____ marketing forms a significant portion of the direct marketing industry. Some organizations attempt to help people opt-out of receiving advertising mail, in many cases motivated by a concern over its negative environmental impact.
   a. Telemarketing
   b. Phishing
   c. Directory Harvest Attack
   d. Direct mail

31. Electronic commerce, commonly known as _____ or eCommerce, consists of the buying and selling of products or services over electronic systems such as the Internet and other computer networks. The amount of trade conducted electronically has grown extraordinarily with wide-spread Internet usage. A wide variety of commerce is conducted in this way, spurring and drawing on innovations in electronic funds transfer, supply chain management, Internet marketing, online transaction processing, electronic data interchange (EDI), inventory management systems, and automated data collection systems.
   a. ADTECH
   b. ACNielsen
   c. AMAX
   d. E-commerce

32. An _____ is the manufacturing of a good or service within a category. Although _____ is a broad term for any kind of economic production, in economics and urban planning _____ is a synonym for the secondary sector, which is a type of economic activity involved in the manufacturing of raw materials into goods and products.

There are four key industrial economic sectors: the primary sector, largely raw material extraction industries such as mining and farming; the secondary sector, involving refining, construction, and manufacturing; the tertiary sector, which deals with services (such as law and medicine) and distribution of manufactured goods; and the quaternary sector, a relatively new type of knowledge _____ focusing on technological research, design and development such as computer programming, and biochemistry.

Chapter 16. Advertising and Public Relations

a. Industry
c. ACNielsen
b. ADTECH
d. AMAX

33. _____s is the social science that studies the production, distribution, and consumption of goods and services. The term _____s comes from the Ancient Greek οá¼°κονομῑα from οá¼¶κος (oikos, 'house') + vÏŒμος (nomos, 'custom' or 'law'), hence 'rules of the house(hold)'. Current _____ models developed out of the broader field of political economy in the late 19th century, owing to a desire to use an empirical approach more akin to the physical sciences.

a. Industrial organization
c. ACNielsen
b. ADTECH
d. Economic

34. _____ is the practice of managing the flow of information between an organization and its publics. _____ - often referred to as _____ - gains an organization or individual exposure to their audiences using topics of public interest and news items that do not require direct payment. Because _____ places exposure in credible third-party outlets, it offers a third-party legitimacy that advertising does not have.

a. Graphic communication
c. Public relations
b. Power III
d. Symbolic analysis

35. _____ refer to a collection of facts usually collected as the result of experience, observation or experiment or a set of premises. This may consist of numbers, words particularly as measurements or observations of a set of variables. _____ are often viewed as a lowest level of abstraction from which information and knowledge are derived.

a. Pearson product-moment correlation coefficient
c. Sample size
b. Data
d. Mean

36. _____ involves disseminating information about a product, product line, brand, or company. It is one of the four key aspects of the marketing mix. (The other three elements are product marketing, pricing, and distribution). P>_____ is generally sub-divided into two parts:

- Above the line _____: Promotion in the media (e.g. TV, radio, newspapers, Internet and Mobile Phones) in which the advertiser pays an advertising agency to place the ad
- Below the line _____: All other _____. Much of this is intended to be subtle enough for the consumer to be unaware that _____ is taking place. E.g. sponsorship, product placement, endorsements, sales _____, merchandising, direct mail, personal selling, public relations, trade shows

a. Promotion
c. Bottling lines
b. Davie Brown Index
d. Cashmere Agency

37. _____ is the deliberate attempt to manage the public's perception of a subject. The subjects of _____ include people (for example, politicians and performing artists), goods and services, organizations of all kinds, and works of art or entertainment.

From a marketing perspective, _____ is one component of promotion.

a. Brando
c. Little value placed on potential benefits
b. Pearson's chi-square
d. Publicity

Chapter 16. Advertising and Public Relations

38. In economics, business, retail, and accounting, a _____ is the value of money that has been used up to produce something, and hence is not available for use anymore. In economics, a _____ is an alternative that is given up as a result of a decision. In business, the _____ may be one of acquisition, in which case the amount of money expended to acquire it is counted as _____.

   a. Variable cost
   b. Fixed costs
   c. Cost
   d. Transaction cost

39. _____ is a way of measuring the success of an online advertising campaign. A CTR is obtained by dividing the number of users who clicked on an ad on a web page by the number of times the ad was delivered (impressions.) For example, if a banner ad was delivered 100 times (impressions delivered) and one person clicked on it (clicks recorded), then the resulting CTR would be 1 percent.

   a. Display advertising
   b. Click-through rate
   c. Web analytics
   d. JICIMS

40. _____ is a branch of philosophy which seeks to address questions about morality, such as how a moral outcome can be achieved in a specific situation (applied _____), how moral values should be determined (normative _____), what moral values people actually abide by (descriptive _____), what the fundamental semantic, ontological, and epistemic nature of _____ or morality is (meta-_____), and how moral capacity or moral agency develops and what its nature is (moral psychology.)

Socrates was one of the first Greek philosophers to encourage both scholars and the common citizen to turn their attention from the outside world to the condition of man. In this view, Knowledge having a bearing on human life was placed highest, all other knowledge being secondary.

   a. ACNielsen
   b. Ethics
   c. ADTECH
   d. AMAX

41. _____ as a legal term refers to promotional statements and claims that express subjective rather than objective views, such that no reasonable person would take literally. _____ is especially featured in testimonials.

In a legal context, the term originated in the English Court of Appeal case Carlill v Carbolic Smoke Ball Company, which centred on whether a monetary reimbursement should be paid when an influenza preventative device failed to work.

   a. Custom media
   b. Heinz pickle pin
   c. Conquesting
   d. Puffery

42. A _____ or personal video recorder (PVR) is a device that records video in a digital format to a disk drive or other memory medium within a device. The term includes stand-alone set-top boxes, portable media players (PMP) and software for personal computers which enables video capture and playback to and from disk. Some consumer electronic manufacturers have started to offer televisions with _____ hardware and software built in to the television itself; LG was first to launch one in 2007.

   a. 6-3-5 Brainwriting
   b. Power III
   c. 180SearchAssistant
   d. Digital video recorder

Chapter 17. Personal Selling and Sales Promotion

1. _____ is a method of direct marketing in which a salesperson solicits to prospective customers to buy products or services, either over the phone or through a subsequent face to face or Web conferencing appointment scheduled during the call.

   _____ can also include recorded sales pitches programmed to be played over the phone via automatic dialing. _____ has come under fire in recent years, being viewed as an annoyance by many.

   a. Telemarketing
   b. Joe job
   c. Directory Harvest Attack
   d. Phishing

2. _____ is a contract between two parties, one being the employer and the other being the employee. An employee may be defined as: 'A person in the service of another under any contract of hire, express or implied, oral or written, where the employer has the power or right to control and direct the employee in the material details of how the work is to be performed.' Black's Law Dictionary page 471 (5th ed. 1979.)
   a. AMAX
   b. ADTECH
   c. Employment
   d. ACNielsen

3. _____ is defined by the American _____ Association as the activity, set of institutions, and processes for creating, communicating, delivering, and exchanging offerings that have value for customers, clients, partners, and society at large. The term developed from the original meaning which referred literally to going to market, as in shopping, or going to a market to sell goods or services.

   _____ practice tends to be seen as a creative industry, which includes advertising, distribution and selling.

   a. Marketing myopia
   b. Customer acquisition management
   c. Product naming
   d. Marketing

4. A _____ or trade mark, identified by the symbols ™ (not yet registered) and ® (registered) business organization or other legal entity to identify that the products and/or services to consumers with which the _____ appears originate from a unique source of origin, and to distinguish its products or services from those of other entities. A _____ is a type of intellectual property, and typically a name, word, phrase, logo, symbol, design, image, or a combination of these elements. There is also a range of non-conventional _____s comprising marks which do not fall into these standard categories.
   a. 180SearchAssistant
   b. Risk management
   c. Trademark
   d. Power III

5. _____ is a trademark law concept permitting the owner of a famous trademark to forbid others from using that mark in a way that would lessen its uniqueness. In most cases, _____ involves an unauthorized use of another's trademark on products that do not compete with, and have little connection with, those of the trademark owner. For example, a famous trademark used by one company to refer to hair care products might be diluted if another company began using a similar mark to refer to breakfast cereals or spark plugs.
   a. Trademark attorney
   b. Federal Bureau of Investigation
   c. Trademark Dilution
   d. Trespass to land

6. _____ is a broad label that refers to any individuals or households that use goods and services generated within the economy. The concept of a _____ is used in different contexts, so that the usage and significance of the term may vary.

Chapter 17. Personal Selling and Sales Promotion

A _____ is a person who uses any product or service.

    a. Consumer
    c. Power III
    b. 6-3-5 Brainwriting
    d. 180SearchAssistant

7. _____ is the study of when, why, how, where and what people do or do not buy products. It blends elements from psychology, sociology, social psychology, anthropology and economics. It attempts to understand the buyer decision making process, both individually and in groups. It studies characteristics of individual consumers such as demographics and behavioural variables in an attempt to understand people's wants. It also tries to assess influences on the consumer from groups such as family, friends, reference groups, and society in general.

    a. Consumer behavior
    c. Consumer confidence
    b. Communal marketing
    d. Multidimensional scaling

8. _____, is a form of Network Marketing (however the terms are often used interchangeably.) It is a marketing strategy that compensates promoters of direct selling companies not only for product sales they personally generate, but also for the sales of others they introduced to the company. The products and company are usually marketed directly to consumers and potential business partners by means of relationship referrals and word of mouth marketing.

    a. Service provider
    c. Cross-selling
    b. Pay to surf
    d. Multi-level marketing

9. A _____ is a statement or claim that a particular event will occur in the future in more certain terms than a forecast. The etymology of this word is Latin . In regards to predicting the future Howard H. Stevenson Says, ' _____ is at least two things: Important and hard.' Important, because we have to act, and hard because we have to realize the future we want, and what is the best way to get there.

    a. 6-3-5 Brainwriting
    c. Prediction
    b. Power III
    d. 180SearchAssistant

10. The term _____ was first coined by New York Times best selling author, Linda Richardson. _____ emphasizes customer needs and meeting those needs with solutions combining products and/or services. A consultative salesperson typically provides detailed instruction or advice on which solution best meets these needs.

    a. Consultative selling
    c. Lead generation
    b. Request for proposal
    d. Sales management

11. _____ refer to a collection of facts usually collected as the result of experience, observation or experiment or a set of premises. This may consist of numbers, words particularly as measurements or observations of a set of variables. _____ are often viewed as a lowest level of abstraction from which information and knowledge are derived.

    a. Pearson product-moment correlation coefficient
    c. Sample size
    b. Mean
    d. Data

12. _____ is a strategic planning method used to evaluate the Strengths, Weaknesses, Opportunities, and Threats involved in a project or in a business venture. It involves specifying the objective of the business venture or project and identifying the internal and external factors that are favorable and unfavorable to achieving that objective. The technique is credited to Albert Humphrey, who led a research project at Stanford University in the 1960s and 1970s using data from Fortune 500 companies.

Chapter 17. Personal Selling and Sales Promotion

a. Product differentiation
c. Market environment
b. Lead scoring
d. SWOT analysis

13. _____ is defined by the Oxford English Dictionary as 'the action or practice of selling among or between established clients, markets, traders, etc.' or 'that of selling an additional product or service to an existing customer'. In practice businesses define _____ in many different ways. Elements that might influence the definition might include: the size of the business, the industry sector it operates within and the financial motivations of those required to define the term.

a. Yield management
c. Service provider
b. Freebie marketing
d. Cross-selling

14. Sales force management systems are information systems used in marketing and management that help automate some sales and sales force management functions. They are frequently combined with a marketing information system, in which case they are often called Customer Relationship Management (CRM) systems.

_____ Systems, typically a part of a company's customer relationship management system, is a system that automatically records all the stages in a sales process.

a. 180SearchAssistant
c. Sales force automation
b. 6-3-5 Brainwriting
d. Power III

15. _____ is a term commonly used to describe commerce transactions between businesses like the one between a manufacturer and a wholesaler or a wholesaler and a retailer i.e both the buyer and the seller are business entity. This is unlike business-to-consumers (B2C) which involve a business entity and end consumer, or business-to-government (B2G) which involve a business entity and government.

The volume of B2B transactions is much higher than the volume of B2C transactions. The primary reason for this is that in a typical supply chain there will be many B2B transactions involving subcomponent or raw materials, and only one B2C transaction, specifically sale of the finished product to the end customer.

a. Social marketing
c. Disruptive technology
b. Customer relationship management
d. Business-to-business

16. Electronic commerce, commonly known as _____ or eCommerce, consists of the buying and selling of products or services over electronic systems such as the Internet and other computer networks. The amount of trade conducted electronically has grown extraordinarily with wide-spread Internet usage. A wide variety of commerce is conducted in this way, spurring and drawing on innovations in electronic funds transfer, supply chain management, Internet marketing, online transaction processing, electronic data interchange (EDI), inventory management systems, and automated data collection systems.

a. ADTECH
c. AMAX
b. E-commerce
d. ACNielsen

17. _____ operations or facilities are commonly called 'distribution centers'. '_____' is the term generally used to describe the process or the work flow associated with the picking, packing and delivery of the packed item(s) to a shipping carrier.

Chapter 17. Personal Selling and Sales Promotion

a. ADTECH
b. ACNielsen
c. AMAX
d. Order processing

18. In economics and sociology, an _____ is any factor (financial or non-financial) that enables or motivates a particular course of action, or counts as a reason for preferring one choice to the alternatives. It is an expectation that encourages people to behave in a certain way. Since human beings are purposeful creatures, the study of _____ structures is central to the study of all economic activity (both in terms of individual decision-making and in terms of co-operation and competition within a larger institutional structure.)

a. AMAX
b. ACNielsen
c. ADTECH
d. Incentive

19. _____ is the physical search for minerals, fossils, precious metals or mineral specimens, and is also known as fossicking.

_____ is synonymous in some ways with mineral exploration which is an organised, large scale and at least semi-scientific effort undertaken by mineral resource companies to find commercially viable ore deposits. To actually be considered a prospector you must become registered as a professional prospector.

a. 180SearchAssistant
b. Power III
c. 6-3-5 Brainwriting
d. Prospecting

20. _____ in organizations and public policy is both the organizational process of creating and maintaining a plan; and the psychological process of thinking about the activities required to create a desired goal on some scale. As such, it is a fundamental property of intelligent behavior. This thought process is essential to the creation and refinement of a plan, or integration of it with other plans, that is, it combines forecasting of developments with the preparation of scenarios of how to react to them.

a. 6-3-5 Brainwriting
b. Power III
c. Planning
d. 180SearchAssistant

21. The _____ is a 1990 United States Federal law. It was signed into law on November 8, 1990 by the president.

The law gives the Food and Drug Administration (FDA) authority to require nutrition labeling of most foods regulated by the Agency; and to require that all nutrient content claims (for example, 'high fiber', 'low fat', etc).

a. Copyright infringement
b. Nutrition Labeling and Education Act
c. Trespass to land
d. Fair Debt Collection Practices Act

22. _____ often refers to either primary or secondary research. Secondary research involves a company using information compiled from various sources, which is about a new or existing product. The advantages of secondary research are that it is relatively cheap and easily accessible.

a. Questionnaire
b. Mystery shoppers
c. Mystery shopping
d. Market Research

23. An _____ is a formal scheme used to promote or encourage specific actions or behavior by a specific group of people during a defined period of time. _____s are particularly used in business management to motivate employees, and in sales in order to attract and retain customers.

Chapter 17. Personal Selling and Sales Promotion

If programs are to be effective, all the factors that affect behavior must be recognized, including: motivation, skills, recognition, an understanding of the goals, and the ability to measure progress.

a. All commodity volume
b. Electronic retailing self-regulation program
c. Advertiser funded programming
d. Incentive program

24. _____ is a branch of philosophy which seeks to address questions about morality, such as how a moral outcome can be achieved in a specific situation (applied _____), how moral values should be determined (normative _____), what moral values people actually abide by (descriptive _____), what the fundamental semantic, ontological, and epistemic nature of _____ or morality is (meta-_____), and how moral capacity or moral agency develops and what its nature is (moral psychology.)

Socrates was one of the first Greek philosophers to encourage both scholars and the common citizen to turn their attention from the outside world to the condition of man. In this view, Knowledge having a bearing on human life was placed highest, all other knowledge being secondary.

a. ACNielsen
b. AMAX
c. ADTECH
d. Ethics

25. In marketing a _____ is a ticket or document that can be exchanged for a financial discount or rebate when purchasing a product. Customarily, _____s are issued by manufacturers of consumer packaged goods or by retailers, to be used in retail stores as a part of sales promotions. They are often widely distributed through mail, magazines, newspapers, the Internet, and mobile devices such as cell phones.

a. Merchandise
b. Marketing communication
c. Merchandising
d. Coupon

26. _____ involves disseminating information about a product, product line, brand, or company. It is one of the four key aspects of the marketing mix. (The other three elements are product marketing, pricing, and distribution). P>_____ is generally sub-divided into two parts:

- Above the line _____: Promotion in the media (e.g. TV, radio, newspapers, Internet and Mobile Phones) in which the advertiser pays an advertising agency to place the ad
- Below the line _____: All other _____. Much of this is intended to be subtle enough for the consumer to be unaware that _____ is taking place. E.g. sponsorship, product placement, endorsements, sales _____, merchandising, direct mail, personal selling, public relations, trade shows

a. Promotion
b. Davie Brown Index
c. Cashmere Agency
d. Bottling lines

27. _____ is one of the four aspects of promotional mix. (The other three parts of the promotional mix are advertising, personal selling, and publicity/public relations.) Media and non-media marketing communication are employed for a pre-determined, limited time to increase consumer demand, stimulate market demand or improve product availability.

a. New Media Strategies
b. Marketing communication
c. Merchandise
d. Sales promotion

Chapter 17. Personal Selling and Sales Promotion

28. _____ are final goods specifically intended for the mass market. For instance, _____ do not include investment assets, like precious antiques, even though these antiques are final goods.

Manufactured goods are goods that have been processed by way of machinery.

- a. Power III
- b. Durable good
- c. Free good
- d. Consumer Goods

29. _____ is one of the four Ps of the marketing mix. The other three aspects are product, promotion, and place. It is also a key variable in microeconomic price allocation theory.
- a. Price
- b. Relationship based pricing
- c. Competitor indexing
- d. Pricing

30. _____ is that part of statistical practice concerned with the selection of individual observations intended to yield some knowledge about a population of concern, especially for the purposes of statistical inference. Each observation measures one or more properties (weight, location, etc.) of an observable entity enumerated to distinguish objects or individuals.
- a. Sports Marketing Group
- b. Richard Buckminster 'Bucky' Fuller
- c. AStore
- d. Sampling

31. A _____, broadcast market, media region, designated market area (DMA), Television Market Area (FCC term) or simply market is a region where the population can receive the same (or similar) television and radio station offerings, and may also include other types of media including newspapers and Internet content. They can coincide with metropolitan areas, though rural regions with few significant population centers can also be designated as markets. Conversely, very large metropolitan areas can sometimes be subdivided into multiple segments.
- a. 180SearchAssistant
- b. Power III
- c. 6-3-5 Brainwriting
- d. Media Market

32. In the United States consumer sales promotions known as _____ or simply sweeps (both single and plural) have become associated with marketing promotions targeted toward both generating enthusiasm and providing incentive reactions among customers by enticing consumers to submit free entries into drawings of chance (and not skill) that are tied to product or service awareness wherein the featured prizes are given away by sponsoring companies. Prizes can vary in value from less than one dollar to more than one million U.S. dollars and can be in the form of cash, cars, homes, electronics, etc.

_____ frequently have eligibility limited by international, national, state, local, or other geographical factors.

- a. Claritas Prizm
- b. Market segment
- c. Commercial planning
- d. Sweepstakes

33. _____ is a form of communication that typically attempts to persuade potential customers to purchase or to consume more of a particular brand of product or service. 'While now central to the contemporary global economy and the reproduction of global production networks, it is only quite recently that _____ has been more than a marginal influence on patterns of sales and production. The formation of modern _____ was intimately bound up with the emergence of new forms of monopoly capitalism around the end of the 19th and beginning of the 20th century as one element in corporate strategies to create, organize and where possible control markets, especially for mass produced consumer goods.

Chapter 17. Personal Selling and Sales Promotion 157

a. Advertising
c. ACNielsen
b. AMAX
d. ADTECH

34. _____ is anything that is generally accepted as payment for goods and services and repayment of debts. The main uses of _____ are as a medium of exchange, a unit of account, and a store of value. Some authors explicitly require _____ to be a standard of deferred payment.
a. Law of supply
c. Leading indicator
b. Microeconomics
d. Money

35. The business terms _____ and pull originated in the logistic and supply chain management, but are also widely used in marketing.

A _____-pull-system in business describes the move of a product or information between two subjects. On markets the consumers usually 'pulls' the goods or information they demand for their needs, while the offerers or suppliers '_____es' them toward the consumers.

a. Completely randomized designs
c. Manufacturers' representatives
b. Gold Key Matching Service
d. Push

36. A trade fair (trade show or expo) is an exhibition organized so that companies in a specific industry can showcase and demonstrate their latest products, service, study activities of rivals and examine recent trends and opportunities. Some trade fairs are open to the public, while others can only be attended by company representatives (members of the trade) and members of the press, therefore _____ are classified as either 'Public' or 'Trade Only'. They are held on a continuing basis in virtually all markets and normally attract companies from around the globe.
a. 180SearchAssistant
c. 6-3-5 Brainwriting
b. Power III
d. Trade shows

37. _____ is a form of intellectual property which gives the creator of an original work exclusive rights for a certain time period in relation to that work, including its publication, distribution and adaptation; after which time the work is said to enter the public domain. _____ applies to any expressible form of an idea or information that is substantive and discrete. Some jurisdictions also recognize 'moral rights' of the creator of a work, such as the right to be credited for the work.
a. Celler-Kefauver Act
c. Reasonable person standard
b. Collective mark
d. Copyright

38. The _____ is a United States copyright law that implements two 1996 treaties of the World Intellectual Property Organization (WIPO.) It criminalizes production and dissemination of technology, devices whether or not there is actual infringement of copyright itself. In addition, the _____ heightens the penalties for copyright infringement on the Internet.
a. Priority right
c. Regulatory
b. Digital Millennium Copyright Act
d. Copyright infringement

39. _____ is a retail channel for the distribution of goods and services. At a basic level it may be defined as marketing and selling products, direct to consumers away from a fixed retail location. Sales are typically made through party plan, one to one demonstrations, and other personal contact arrangements.
a. 180SearchAssistant
c. Direct selling
b. Power III
d. 6-3-5 Brainwriting

Chapter 18. Price Concepts and Approaches

1. A _____ is a type of wholesale merchant business that buys goods and bulk products from importers, other wholesalers and then sells to retailers. _____s can deal in any commodity destined for the retail market. Typical categories are food, lumber, hardware, fuel, and textiles.
   - a. Tacit collusion
   - b. Refusal to deal
   - c. Chief privacy officer
   - d. Jobbing house

2. _____ is one of the four Ps of the marketing mix. The other three aspects are product, promotion, and place. It is also a key variable in microeconomic price allocation theory.
   - a. Competitor indexing
   - b. Relationship based pricing
   - c. Pricing
   - d. Price

3. A _____ is a plan of action designed to achieve a particular goal.

   _____ is different from tactics. In military terms, tactics is concerned with the conduct of an engagement while _____ is concerned with how different engagements are linked.
   - a. 6-3-5 Brainwriting
   - b. 180SearchAssistant
   - c. Power III
   - d. Strategy

4. _____ is a strategic planning method used to evaluate the Strengths, Weaknesses, Opportunities, and Threats involved in a project or in a business venture. It involves specifying the objective of the business venture or project and identifying the internal and external factors that are favorable and unfavorable to achieving that objective. The technique is credited to Albert Humphrey, who led a research project at Stanford University in the 1960s and 1970s using data from Fortune 500 companies.
   - a. Market environment
   - b. Product differentiation
   - c. SWOT analysis
   - d. Lead scoring

5. In economics, '_____' can refer to any kind of predatory pricing. However, the word is now generally used only in the context of international trade law, where _____ is defined as the act of a manufacturer in one country exporting a product to another country at a price which is either below the price it charges in its home market or is below its costs of production. The term has a negative connotation, but advocates of free markets see '_____' as beneficial for consumers and believe that protectionism to prevent it would have net negative consequences.
   - a. Hawkers
   - b. Gold Key Matching Service
   - c. Sample sales
   - d. Dumping

6. _____ in economics and business is the result of an exchange and from that trade we assign a numerical monetary value to a good, service or asset. If I trade 4 apples for an orange, the _____ of an orange is 4 - apples. Inversely, the _____ of an apple is 1/4 oranges.
   - a. Pricing
   - b. Discounts and allowances
   - c. Price
   - d. Contribution margin-based pricing

7. A _____ is a tax imposed on goods when they are moved across a political boundary. They are usually associated with protectionism, the economic policy of restraining trade between nations. For political reasons, _____s are usually imposed on imported goods, although they may also be imposed on exported goods.
   - a. Fiscal policy
   - b. Power III
   - c. Monetary policy
   - d. Tariff

Chapter 18. Price Concepts and Approaches

8. The _____ of 1936 (or Anti-Price Discrimination Act, 15 U.S.C. § 13) is a United States federal law that prohibits what were considered, at the time of passage, to be anticompetitive practices by producers, specifically price discrimination. It grew out of practices in which chain stores were allowed to purchase goods at lower prices than other retailers.

a. Trademark infringement
b. Fair Debt Collection Practices Act
c. Registered trademark symbol
d. Robinson-Patman Act

9. _____ is a broad label that refers to any individuals or households that use goods and services generated within the economy. The concept of a _____ is used in different contexts, so that the usage and significance of the term may vary.

A _____ is a person who uses any product or service.

a. 180SearchAssistant
b. Power III
c. 6-3-5 Brainwriting
d. Consumer

10. _____ are final goods specifically intended for the mass market. For instance, _____ do not include investment assets, like precious antiques, even though these antiques are final goods.

Manufactured goods are goods that have been processed by way of machinery.

a. Free good
b. Durable good
c. Power III
d. Consumer Goods

11. An _____ is the manufacturing of a good or service within a category. Although _____ is a broad term for any kind of economic production, in economics and urban planning _____ is a synonym for the secondary sector, which is a type of economic activity involved in the manufacturing of raw materials into goods and products.

There are four key industrial economic sectors: the primary sector, largely raw material extraction industries such as mining and farming; the secondary sector, involving refining, construction, and manufacturing; the tertiary sector, which deals with services (such as law and medicine) and distribution of manufactured goods; and the quaternary sector, a relatively new type of knowledge _____ focusing on technological research, design and development such as computer programming, and biochemistry.

a. AMAX
b. ADTECH
c. ACNielsen
d. Industry

12. _____ is defined by the American _____ Association as the activity, set of institutions, and processes for creating, communicating, delivering, and exchanging offerings that have value for customers, clients, partners, and society at large. The term developed from the original meaning which referred literally to going to market, as in shopping, or going to a market to sell goods or services.

_____ practice tends to be seen as a creative industry, which includes advertising, distribution and selling.

a. Marketing myopia
b. Customer acquisition management
c. Product naming
d. Marketing

Chapter 18. Price Concepts and Approaches

13. The _____ is generally accepted as the use and specification of the four p's describing the strategic position of a product in the marketplace. One version of the origins of the _____ starts in 1948 when James Culliton said that a marketing decision should be a result of something similar to a recipe. This version continued in 1953 when Neil Borden, in his American Marketing Association presidential address, took the recipe idea one step further and coined the term 'Marketing-Mix'.
    a. Power III
    b. 180SearchAssistant
    c. 6-3-5 Brainwriting
    d. Marketing mix

14. _____ is the use of marginal concepts within economics. (Marginal concepts are associated with a specific change in the quantity used of a good or of a service, as opposed to some notion of the over-all significance of that class of good or service, or of some total quantity thereof.) The central concept of _____ proper is that of marginal utility, but marginalists following the lead of Alfred Marshall were further heavily dependent upon the concept of marginal physical productivity in their explanation of cost; and the neoclassical tradition that emerged from British _____ generally abandoned the concept of utility and gave marginal rates of substitution a more fundamental rôle in analysis.
    a. 6-3-5 Brainwriting
    b. Power III
    c. 180SearchAssistant
    d. Marginalism

15. In economics, _____ is the process by which a firm determines the price and output level that returns the greatest profit. There are several approaches to this problem. The total revenue--total cost method relies on the fact that profit equals revenue minus cost, and the marginal revenue--marginal cost method is based on the fact that total profit in a perfectly competitive market reaches its maximum point where marginal revenue equals marginal cost.
    a. 180SearchAssistant
    b. Profit margin
    c. Power III
    d. Profit maximization

16. A personal and cultural _____ is a relative ethic _____, an assumption upon which implementation can be extrapolated. A _____ system is a set of consistent _____s and measures that is soo not true. A principle _____ is a foundation upon which other _____s and measures of integrity are based.
    a. Perceptual maps
    b. Supreme Court of the United States
    c. Package-on-Package
    d. Value

17. In economics, business, retail, and accounting, a _____ is the value of money that has been used up to produce something, and hence is not available for use anymore. In economics, a _____ is an alternative that is given up as a result of a decision. In business, the _____ may be one of acquisition, in which case the amount of money expended to acquire it is counted as _____.
    a. Cost
    b. Variable cost
    c. Transaction cost
    d. Fixed costs

18. _____ is the practice of individuals including commercial businesses, governments and institutions, facilitating the sale of their products or services to other companies or organizations that in turn resell them, use them as components in products or services they offer _____ is also called business-to-_____ for short. (Note that while marketing to government entities shares some of the same dynamics of organizational marketing, B2G Marketing is meaningfully different.)
    a. Law of disruption
    b. Disruptive technology
    c. Mass marketing
    d. Business marketing

19. The _____ is a 1990 United States Federal law. It was signed into law on November 8, 1990 by the president.

Chapter 18. Price Concepts and Approaches

The law gives the Food and Drug Administration (FDA) authority to require nutrition labeling of most foods regulated by the Agency; and to require that all nutrient content claims (for example, 'high fiber', 'low fat', etc).

a. Trespass to land
b. Nutrition Labeling and Education Act
c. Copyright infringement
d. Fair Debt Collection Practices Act

20. In mathematics, an _____, or central tendency of a data set refers to a measure of the 'middle' or 'expected' value of the data set. There are many different descriptive statistics that can be chosen as a measurement of the central tendency of the data items.

An _____ is a single value that is meant to typify a list of values.

a. Average
b. AMAX
c. ACNielsen
d. ADTECH

21. In economics, _____ is equal to total cost divided by the number of goods produced (the output quantity, Q.) It is also equal to the sum of average variable costs (total variable costs divided by Q) plus average fixed costs (total fixed costs divided by Q.) _____s may be dependent on the time period considered (increasing production may be expensive or impossible in the short term, for example.)

a. Average variable cost
b. ACNielsen
c. ADTECH
d. Average cost

22. _____ is a rivalry between individuals, groups, nations for territory, a niche, or allocation of resources. It arises whenever two or more parties strive for a goal which cannot be shared. _____ occurs naturally between living organisms which co-exist in the same environment.

a. Price fixing
b. Non-price competition
c. Price competition
d. Competition

23. _____ is the study of when, why, how, where and what people do or do not buy products. It blends elements from psychology, sociology, social psychology, anthropology and economics. It attempts to understand the buyer decision making process, both individually and in groups. It studies characteristics of individual consumers such as demographics and behavioural variables in an attempt to understand people's wants. It also tries to assess influences on the consumer from groups such as family, friends, reference groups, and society in general.

a. Consumer behavior
b. Communal marketing
c. Consumer confidence
d. Multidimensional scaling

24. In economics, _____ is the desire to own something and the ability to pay for it. The term _____ signifies the ability or the willingness to buy a particular commodity at a given point of time.

a. Market system
b. Discretionary spending
c. Demand
d. Market dominance

Chapter 18. Price Concepts and Approaches

25. _____s is the social science that studies the production, distribution, and consumption of goods and services. The term _____s comes from the Ancient Greek οἰκονομία from οἶκος (oikos, 'house') + νόμος (nomos, 'custom' or 'law'), hence 'rules of the house(hold)'. Current _____ models developed out of the broader field of political economy in the late 19th century, owing to a desire to use an empirical approach more akin to the physical sciences.

   a. Industrial organization   b. Economic
   c. ACNielsen   d. ADTECH

26. In economics, _____ are business expenses that are not dependent on the activities of the business They tend to be time-related, such as salaries or rents being paid per month. This is in contrast to variable costs, which are volume-related (and are paid per quantity.)

In management accounting, _____ are defined as expenses that do not change in proportion to the activity of a business, within the relevant period or scale of production.

   a. Variable cost   b. Marginal cost
   c. Transaction cost   d. Fixed costs

27. In economics and finance, _____ is the change in total cost that arises when the quantity produced changes by one unit. It is the cost of producing one more unit of a good. Mathematically, the _____ function is expressed as the first derivative of the total cost (TC) function with respect to quantity (Q.)

   a. Transaction cost   b. Variable cost
   c. Marginal cost   d. Fixed costs

28. _____ is a common market form. Many markets can be considered monopolistically competitive, often including the markets for restaurants, cereal, clothing, shoes and service industries in large cities. Short-run equilibrium of the firm under _____

Monopolistically competitive markets have the following characteristics:

- There are many producers and many consumers in a given market, and no business has total control over the market price.
- Consumers perceive that there are non-price differences among the competitors' products.
- There are few barriers to entry and exit.
- Producers have a degree of control over price.

Long-run equilibrium of the firm under _____

The characteristics of a monopolistically competitive market are almost the same as in perfect competition, with the exception of heterogeneous products, and that _____ involves a great deal of non-price competition (based on subtle product differentiation.) A firm making profits in the short run will break even in the long run because demand will decrease and average total cost will increase.

   a. Gross domestic product   b. Monopolistic competition
   c. Recession   d. Macroeconomics

Chapter 18. Price Concepts and Approaches 163

29. An _____ is a market form in which a market or industry is dominated by a small number of sellers (oligopolists.) Because there are few participants in this type of market, each oligopolist is aware of the actions of the others. The decisions of one firm influence, and are influenced by, the decisions of other firms.
  a. ACNielsen
  b. Oligopoly
  c. AMAX
  d. ADTECH

30. In economics, and cost accounting, _____ describes the total economic cost of production and is made up of variable costs, which vary according to the quantity of a good produced and include inputs such as labor and raw materials, plus fixed costs, which are independent of the quantity of a good produced and include inputs (capital) that cannot be varied in the short term, such as buildings and machinery. _____ in economics includes the total opportunity cost of each factor of production in addition to fixed and variable costs.

The rate at which _____ changes as the amount produced changes is called marginal cost.

  a. Household production function
  b. Hoarding
  c. Product proliferation
  d. Total cost

31. _____s are used in open sentences. For instance, in the formula x + 1 = 5, x is a _____ which represents an 'unknown' number. _____s are often represented by letters of the Roman alphabet, or those of other alphabets, such as Greek, and use other special symbols.
  a. Personalization
  b. Book of business
  c. Variable
  d. Quantitative

32. _____s are expenses that change in proportion to the activity of a business. In other words, _____ is the sum of marginal costs. It can also be considered normal costs.
  a. Transaction cost
  b. Fixed costs
  c. Marginal cost
  d. Variable cost

33. In economics, _____ is the ratio of the percent change in one variable to the percent change in another variable. It is a tool for measuring the responsiveness of a function to changes in parameters in a relative way. Commonly analyzed are _____ of substitution, price and wealth.
  a. Opinion leadership
  b. Intellectual property
  c. ACNielsen
  d. Elasticity

34. A _____ or trade mark, identified by the symbols â„¢ (not yet registered) and Â® (registered) business organization or other legal entity to identify that the products and/or services to consumers with which the _____ appears originate from a unique source of origin, and to distinguish its products or services from those of other entities. A _____ is a type of intellectual property, and typically a name, word, phrase, logo, symbol, design, image, or a combination of these elements. There is also a range of non-conventional _____s comprising marks which do not fall into these standard categories.
  a. Power III
  b. Risk management
  c. 180SearchAssistant
  d. Trademark

Chapter 18. Price Concepts and Approaches

35. _____ is a trademark law concept permitting the owner of a famous trademark to forbid others from using that mark in a way that would lessen its uniqueness. In most cases, _____ involves an unauthorized use of another's trademark on products that do not compete with, and have little connection with, those of the trademark owner. For example, a famous trademark used by one company to refer to hair care products might be diluted if another company began using a similar mark to refer to breakfast cereals or spark plugs.
   a. Federal Bureau of Investigation
   b. Trademark Dilution
   c. Trademark attorney
   d. Trespass to land

36. A _____ is the price one pays as remuneration for services, especially the honorarium paid to a doctor, lawyer, consultant, or other member of a learned profession. _____s usually allow for overhead, wages, costs, and markup.

   Traditionally, professionals in Great Britain received a _____ in contradistinction to a payment, salary, or wage, and would often use guineas rather than pounds as units of account.

   a. Price shading
   b. Transfer pricing
   c. Price war
   d. Fee

37. _____ is a pricing method used by companies. It is used primarily because it is easy to calculate and requires little information. There are several varieties, but the common thread in all of them is that one first calculates the cost of the product, then includes an additional amount to represent profit.
   a. Relationship based pricing
   b. Loss leader
   c. Break even analysis
   d. Cost-plus pricing

38. A _____ is a collection of symbols, experiences and associations connected with a product, a service, a person or any other artifact or entity.

   _____s have become increasingly important components of culture and the economy, now being described as 'cultural accessories and personal philosophies'.

   Some people distinguish the psychological aspect of a _____ from the experiential aspect.

   a. Brandable software
   b. Brand equity
   c. Store brand
   d. Brand

39. The _____ is a database of consumer perception of brands created and managed by BrandAsset Consulting, a division of Young ' Rubicam Brands to provide information to enable firms to improve the marketing decision-making process and to manage brands better. _____ and _____ also describe the Y'R group managing the database.

   _____ measures the value of a brand along four dimensions: 'Differentiation,' 'Relevance,' 'Esteem,' and 'Knowledge.' Differentiation and Relevance build up to 'Brand Strength.' Esteem and Knowledge are used to calculate 'Brand Stature.' _____ defines these terms as follows.

   a. Target audience
   b. Brand Asset Valuator
   c. Targeted advertising
   d. Hoover free flights promotion

Chapter 18. Price Concepts and Approaches

40. The break-even point for a product is the point where total revenue received equals the total costs associated with the sale of the product (TR=TC.) A break-even point is typically calculated in order for businesses to determine if it would be profitable to sell a proposed product, as opposed to attempting to modify an existing product instead so it can be made lucrative. _____ can also be used to analyse the potential profitability of an expenditure in a sales-based business.

In _____, margin of safety is how much output or sales level can fall before a business reaches its break-even point (BEP).

a. Contribution margin-based pricing
c. Pay Per Sale
b. Price skimming
d. Break even analysis

41. _____ is the process of understanding, anticipating and influencing consumer behavior in order to maximize revenue or profits from a fixed, perishable resource This process was first discovered by Dr. Matt H. Keller. The challenge is to sell the right resources to the right customer at the right time for the right price. This process can result in price discrimination, where a firm charges customers consuming otherwise identical goods or services a different price for doing so.

a. Yield management
c. Cross-selling
b. Service provider
d. Multi-level marketing

42. _____ is a form of communication that typically attempts to persuade potential customers to purchase or to consume more of a particular brand of product or service. 'While now central to the contemporary global economy and the reproduction of global production networks, it is only quite recently that _____ has been more than a marginal influence on patterns of sales and production. The formation of modern _____ was intimately bound up with the emergence of new forms of monopoly capitalism around the end of the 19th and beginning of the 20th century as one element in corporate strategies to create, organize and where possible control markets, especially for mass produced consumer goods.

a. ACNielsen
c. AMAX
b. ADTECH
d. Advertising

Chapter 19. Pricing Strategies

1. _____ is one of the four Ps of the marketing mix. The other three aspects are product, promotion, and place. It is also a key variable in microeconomic price allocation theory.

   a. Price
   c. Relationship based pricing
   b. Pricing
   d. Competitor indexing

2. A _____ is a plan of action designed to achieve a particular goal.

   _____ is different from tactics. In military terms, tactics is concerned with the conduct of an engagement while _____ is concerned with how different engagements are linked.

   a. 6-3-5 Brainwriting
   c. 180SearchAssistant
   b. Strategy
   d. Power III

3. _____ is defined by the American _____ Association as the activity, set of institutions, and processes for creating, communicating, delivering, and exchanging offerings that have value for customers, clients, partners, and society at large. The term developed from the original meaning which referred literally to going to market, as in shopping, or going to a market to sell goods or services.

   _____ practice tends to be seen as a creative industry, which includes advertising, distribution and selling.

   a. Customer acquisition management
   c. Marketing myopia
   b. Product naming
   d. Marketing

4. The _____ is a marketing term and refers to all of the forces outside of marketing that affect marketing management's ability to build and maintain successful relationships with target customers. The _____ consists of both the macroenvironment and the microenvironment.

   The microenvironment refers to the forces that are close to the company and affect its ability to serve its customers.

   a. Business-to-consumer
   c. Psychographic
   b. Market environment
   d. Customer franchise

5. A _____ is a collection of symbols, experiences and associations connected with a product, a service, a person or any other artifact or entity.

   _____s have become increasingly important components of culture and the economy, now being described as 'cultural accessories and personal philosophies'.

   Some people distinguish the psychological aspect of a _____ from the experiential aspect.

   a. Brandable software
   c. Store brand
   b. Brand equity
   d. Brand

6. The _____ is a database of consumer perception of brands created and managed by BrandAsset Consulting, a division of Young ' Rubicam Brands to provide information to enable firms to improve the marketing decision-making process and to manage brands better. _____ and _____ also describe the Y'R group managing the database.

Chapter 19. Pricing Strategies 167

_____ measures the value of a brand along four dimensions: 'Differentiation,' 'Relevance,' 'Esteem,' and 'Knowledge.' Differentiation and Relevance build up to 'Brand Strength.' Esteem and Knowledge are used to calculate 'Brand Stature.' _____ defines these terms as follows.

a. Targeted advertising
b. Target audience
c. Hoover free flights promotion
d. Brand Asset Valuator

7. _____ is a method of direct marketing in which a salesperson solicits to prospective customers to buy products or services, either over the phone or through a subsequent face to face or Web conferencing appointment scheduled during the call.

_____ can also include recorded sales pitches programmed to be played over the phone via automatic dialing. _____ has come under fire in recent years, being viewed as an annoyance by many.

a. Directory Harvest Attack
b. Telemarketing
c. Joe job
d. Phishing

8. An _____ is the manufacturing of a good or service within a category. Although _____ is a broad term for any kind of economic production, in economics and urban planning _____ is a synonym for the secondary sector, which is a type of economic activity involved in the manufacturing of raw materials into goods and products.

There are four key industrial economic sectors: the primary sector, largely raw material extraction industries such as mining and farming; the secondary sector, involving refining, construction, and manufacturing; the tertiary sector, which deals with services (such as law and medicine) and distribution of manufactured goods; and the quaternary sector, a relatively new type of knowledge _____ focusing on technological research, design and development such as computer programming, and biochemistry.

a. ADTECH
b. ACNielsen
c. AMAX
d. Industry

9. _____ refer to a collection of facts usually collected as the result of experience, observation or experiment or a set of premises. This may consist of numbers, words particularly as measurements or observations of a set of variables. _____ are often viewed as a lowest level of abstraction from which information and knowledge are derived.

a. Mean
b. Pearson product-moment correlation coefficient
c. Sample size
d. Data

10. _____ is the pricing technique of setting a relatively low initial entry price, often lower than the eventual market price, to attract new customers. The strategy works on the expectation that customers will switch to the new brand because of the lower price. _____ is most commonly associated with a marketing objective of increasing market share or sales volume, rather than to make profit in the short term.

a. Competitor indexing
b. Fee
c. Price war
d. Penetration pricing

Chapter 19. Pricing Strategies

11. _____ often refers to either primary or secondary research. Secondary research involves a company using information compiled from various sources, which is about a new or existing product. The advantages of secondary research are that it is relatively cheap and easily accessible.
    a. Mystery shopping
    b. Mystery shoppers
    c. Questionnaire
    d. Market Research

12. A _____ or trade mark, identified by the symbols â"¢ (not yet registered) and Â® (registered) business organization or other legal entity to identify that the products and/or services to consumers with which the _____ appears originate from a unique source of origin, and to distinguish its products or services from those of other entities. A _____ is a type of intellectual property, and typically a name, word, phrase, logo, symbol, design, image, or a combination of these elements. There is also a range of non-conventional _____s comprising marks which do not fall into these standard categories.
    a. Power III
    b. 180SearchAssistant
    c. Risk management
    d. Trademark

13. Competitiveness is a comparative concept of the ability and performance of a firm, sub-sector or country to sell and supply goods and/or services in a given market. Although widely used in economics and business management, the usefulness of the concept, particularly in the context of national competitiveness, is vigorously disputed by economists, such as Paul Krugman .

The term may also be applied to markets, where it is used to refer to the extent to which the market structure may be regarded as perfectly _____.

    a. Geographical pricing
    b. Customs union
    c. Free trade zone
    d. Competitive

14. The _____ is a 1990 United States Federal law. It was signed into law on November 8, 1990 by the president.

The law gives the Food and Drug Administration (FDA) authority to require nutrition labeling of most foods regulated by the Agency; and to require that all nutrient content claims (for example, 'high fiber', 'low fat', etc).

    a. Trespass to land
    b. Fair Debt Collection Practices Act
    c. Copyright infringement
    d. Nutrition Labeling and Education Act

15. The (manufacturer's) suggested retail price (MSRP or SRP), _____ or recommended retail price (RRP) of a product is the price the manufacturer recommends that the retailer sell it for. The intention was to help to standardize prices among locations. While some stores always sell at, or below, the suggested retail price, others do so only when items are on sale or closeout.
    a. Predatory pricing
    b. 180SearchAssistant
    c. Power III
    d. List price

16. _____ is an economic concept with commonplace familiarity. It is the price that a good or service is offered at, or will fetch, in the marketplace. It is of interest mainly in the study of microeconomics.
    a. Power III
    b. Forward market
    c. Market price
    d. Market maker

Chapter 19. Pricing Strategies

17. _____ in economics and business is the result of an exchange and from that trade we assign a numerical monetary value to a good, service or asset. If I trade 4 apples for an orange, the _____ of an orange is 4 - apples. Inversely, the _____ of an apple is 1/4 oranges.
   a. Discounts and allowances
   b. Pricing
   c. Contribution margin-based pricing
   d. Price

18. A _____ is an amount paid by way of reduction, return, or refund on what has already been paid or contributed. It is a type of sales promotion marketers use primarily as incentives or supplements to product sales. The mail-in _____ is the most common.
   a. Personalization
   b. Rebate
   c. Lifestyle city
   d. Strand

19. _____ is a broad label that refers to any individuals or households that use goods and services generated within the economy. The concept of a _____ is used in different contexts, so that the usage and significance of the term may vary.

   A _____ is a person who uses any product or service.

   a. 6-3-5 Brainwriting
   b. Power III
   c. 180SearchAssistant
   d. Consumer

20. _____ is the study of the Earth and its lands, features, inhabitants, and phenomena. A literal translation would be 'to describe or write about the Earth'. The first person to use the word '_____' was Eratosthenes.
   a. Power III
   b. 6-3-5 Brainwriting
   c. 180SearchAssistant
   d. Geography

21. _____ is the study of when, why, how, where and what people do or do not buy products. It blends elements from psychology, sociology, social psychology, anthropology and economics. It attempts to understand the buyer decision making process, both individually and in groups. It studies characteristics of individual consumers such as demographics and behavioural variables in an attempt to understand people's wants. It also tries to assess influences on the consumer from groups such as family, friends, reference groups, and society in general.
   a. Communal marketing
   b. Consumer confidence
   c. Consumer behavior
   d. Multidimensional scaling

22. _____ is the process of understanding, anticipating and influencing consumer behavior in order to maximize revenue or profits from a fixed, perishable resource This process was first discovered by Dr. Matt H. Keller. The challenge is to sell the right resources to the right customer at the right time for the right price. This process can result in price discrimination, where a firm charges customers consuming otherwise identical goods or services a different price for doing so.
   a. Yield management
   b. Multi-level marketing
   c. Cross-selling
   d. Service provider

Chapter 19. Pricing Strategies

23. _____ - Prices increase as shipping distances increase. This is sometimes done by drawing concentric circles on a map with the plant or warehouse at the center and each circle defining the boundary of a price zone. Instead of using circles, irregularly shaped price boundaries can be drawn that reflect geography, population density, transportation infrastructure, and shipping cost. The term '_____' can also refer to the practice of setting prices that reflect local competitive conditions, i.e., the market forces of supply and demand, rather than actual cost of transportation.

_____, as practiced in the gasoline industry in the United States, is the pricing of gasoline based on a complex and secret weighting of factors, such as the number of competing stations, number of vehicles, average traffic flow, population density, and geographic characteristics. This can result in two branded gas stations only a few miles apart selling gasoline at a price differential of as much as $0.50 per gallon.

a. Safeguard
c. Countervailing duties
b. Geographical pricing
d. Zone pricing

24. _____ or price ending is a marketing practice based on the theory that certain prices have a psychological impact. The retail prices are often expressed as 'odd prices': a little less than a round number, e.g. $19.99 or £6.95 (but not necessarily mathematically odd, it could also be 2.98.) The theory is this drives demand greater than would be expected if consumers were perfectly rational.

a. Supplier diversity
c. Chain stores
b. First-mover advantage
d. Psychological pricing

25. A _____ or leader is a product sold at a low price (at cost or below cost) to stimulate other, profitable sales. It is a kind of sales promotion, in other words marketing concentrating on a pricing strategy. The price can even be so low that the product is sold at a loss.

a. Penetration pricing
c. Resale price maintenance
b. Price shading
d. Loss leader

26. _____ is a term commonly used to describe commerce transactions between businesses like the one between a manufacturer and a wholesaler or a wholesaler and a retailer i.e both the buyer and the seller are business entity.This is unlike business-to-consumers (B2C) which involve a business entity and end consumer, or business-to-government (B2G) which involve a business entity and government.

The volume of B2B transactions is much higher than the volume of B2C transactions. The primary reason for this is that in a typical supply chain there will be many B2B transactions involving subcomponent or raw materials, and only one B2C transaction, specifically sale of the finished product to the end customer.

a. Business-to-business
c. Social marketing
b. Customer relationship management
d. Disruptive technology

27. Electronic commerce, commonly known as _____ or eCommerce, consists of the buying and selling of products or services over electronic systems such as the Internet and other computer networks. The amount of trade conducted electronically has grown extraordinarily with wide-spread Internet usage. A wide variety of commerce is conducted in this way, spurring and drawing on innovations in electronic funds transfer, supply chain management, Internet marketing, online transaction processing, electronic data interchange (EDI), inventory management systems, and automated data collection systems.

a. ACNielsen
b. E-commerce
c. AMAX
d. ADTECH

28. _____ is a strategic planning method used to evaluate the Strengths, Weaknesses, Opportunities, and Threats involved in a project or in a business venture. It involves specifying the objective of the business venture or project and identifying the internal and external factors that are favorable and unfavorable to achieving that objective. The technique is credited to Albert Humphrey, who led a research project at Stanford University in the 1960s and 1970s using data from Fortune 500 companies.

a. SWOT analysis
b. Lead scoring
c. Product differentiation
d. Market environment

29. _____ is a technique used in propaganda and advertising. Also known as association, this is a technique of projecting positive or negative qualities (praise or blame) of a person, entity, object, or value (an individual, group, organization, nation, patriotism, etc.) to another in order to make the second more acceptable or to discredit it.

a. Supplier
b. Micro ads
c. Sexism,
d. Transfer

30. _____ refers to the pricing of contributions (assets, tangible and intangible, services, and funds) transferred within an organization. For example, goods from the production division may be sold to the marketing division, or goods from a parent company may be sold to a foreign subsidiary. Since the prices are set within an organization (i.e. controlled), the typical market mechanisms that establish prices for such transactions between third parties may not apply.

a. Fee
b. Discounts and allowances
c. Price skimming
d. Transfer pricing

31. _____ is a marketing strategy that involves offering several products for sale as one combined product. This strategy is very common in the software business (for example: bundle a word processor, a spreadsheet, and a database into a single office suite), in the cable television industry (for example, basic cable in the United States generally offers many channels at one price), and in the fast food industry in which multiple items are combined into a complete meal. A bundle of products is sometimes referred to as a package deal or a compilation or an anthology.

a. Technology acceptance model
b. Product bundling
c. Primary research
d. Psychographic

32. In marketing and strategy, _____ refers to a reduction in the sales volume, sales revenue, or market share of one product as a result of the introduction of a new product by the same producer.

For example, if Coca Cola were to introduce a similar product (say, Diet Coke or Cherry Coke), this new product could take some of the sales away from the original Coke. _____ is a key consideration in product portfolio analysis.

a. Business-to-consumer
b. Marketing
c. Co-marketing
d. Cannibalization

33. _____s are Web-based intelligent software applications that can help online shoppers find lower price for commodities or services. Price comparison services was the earliest service a _____ provides. To search the price of a particular item, a _____ would search multiple online stores based on the keyword the online shopper provides.

a. Book of business
b. Comparison-Shopping agent
c. Net Promoter^R score
d. Distribution

ANSWER KEY

Chapter 1
1. a	2. b	3. b	4. a	5. d	6. d	7. d	8. d	9. a	10. a
11. d	12. b	13. c	14. d	15. d	16. b	17. c	18. a	19. d	20. c
21. c	22. d	23. b	24. d	25. a	26. a	27. a	28. b	29. c	30. c
31. b	32. d	33. d	34. c	35. d	36. d	37. c	38. d	39. c	40. d
41. c	42. c	43. d	44. c	45. d	46. d	47. c	48. b	49. b	

Chapter 2
1. d	2. c	3. d	4. d	5. a	6. d	7. d	8. d	9. b	10. b
11. a	12. a	13. d	14. c	15. b	16. d	17. b	18. d	19. c	20. c
21. d	22. b	23. d	24. d	25. d	26. b	27. c	28. d	29. d	30. d
31. b	32. c	33. d	34. d	35. d	36. b	37. d	38. b	39. a	40. c
41. d	42. a	43. c	44. c						

Chapter 3
1. b	2. c	3. d	4. d	5. d	6. c	7. b	8. d	9. d	10. d
11. d	12. c	13. d	14. c	15. d	16. d	17. a	18. b	19. d	20. d
21. d	22. d	23. d	24. b	25. c	26. d	27. c	28. d	29. b	30. d
31. d	32. c	33. d	34. a	35. a	36. b	37. a	38. d	39. d	40. b
41. a	42. d	43. b	44. d	45. d	46. d	47. c	48. d	49. d	

Chapter 4
1. a	2. d	3. d	4. d	5. b	6. d	7. d	8. b	9. d	10. b
11. d	12. c	13. a	14. c	15. a	16. b	17. a	18. d	19. d	20. a
21. a	22. d	23. d	24. a	25. d	26. d	27. c	28. c	29. a	30. c
31. d	32. d	33. a	34. a	35. b	36. c	37. d	38. c	39. d	40. d

Chapter 5
1. d	2. a	3. a	4. d	5. a	6. b	7. d	8. a	9. b	10. b
11. d	12. c	13. d	14. d	15. a	16. d	17. b	18. d	19. a	20. d
21. a	22. d	23. b	24. b	25. d	26. d	27. d	28. d	29. d	30. a
31. d	32. a	33. c	34. c	35. a	36. b				

Chapter 6
1. d	2. b	3. d	4. d	5. d	6. b	7. b	8. c	9. a	10. a
11. a	12. a	13. d	14. a	15. d	16. c	17. d	18. a	19. b	20. d
21. c	22. b	23. b	24. a	25. d	26. c	27. a	28. a	29. d	30. c
31. c	32. d								

Chapter 7
1. d	2. d	3. c	4. d	5. d	6. c	7. d	8. a	9. d	10. c
11. d	12. a	13. b	14. a	15. d	16. c	17. d	18. a	19. d	20. d
21. a	22. a	23. d	24. d	25. a	26. a	27. a	28. b	29. a	30. d
31. b	32. d	33. d	34. b	35. d	36. c	37. d	38. d	39. a	40. d
41. d	42. d	43. b	44. d	45. c	46. d	47. a			

Chapter 8

1. d	2. d	3. a	4. d	5. d	6. b	7. a	8. c	9. a	10. c
11. d	12. a	13. a	14. d	15. b	16. d	17. a	18. d	19. d	20. d
21. a	22. d	23. d	24. c	25. d	26. d	27. d	28. d	29. c	30. a
31. b	32. a	33. c	34. d	35. a	36. c	37. a	38. b	39. d	40. a
41. b	42. d	43. d	44. d	45. d	46. d				

Chapter 9

1. d	2. b	3. d	4. d	5. c	6. c	7. a	8. b	9. a	10. d
11. a	12. c	13. c	14. a	15. d	16. a	17. d	18. d	19. d	20. d
21. a	22. d	23. d	24. d	25. d	26. a	27. c	28. c	29. d	30. a
31. d	32. d	33. d	34. b						

Chapter 10

1. d	2. c	3. d	4. a	5. c	6. d	7. d	8. c	9. d	10. c
11. a	12. d	13. b	14. d	15. d	16. d	17. b	18. a	19. d	20. d
21. d	22. a	23. b	24. d	25. d	26. d	27. d	28. b	29. d	30. d
31. a	32. c	33. c	34. d	35. d	36. d	37. d	38. d	39. b	40. a
41. a	42. d	43. a	44. d	45. d					

Chapter 11

1. b	2. a	3. d	4. d	5. a	6. d	7. b	8. d	9. d	10. d
11. b	12. c	13. d	14. b	15. d	16. c	17. b	18. d	19. d	20. b
21. b	22. b	23. d	24. d	25. d	26. c	27. a	28. d	29. c	30. a

Chapter 12

1. c	2. d	3. c	4. c	5. a	6. d	7. c	8. a	9. d	10. a
11. d	12. d	13. b	14. b	15. d	16. c	17. d	18. c	19. b	20. c
21. a	22. d	23. a	24. b	25. a	26. d	27. d	28. b	29. c	30. c
31. d	32. d	33. a	34. c	35. b	36. d	37. a	38. d	39. d	40. c
41. d	42. d	43. a	44. c	45. d	46. c	47. b			

Chapter 13

1. d	2. d	3. d	4. a	5. d	6. d	7. d	8. a	9. b	10. a
11. d	12. c	13. d	14. a	15. b	16. d	17. a	18. d	19. d	20. d
21. d	22. c	23. d	24. d	25. a	26. b	27. b	28. b	29. c	30. b
31. b	32. a	33. c	34. a	35. a	36. d	37. d	38. b	39. d	40. d
41. d	42. d	43. d	44. d	45. a	46. d	47. d	48. a	49. d	50. b

ANSWER KEY

Chapter 14

1. b	2. a	3. b	4. d	5. a	6. b	7. a	8. a	9. c	10. b
11. d	12. b	13. b	14. b	15. d	16. c	17. d	18. d	19. b	20. b
21. b	22. c	23. d	24. c	25. c	26. d	27. d	28. a	29. d	30. c
31. d	32. d	33. d	34. c	35. b	36. b	37. a	38. d	39. d	40. d
41. c	42. c	43. d	44. b	45. c	46. d	47. d	48. c	49. a	50. c
51. d	52. a	53. d	54. d						

Chapter 15

1. c	2. a	3. b	4. b	5. d	6. c	7. d	8. d	9. d	10. c
11. d	12. d	13. d	14. d	15. d	16. d	17. d	18. d	19. d	20. d
21. b	22. c	23. d	24. c	25. d	26. a	27. c	28. c	29. c	30. a
31. d	32. d	33. a	34. d	35. a	36. d	37. d	38. d	39. d	40. b
41. d	42. d	43. c	44. c	45. d	46. d	47. b	48. d	49. b	50. d
51. b	52. a	53. c	54. d	55. d	56. d	57. d	58. d		

Chapter 16

1. a	2. d	3. d	4. b	5. d	6. d	7. b	8. b	9. a	10. c
11. d	12. d	13. d	14. d	15. c	16. a	17. b	18. d	19. c	20. c
21. d	22. d	23. d	24. b	25. b	26. d	27. d	28. b	29. d	30. d
31. d	32. a	33. d	34. c	35. b	36. a	37. d	38. c	39. b	40. b
41. d	42. d								

Chapter 17

1. a	2. c	3. d	4. c	5. c	6. a	7. a	8. d	9. c	10. a
11. d	12. d	13. d	14. c	15. d	16. b	17. d	18. d	19. d	20. c
21. b	22. d	23. d	24. d	25. d	26. a	27. d	28. d	29. d	30. d
31. d	32. d	33. a	34. d	35. d	36. d	37. d	38. b	39. c	

Chapter 18

1. d	2. c	3. d	4. c	5. d	6. c	7. d	8. d	9. d	10. d
11. d	12. d	13. d	14. d	15. d	16. d	17. a	18. d	19. b	20. a
21. d	22. d	23. a	24. c	25. b	26. d	27. c	28. b	29. b	30. d
31. c	32. d	33. d	34. d	35. b	36. d	37. d	38. d	39. b	40. d
41. a	42. d								

Chapter 19

1. b	2. b	3. d	4. b	5. d	6. d	7. b	8. d	9. d	10. d
11. d	12. d	13. d	14. d	15. d	16. c	17. d	18. b	19. d	20. d
21. c	22. a	23. d	24. d	25. d	26. a	27. b	28. a	29. d	30. d
31. b	32. d	33. b							